"*A warm-hearted journey into your soul, offering what may be the first true understanding of the voices in your head.*"

-- Joanne Shwed, editor and interior designer

HOW
TO BE
HAPPY

AS TOLD BY THE MILLION STARS

RITA ISSA

HOW TO BE HAPPY
AS TOLD BY THE MILLION STARS

Balboa Press books may be ordered through booksellers or by contacting:

Balboa Press
A Division of Hay House
1663 Liberty Drive
Bloomington, IN 47403
www.balboapress.com
1-(877) 407-4847

Editing, interior design, and layout by Joanne Shwed, Backspace Ink
(www.backspaceink.com)

For information on How to be Happy, please visit www.RitaIssa.com

Printed in the United States of America.

ISBN: 978-1-4525-7843-9 (sc)
ISBN: 978-1-4525-7845-3 (hc)
ISBN: 978-1-4525-7844-6 (e)

Library of Congress Control Number: 2013913240

Balboa Press rev. date: 8/26/2013

This book is dedicated to you.

CHAPTER ONE

Needs and I-Haves

"Up there! *Look up there!*"

I pointed to the endless, bright sky on that clear summer night.

My little Dunia and I sat on the swing in our beautiful august backyard. We sang our favorite songs, giggled, and pretended that the loud cicada orchestra in the background was playing just for us. When we sang they quieted down and when we stopped they sang louder, but often they got confused!

"Look at the million stars shining up there!" I said.

Dunia's wide-open eyes looked up and gazed in amazement. Then she turned to me and, with her curious five-year-old tiny voice, asked, "After we die and go to heaven, do you think we'll be together?"

Not waiting for an answer, she went on.

"Will you look the same? Will I recognize you?"

One more time, and before I got a chance to say anything, she continued.

"Will you recognize me?"

She stared at me, and I felt a chill overwhelm my body.

"Of *course* I will," I responded as successfully as my words could hide my choking voice, and as much as the discreet tears could cover my surprise and sadness.

With no hesitation, and almost no doubt, I pretended that her questions were common and my answers obvious and easy.

"Of course we'll be together. We'll live, eat, and sleep together. We'll play, laugh, dance, and sing, just like we're doing right now!"

I'd like to believe that the disguised certainty of my answer satisfied her curiosity, and reassured and comforted her, at least for a while.

After I tucked Dunia in bed, I stepped back outside. The cicadas were still celebrating their happening lazy life, loud and happy!

I lay down on the swing, staring back at the infinite sparkles way up in the eternal distance. The warm breeze had calmed down a little, but I could still feel it wrapping itself around me, caressing me with its heavenly softness.

Slowly, the singing quieted. Everyone and everything went to sleep, safe in the arms of the night, except the million stars that shone brighter and brighter.

There was silence all around.

All of a sudden, Dunia's concerned questions echoed in my mind. Then, one after the other, my own oh-so-familiar questions started to wake up and parade themselves, some mysteriously carrying me back to Dunia's age, maybe even earlier.

"Where do I come from? Where am I going? What am I doing here? What do I want? Who am I? *Who* am I?"

"You are a great Human Being!"

"I am a great Human Being," I repeated.

"You are a great Human Being!"

"I know I am," I proudly agreed.

Suddenly, I froze.

"*Wait* a minute!" I thought. "Who's talking to me?"

Afraid to be seen or heard, I managed to hold my breath, but my heart betrayed me. It was beating so fast and loudly that I could clearly hear it myself.

I hesitated for a moment, then cautiously sat up and dared to mumble, "Who's *there*?"

"Up here! *Look up here!*"

"Look up *where*?" I silently thought. "I'm outside in my backyard. Nothing is above me but the deep sky!"

Giving up like a prey at the mercy of its fate, I rolled my eyes up while my head remained lowered with fear.

"Do not be afraid."

"Who are you? *Where* are you?"

As I finished asking these questions, I felt something softly touch my chin and gently lift my head.

I looked up and witnessed the biggest, brightest star I had ever seen in my life!

"Who *are* you?" I repeated in disbelief. "Are you talking to *me*?"

With the greatest twinkle, the star winked straight at me and spoke.

"Call me Starry. I heard you wonder about who you are."

"Yes!" I answered, in a trembling voice, and then thought, "Is a star really *talking* to me?"

Despite my fear, I continued.

"You said that I'm a great Human Being."

"Yes."

"Is this supposed to be a revelation?"

Starry responded with a comforting voice.

"There are moments in your life when you forget who you are. Tonight, I will remind you. Tomorrow, you will remind another Human Being who forgot."

At that point, it strangely felt like I was conversing with an old, familiar friend. With my fear mysteriously melting away, and with a curious trust, I asked, "What do you want to remind me of?"

"When your journey on Earth began," Starry said, "you had a body—a Human's body, with tiny, delicate fingers and toes; a perfect count that made your parents happy. You had the softest skin and the most intoxicating baby smell."

"Intoxicating! You can say *that* again!"

These words came in a different voice. I wasn't sure who it was, but Starry seemed to ignore them, and she continued to speak.

"You had beautiful, bright eyes that saw nothing and everything. You had little ears and a little bud of a nose.

"You had precious, tiny lips that knew almost no rest. Every waking moment, they were either taking or giving. Your angelic and contagious smiles poured intense pleasure and pure love into

4

every heart. Your honest giggles put a smile on every face around you, especially the faces of people who needed it the most.

"Your lips allowed you to receive life and, when you needed something, they got busy asking for it, and those requests left no one nearby indifferent."

More words from the strange voice zoomed across the sky.

"Cute baby! Look at that baby. So *cute*! Your lips might've been precious and tiny, but your voice was giant. *Giant*! Do you remember all my sleepless days and nights? I sure do!"

"What was *that*?" I asked, startled.

"It's me, Shooter! I shoot up and across, and help Starry's messages get across ..."

"Shooter! Perhaps you should slow down for tonight," Starry warned, even though she knew that her warning was a complete failure. It reminded me of my warnings to Dunia and those numerous times I would count to three ... 10 times in a row!

Starry then reassured me.

"Do not worry! Shooter will be running around all night. I have to admit, though, that he is right. Your voice *was* very loud! When you needed something, everyone around you knew about it, and someone had to answer and help satisfy your need.

"When you were hungry, you cried until you ate. When you were thirsty, you cried until you drank. When you were sleepy, you cried until you slept. When you had pain, you cried until you had relief. When you felt scared, you cried until you felt safe. When you needed love, you cried until you received love.

"You instinctively felt your every need and, very quickly, you became an expert at expressing it."

"Expressing it very *loudly*," added Shooter.

5

"In that way," Starry continued, "you became an expert at getting the I-have that satisfied your need, regardless of how this I-have was provided or who provided it for you."

✦

"My *I-have*?"

"Your needs are something you feel. No matter how often you try to resist them, you cannot stop them from coming to you. Trying to ignore them or to get rid of them is useless, and fighting them will only exhaust you because your needs always win. They stick around and never leave.

"You think that they bother you and insist on annoying you. You feel that they harass you, maybe even drive you crazy. You say that they stress you out and make you feel unhappy. Despite that, your needs never give up on you."

"Never give up on me? You mean they never give up."

"Your needs never give up *on* you," Starry affirmed.

"I don't understand! When someone or something doesn't give up on me, it's usually because they care about me and are good to me."

"Needs care about you. In fact, they care a lot. They are very good to you."

"How can they be good to me when all they do is make me feel unhappy?"

"Needs *are* good to you," Starry repeated. "Every need is a 'blessing in disguise'—as Human words say. The secret is for you not to be intimidated or fooled by the disguise—the apparent pain and unhappiness under which the need sometimes hides. Taking the time to look beyond the disguise, see what each need shows

6

you, and listen to what it tells you allows you to understand how this need wants to be satisfied.

"Each need carries an important message. Understanding the language your need speaks beyond all Human words and figuring out its message helps you decide your destination and set your next goal. The message acts like a light that guides you in the dark. It helps unfold the nature of the next step you will be taking in your life and clarify its direction. From one need to the other, and from one step to the next, your life is in constant evolution.

"You identify which one of your unmet needs is responsible for the unhappiness you feel in the present moment. Once you do, you take action—receive or give something—and collect what satisfies this need. Once satisfied, the need vanishes, leaving behind a great energy of happiness that pushes you forward on the path of your ongoing evolution. This energy liberates you and prepares you for the next step in your life.

"What you collect from receiving or giving is an 'I-have.' Your collection of I-haves is your source of love, safety, and happiness."

Shooter said that where there's a need, there's an I-have. First, I feel my need and identify it. Then, I find an I-have that satisfies it. Once satisfied, this need will not annoy or harass me anymore. It will no longer drive me crazy, stress me out, or make me feel unhappy. Instead, my satisfied need liberates me and, alongside my collected I-have, it energizes me. Off I go to my next adventure—feeling and identifying a need, and collecting an I-have.

✦

"You realize that, for us Humans, it's not always possible to collect all the I-haves that satisfy all our needs."

"Every Human has a story and so do you," Starry said. "Your story influences the variety of your needs. It sets their priority level and the degree of their importance inside your life. One after the other, and at the pace of your own story, you collect the I-haves that satisfy those needs, whether they are needs that you create for yourself or ones that life creates for you."

"Sometimes," I interrupted, "I can easily identify a need. For example, when I'm hungry, I know that I need to eat. When I'm thirsty, I know that I need to drink. My *problem* is when I know that I need *something* but just can't figure out what it is. It's difficult to always identify my needs. Sometimes, I'm not sure what the need is but, more often, I have no clue! All I know and am sure of is that I feel unhappy."

"What you are saying about your need or *problem*—as Human words call it—is true. Some needs are rather easy to identify, such as many of your physical survival needs—what your body requires to assure its survival and function. When you are hungry or thirsty, for example, your body informs you about its need for food or water. On the other hand, other physical as well as many mental and emotional needs are more difficult to identify.

"While common to many Humans, physical, mental, and emotional needs are personal to each Human and relative to each Human's story, just like your needs are personal to you and relative to your story—your story of Here and Now, as well as the story you came with, and the one you came into."

✪

"The story I came *with*?" I asked.

"When you are born," Starry answered, "you have a body, a mind, and emotions. You have a character, weaknesses, difficulties, strengths, talents, gifts, and dreams. Some people argue that these are genetic. Some believe in luck, fate, destiny, karma, or even a past life. Regardless, it is the story you came with."

"And the story I came *into*?"

"You are born within a family, through a mother and a father. You may have one or more caregivers. You have a place where you arrive and refer to as 'home.' Regardless of the details, it is the story you came into.

"Your story is unique to you," she continued, "just like every Human's story is unique to them. It is the only story you have and will ever have during your Human life.

"Different factors influence your story, such as your physical, mental, and emotional health. People around you, as well as those whom you have never met and those whom you may or will never meet—along with *their* own stories—also influence your story."

Shooter gave many examples of these people: caregivers, parents, family, siblings, relatives, friends, teachers, neighbors, colleagues, idols, role models, religious or political leaders, media people, ancestors, people from history, a movie character, or a hero from a book.

"Your story is influenced by places, conditions, circumstances, events, and situations," Starry added. "Your knowledge, education, and countless experiences affect your story. Let us not forget your thoughts, decisions, choices, words, actions, efforts, achievements, successes, failures, and disappointments. Life's opportunities and fortunes as well as its challenges, obstacles, difficulties, lessons, and messages all influence your story. Your Human chronological age and different stages of your Human life also play an important role in determining your story.

"All of these factors—among other ones—affect your story. Your story affects your emotions. Your emotions affect your needs. Factors change all the time; therefore, your needs change all the time."

✦

"This must be why there are so many needs that I cannot identify!"

"Some needs clearly belong to your story. There are needs that you create for yourself, and others that life creates for you.

"There are people—most likely your parents—who identified some of your needs, maybe even created them for you, sometimes purposely out of love and concern. Other times, they may have mistaken some of *their* needs for yours. They set many of your goals. Your job was simply to work hard towards these goals and reach them."

Shooter reminded me of the times when I was told that I needed to eat to grow. I needed to get dressed on my own like a big kid. I needed to become responsible and clean my room. I needed to study hard, graduate, and get a degree and a job. I needed to marry and start a family. I needed to do this ... I needed to do that ...

"So, you ate and you grew," Starry continued. "You got dressed like a big kid. You became responsible and cleaned your room. You studied hard, graduated, and got a degree and a job. You married and started a family.

"Then, one day, the goals were no longer preset for you. All of a sudden, you were on your own. *Now* what? Where do you go from here? Where do you *want* to go?

"Reaching a goal may not be easy, but identifying a need and setting a goal can also be difficult. This is why, among other reasons, you often go on living with routine needs and goals.

"Sooner or later, somewhere along the way, you start feeling your *original* needs—the ones that belong to your own story and had never left but which you had instead put behind other needs. You keep feeling your original needs, trying to see what they are showing you and listen to what they are telling you, until you understand what they want you to know, take action, and satisfy them."

"See? Listen? Understand?" I wondered.

"Emotions are often complex," Starry said. "Therefore, a need could also be complex. While you feel and identify a need—or at least *think* that you do—others are felt and confuse you all over again.

"The nature, source, and cause of a need are sometimes easy to understand, but often they remain a complete mystery. When you cannot understand them, just feel the need itself."

"How do I do *that*?"

"Keep it simple. Narrow the needs quest to one question: How am I feeling right now? You can reduce this question to one word: *Feel?* Then, narrow the answer to: happy or unhappy."

Shooter said that I can match happy with a green color (happy-green) and unhappy with a red color (unhappy-red). He said that traffic lights inspired the colors. Green means go ahead, move on, and the coast is clear. Red means stop, watch and see, listen, and understand.

"A happy or an unhappy feeling is the translation of one or many emotions," Starry explained. "These emotions will help you identify the need that is calling you and wants to be satisfied in the present moment."

Shooter described many of the endless emotions that could be translated by an unhappy feeling, such as sad, guilty, sorry, remorseful, regretful, hurting, frustrated, resentful, bitter, vengeful, anxious, scared, angry, upset, overwhelmed, stressed, worried, confused, tired, numb, discouraged, depressed, embarrassed, disappointed, lonely, nostalgic, longing, bored, stuck, empty, misunderstood, unrecognized, unappreciated, and unloved.

"Regardless of the emotion," continued Starry, "and regardless of the need's nature, source, or cause, a happy or an unhappy feeling is common to all Humans."

Shooter said that it doesn't matter if the person is young or old, if they are a man or a woman, what they look like, what their skin color is, which country they come from or where they live, what language they speak, to what God they pray, or if they don't pray at all. It makes no difference who their parents are, what their job or title is, or how much or little money they have. It makes no difference what their Human story is.

A happy or an unhappy feeling cannot tell the difference. A happy feeling means that the need is satisfied while an unhappy feeling means that the need is not satisfied.

"After you have asked *Feel?*" Starry resumed, "and answered happy-green or unhappy-red, go to the Needs chart.

"The Needs chart is a user-friendly tool that helps you identify which need is lacking satisfaction and talking to you through your unhappy-red feeling.

"Different physical, mental, and emotional needs are common to many Humans, but are not necessarily felt at the same time, in the same order, or at the same priority level or degree of importance by all Humans. Some needs are intertwined—they complement or depend on each other. Needs change over time.

"For those reasons—among other ones—the needs on the chart are not listed in any specific order. The chart displays the most common needs in a simple and clear way."

"What does the Needs chart look like?"

"Up here! *Look up here!*" Shooter shouted.

I looked up. A shower of a million stars lit up the sky! One after the other, they gracefully moved around and lined up, creating magnificent pictures. I watched them display themselves to me. Each star filled its perfect spot and did exactly what it was designed to do.

Starry explained that the stars are gathered in different groups, just to make it simple to understand and easy to remember.

"There it is! Do you *see* it?" Shooter asked.

"Wow!" I exclaimed, both amazed and excited. "This is a *miracle!*"

The sky was spectacular. It was the most beautiful painting I had ever watched "in the making." It was so alive, as if each star were a magical character in a play!

There it was ... the Needs chart—*my* Needs chart—as told by the million stars.

✪ ✪ ✪

My Needs Chart

1. *My physical needs to receive an I-have* are, among others:

    - My physical *survival* needs to breathe, drink, eat, rest, sleep, stay warm, be dressed, have shelter, be healthy, and have a disease-free and pain-free body that moves and functions freely

    - My physical *basic* needs to breathe clean air, drink clean water, eat basic food, and have shelter where basic services are available, such as clean running water and power; work; have income—money, investments, benefits, insurance, savings, a retirement plan, and a financial safety net; be debt free and own a house, a car, and other material possessions; live in a stable, safe, and peaceful environment, neighborhood, and country where there is no harm, accidents, violence, crime, war, or natural disasters; live in a place where there is a system for justice, law, order, defense, human rights protection, and a fair and strong government; be intimate, and receive physical affection: touch, hug, kiss, be touched, be hugged, and be kissed; reproduce; and receive medical care, and physical help and support when needed

2. *My mental needs to receive an I-have* are, among others, to:

   - Have and develop my intelligence and memory, and be able to remember and forget; learn something new, understand, and seek answers and knowledge; research, explore, and discover the truth; study, educate myself, read, and watch documentaries; travel and expand; make progress; and receive mental help and support when needed

3. *My emotional needs to receive an I-have* are, among others, to:

   - Have a Human identity, and to have and know my full name; my exact date and place of birth; my gender and sexual orientation; my personality, character, habits, hobbies, gifts, talents, strengths, and weaknesses; and my role, function, and job

   - Identify my needs, and collect the satisfying I-haves; know the truth of the story I came with; my dreams, passions, and aspirations; where I came from and where I am going; and my life's mission and purpose

- Know the truth of the story I came into; who my mother and father are, what they look and are like, and who I look and am like; to whom and where I belong; the background and history of my roots; my family history and heredity factors; what my story looked like, especially my childhood; my ancestors and what their stories looked like; and my country, nationality, ethnicity, race, culture, language, and religion and belief system

- Have and belong to my family; live with, be close to, and spend quality time with my loved ones, such as my parents, siblings, relatives, relationship partner, children, and people whose story looks like mine; celebrate traditions and enjoy the comforts of the familiar; experience pleasant surprises; socialize with my friends, colleagues, neighbors, and community members; establish contact, interact, and exchange with people in a group activity, a social event, or a team at work; have fellowship and public relations; and have and belong to a network

- Experience romance; fall and be in love; marry; have children; have privacy and spend some time alone; have companionship and not be lonely; keep in touch, converse, communicate, talk, express myself, and confide in someone; and receive emotional help and support when needed

- Be close to nature and animals; live in a clean, beautiful environment, and be surrounded with a beautiful setting at home, at work, and in my neighborhood

- Have good looks and a nice appearance, be attractive and desired, and fit in; eat right, sleep well, and exercise; take a break and relax; feel a constant sense of well-being; live a regret-free, resentment-free, fear-free, stress-free, worry-free, and comfortable life; have a sense of humor, laugh, and have fun; enjoy life's abundant delights, and indulge my senses through what I see, hear, smell, taste, and touch and feel; enjoy leisure time, hobbies, activities, sports, games, and adventures

- Be creative; express myself in different ways, such as through music (listen, play, write, sing, or dance), art (read, write, speak, paint, draw, color, sculpt, act, or cook), and beauty (photograph, garden, decorate, renovate, or build); be spontaneous; experience something new; know, predict, guarantee the future, and prevent problems; have a new challenge and goal, meet this challenge, and reach this goal; have a variety of ideas and projects; have an abundance of options, and sometimes have only one obvious choice; have freedom of expression, words, choice, decision, and action; have independence and autonomy; have power and be in control; compete and win; achieve success, be better, and be the best; gain respect and esteem; earn a good reputation; receive attention and admiration and feel important; be heard, recognized, understood, acknowledged, accepted, valued, and wanted; and receive affection, care, and love

4. *My emotional needs to give an I-have* are, among others, to:

- Give love; contribute and give back; listen; be tolerant and kind; teach, improve, motivate, and guide; organize something; support, help, solve problems, and rescue; share, donate, volunteer, and do humanitarian work; dream, invent, and implement something new; make a difference through my work and my words, gestures, and actions; achieve something; accomplish my mission; and make a unique contribution to this world—one that will leave *my* eternal signature

5. *My need to be completely fulfilled and truly happy* are, among others, to:

- Become aware of my thoughts, organize and control them, and enjoy the stillness of my mind
- Become aware of my past, and accept, forgive, thank, and release it
- Trust my future instead of fearing it or expecting it to save me
- Have faith, meditate, pray, and connect with God
- Constantly grow and glow
- Live Here and Now
- Be happy Here and Now

I contemplated my Needs chart. Then, slowly, the glittering stars vanished, one after the other, ending this magnificent parade. I was speechless!

"Did you understand what the stars tried to show and tell you?" Shooter asked.

Not getting any reaction from me, he continued.

"Hey! Are you *okay?*"

This question brought me back to Earth. I tried to answer.

"I ... I'm ... I don't know ... *Wow!* I feel like I just went to the twilight and back. That was absolutely *incredible!*"

"Do you think you understand what the twilight tried to show and tell you?" he repeated.

Not quite sure of the answer, I replied with my own question.

"How do I use the Needs chart?"

"Keep the chart in a visible place," Starry answered, "where you can quickly and easily refer to it, for example, on a wall or the back of a door. You can also keep it in a box—your Precious Box, with other tools you will collect along the way. These tools will remind you of the great Human Being that you are. You will refer to this box and use these tools when you need them.

"The Needs chart will be one of these many tools. Read it, and feel welcome to add a personal need not already listed. Read, and feel happy or unhappy.

"When you feel happy-green, smile and read on. When you feel unhappy-red, stop and take note of that specific need. Either circle it on the chart itself or make a separate note to keep the chart clear for future referrals.

"At first, you may not easily be aware of your happy-green or unhappy-red feeling. Read the chart on a regular basis. You will be surprised at how clearly and quickly you will be able to see, hear, and feel the need that is calling you. You will understand the language that a need speaks beyond all Human words, and you will be able to figure out the message it has for you. You will be able to identify the need that wants your attention and care, for the time being."

Shooter told me to read the chart in the same way I walk through the aisles of a grocery store: Examine the goods and choose what appeals to me. He said to read the needs on this chart, one need at a time, and feel happy or unhappy.

"Read and feel," Starry continued. "Do not think with your mind. Do not go into the details of your thoughts or emotions. Do not analyze what, why, where, when, who, or how, and do not elaborate. Do not judge and do not label. Just feel happy-green or unhappy-red, and note the need that makes you feel unhappy-red.

"The body is able to express a happy or an unhappy feeling with a language it speaks beyond all Human words. When the feeling is happy-green, the muscles are relaxed. When the feeling is unhappy-red, the body reacts and expresses this unhappiness with a discreet change in the breathing and heartbeat, often accompanied by a subtle, uncomfortable muscle tension that feels like a knot in one or more parts of the body—most commonly the throat, chest, or stomach.

"There are times when the unhappy-red feeling is more intense, and different parts of the body develop other symptoms, such as tears, a choking sensation, heart palpitations, or stomach cramps.

"When reading a specific need makes you feel unhappy-red, stop and make note of it. Identifying the unsatisfied need is solving half of the *problem*—as Human words call it.

"Then, resume reading if the intensity of your reaction allows you to do so. When you read the Needs chart, you will become aware of the numerous satisfied needs in your life, and you will be grateful for them.

"Your needs—the ones that are satisfied as well as the unmet ones that are calling you—build your comfort zone, your balance equation, or your balance pie."

"Up here! *Look up here!*" Shooter shouted.

I looked up and saw a picture glow in the sky.

✮ ✮ ✮

$a + b + c + d + e + ... = my\ comfort\ zone = my\ balance\ equation$

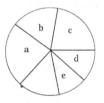

my balance pie

✮ ✮ ✮

"Each letter of your equation and each slice of your pie represents one of your needs," Starry explained. "Your equation is personal to you, and so is your pie."

"What is your equation today?" Shooter asked. "Let the million stars and your Needs chart help you write it down. How big is each slice of your pie and what flavor is it? Let them show and tell you.

"Keep your equation and pie in your Precious Box," he added. "Refer to them when you feel that you are no longer 'balanced,' and update them when necessary."

"Your life is in constant evolution," reminded Starry. "All along your life's journey, different needs arise while others disappear. Your needs today are different from yesterday's needs. They are also different from tomorrow's needs.

"Some needs regularly come back and others seldom do. There are needs that, once satisfied, leave and never come back. Some needs have to be satisfied on a continual basis and some in a cyclical way. Some needs are satisfied partially or completely, and temporarily or permanently. Other needs may never be satisfied in the way that you would like.

"Remember that needs are affected by emotions. Emotions are affected by the Human story. The Human story is affected by factors that change all the time. Therefore, needs change all the time."

"What's the purpose of living with needs that change all the time?" I asked.

"Everyone and everything changes; that's being alive!" Shooter announced. "As long as your needs are changing, there's no problem; it when they *stop* changing that you should start worrying!"

Starry laughed.

"The ultimate purpose of your life is for you to be happy Here and Now," she said, "being exactly where you are, and doing exactly what you are doing—just like a star in a million!

"One of life's purposes is for you to satisfy the need that will speak after you have finished satisfying another one.

"Thanks to needs that change all the time, your life is in constant evolution.

"When you feel unhappy, refer to your Needs chart and feel, identify, and express your physical, mental, or emotional unmet need calling for your attention and assistance, and then collect the I-have that would satisfy it."

"Just like your precious lips once expressed loudly and beyond all Human words and sounds," Shooter said, "and just like you managed to collect the I-have that satisfied your need, one way or another, bringing yourself back to your comfort zone."

"*My* comfort zone is never comfortable enough," I complained. "*My* I-haves are never enough for me to feel happy."

"Each Human has their personal comfort zone for the variety of their needs," Starry said. "Different I-haves are collected to satisfy those needs.

"Sometimes, needs are reduced to those of survival, and the Human lives happily with a small number of I-haves in order to satisfy one ultimate need. Sometimes, an I-have is rejected, whether temporarily or permanently, in order to satisfy a more important need.

"Some I-haves are collected to ensure a high level of safety and security for today, tomorrow, and maybe years ahead. Some are collected and used as a substitute for others. Some I-haves are used to build a protective shield that covers up and numbs a pain caused by a different need that hides deeply inside.

"At times, many I-haves are collected in order to have more—or have the most—hoping, assuming, and being comforted that, if the Human has more, then they will *be* more accepted, recognized, appreciated, respected, admired, and ultimately more loved. 'I have more' is interpreted as 'I am important, I am good enough, I am worthy of being loved, and I am loved.'

"Other times, I-haves are collected because the Human loves to feel the pure pleasures and the vibrant physical, mental, and emotional sensations—a delightful variety of experiences filled with beauty, comfort, and luxury to indulge the body, mind, and emotions."

"Sometimes," I sarcastically added, "I-haves are collected simply because the *Human* is superficial, materialistic, shallow, and empty on the inside."

"Good one, Genius!" Shooter said.

"Who's Genius?" I asked.

"*Shooter!*" warned Starry. "It is time to go."

"Already? Can't a star tell a joke around here?"

Disregarding Shooter's words, Starry continued.

"Look at the world around you. God created an abundant world and made it available for you. God wants you rich. He blessed you with abundance because He wants you to have it.

"Do not judge abundance. Do not refuse or reject it, and do not feel guilty about having it. The story you came with and the one you came into, as well as the life happening inside and around you Here and Now, offer you abundant opportunities to collect many I-haves. Welcome these opportunities and I-haves and gladly enjoy them.

"Attract abundance to your life. Abundance helps satisfy your basic as well as your not-so-basic needs to receive. You then become physically, mentally, and emotionally available to satisfy your need to give back to others and to contribute to the world. Giving back blesses you with an indescribable feeling of fulfillment and true happiness."

Shooter compared this to a little seed that needs to receive the right elements to grow into a little plant. Although it starts giving back early in its tender life, the more air, light, water, and rich soil nutrients this little plant receives, the more it grows and abundantly gives back lush leaves, pretty flowers, and healthy and tasty fruit.

He then gave the example of the time when my friend Susan needed my emotional and financial support, which I could not give her because I had lost my job and was scared and worried about paying my own bills. However, when I started working again, I was able to give her my support and lend her money.

"The more abundant your I-haves are," Starry continued, "the easier it becomes for you to share and give back to another Human who, in their turn, can now satisfy their need to receive, and then become able to give back. Attracting abundance becomes your duty in keeping this energy cycle of receiving and giving going around in the world."

I pondered this, and then admitted, "I never really thought of it that way."

Starry said nothing. I waited, expecting her or Shooter to make a comment. I waited a little more, wondering why they were not saying anything.

Starry and Shooter were gone.

The softness of dawn had slowly started to highlight the beautiful and abundant world around me, as if to confirm Starry's words. It was the last thing I saw before I fell asleep.

The next thing I knew were Dunia's little hands on my face and her sweet good-morning kiss on my nose. I opened my eyes. Her precious face was there, waiting for me to wake up. She was watching me, with deep love shining through her eyes, and she softly smiled.

"I was looking for you, Mommy. I called you but you didn't hear me."

I smiled back and tapped a few times on the empty spot next to me.

"Come up and lie down here," I whispered.

She climbed up and cuddled tightly against me. I put my arm around her and swung into the morning's delicate light, welcomed by the birds' singing ceremony.

I wasn't sure what had happened during the night and, honestly, I wasn't sure if I *wanted* to know.

CHAPTER TWO

I-Haves and I-Am

Throughout the day, I felt as if I were in a daze. I wondered if it was because I had not slept all night and was tired or because I really had a conversation with a star ... *with a star!*

I kept waiting for Starry to give me a sign.

Nothing.

"I must be going crazy," I thought. "I'm sure I was dreaming. That's *it*! It was definitely a dream."

Despite my conclusion, I was excited when night finally came so I could go outside and find Starry waiting to tell me more. At the same time, I was scared to find out that a star would actually be *waiting* for me!

After Dunia went to sleep, I stepped outside and sat on the swing. I watched the stars and waited ...

"I am happy to see you again!"

"Yes!" I thought. "Yes, *yes*, YES!"

Pretending to be cool, and forgetting that Starry could hear every thought, I said, "Good evening!"

"Did you have a good day?" she asked.

"Yes, I did. Dunia and I spent most of the day together. I'm still off work for my summer vacation and she'll be going to school soon. We went shopping for some school stuff, you know ..."

"'You *know*'?" I thought. "What a stupid thing to say! What does Starry know about school stuff and, if she did, why would she care anyway?"

Attempting to remediate what I just said, I asked her another question.

"Did you rest?"

"Yes, I did. Thank you for asking."

"Did Shooter also rest?"

"Oh, yes!" she laughed. "He was exhausted from running around all night."

"I can imagine!" I added, not knowing what to say next. I mean, really ... what exactly *do* you ask a star? "What would you like to drink?"

I heard Starry giggle but she said nothing.

At the risk of sounding rude, I went straight to the point and to what I had waited all day to ask her.

"Starry, you taught me last night how to identify a need calling me when it lacks an I-have necessary to satisfy it. You told me to ask myself *Feel?*, answer happy-green or unhappy-red, and then refer to my Needs chart. Would you now tell me how to identify and collect this I-have?"

28

"Some needs are obvious," she answered, "and their satisfying I-haves are somewhat easy to identify and collect. When trying to satisfy a need is more difficult, different ways can help, such as the *5W2H-O&D* technique.

"This technique helps you ask yourself the appropriate questions and find many answers. It will lead you to identify and collect the I-have that will satisfy your need. It is a very simple technique. All you need are a paper and two different color pens—blue and red, for example.

"*5W2H-O&D* sometimes allows you to get answers rather quickly and on your own; other times, you might need the assistance of someone whom you trust and who would love to see you happy. This person could be a loved one, a relative, a friend, a colleague, or maybe someone you know who has already collected an I-have that satisfied a similar need, and who would genuinely advise you and share their answers, experience, and tips with you.

"You can get the help and expertise of a professional in the field, a consultant, a mentor, a therapist, a religious or spiritual guide, or a person within a specialized association, organization, or study club.

"Sometimes, the simple act of talking to someone can help you identify the I-have—as well as the need—and offer you great relief from your unhappy feeling.

"You can also turn to a source of information that might help you, such as a course, an article in a book, or the Internet."

"What is this *5W2H-O&D* technique about and how can I use it?"

"*5W* stands for five questions that start with the letter *W*," Starry elaborated. "They are *What?*, *Why?*, *Where?*, *When?*, and *Who?*

"*2H* stands for two questions that start with the letter *H*. They are *How?* and *How much?*

"*O* stands for this question: "What are my satisfying I-have options?" The answer to *O* displays the one or more satisfying I-have options of which you think, hear, or dream, and for which you will research, query, and collect more information, using the help of *Where?*, *When?*, *Who?*, *How?*, and *How much?*

"*D* stands for the date you set to actually start taking action and collecting the I-have you choose to collect among others.

"You gather the information and then try to find the most convenient answers to the *W*, *H*, and *O* questions. You do that to the best of your knowledge and abilities for the time being. You do that, in no specific order, since laying out the different options for *O* and answering one *W* or *H* question before another one makes finding the most convenient I-have option much easier, especially when there is more than one option from which to choose.

"One or more questions may not have an appropriate or perfect answer, or there might be an answer you cannot find. Ask the question, note it in your agenda, and leave it alone for now. Let the answer find itself whenever it is time for it to do so. Just skip this particular question and move on to the next one. You might want to go back to it later and verify if the answer is there, if it needs more time to reveal itself, or if the question or answer no longer makes a difference."

✿

"Now, go in the house and get the paper and the blue and red pens," Shooter said.

"You mean I'm *really* going to take notes?"

"Yes, you're going to take notes. Now *go!*"

I got up, hesitating and thinking, "What if I come back and Starry and Shooter are gone?"

"We're not going anywhere, Genius!"

Despite Shooter's reassuring words, I ran in and out of the house as quickly as I could.

"I'm ready. I have the paper and pens right here."

"Great! Now, name one need for which you'd like to find a satisfying I-have," Shooter said. "Name one situation or *problem* for which you want to find a solution."

"*One*? I have a lot more than just one problem!" I admitted, discouraged. "Let's see ... my problem is my social life, which is pretty boring. No wait ... my problem is that I'm tired from always running around. No, no, wait again! It's my job. I want to change my job ... actually, change my whole career!"

"We are going to practice the *5W2H-O&D* technique," Starry proposed, "one situation—or *problem*—at a time. You will ask the *5W2H-O* questions, and then use your blue pen to write down the answers.

"Let us start with the first example and the first *W* question: *What?* The answer to *What?* is the title or brief description of your present situation or problem. What is your answer to *What?*"

"My answer to *What?* is 'my social life is boring,'" I said.

"The second *W* question is *Why?*" Starry continued. "The answer to *Why?* often starts with 'I want to satisfy my need to ...' You can use the help of the Needs chart to find this need and complete the sentence. For the first example, what is your answer to *Why?*"

"My answer to *Why?* is 'To satisfy my emotional need to socialize.'"

"What is your answer to *Where?*" she asked.

"Uh ... let me see ... um ..."

"Since the answer to *O* displays the different satisfying I-have options," she intervened, "and since, in the case of this example, you have more than one option from which to choose, you can answer *O* before *Where?*

"Remember that you answer the *5W2H-O* questions in no particular order. Skip a question for which you cannot yet find an answer. For this example, and for those same reasons, you will also skip *When?*, *Who?*, *How?*, and *How much?*, and go straight to *O*.

"What are your satisfying I-have options? This question can even be reduced to one word: *Options?*"

"I'd like to participate in a group activity," I said. "I have two options that often cross my mind: (1) dance the tango; or (2) play cards."

"What is your answer to *Where?*"

"For my first option, which is to dance the tango, I can start by learning to dance. I can either go to the new dance school that opened on Second Street last month, or go online to find other dance schools in the area. For my second option, which is to play cards, I could play here at home or discuss rotating houses with whomever will be playing."

"What is your answer to *When?*"

"For the tango, I'll go online or call or visit the schools and find out about the schedule. For playing cards, I can either play on Tuesday or Thursday night since I get off work a little earlier."

"What is your answer to *Who?*"

"For the tango, it's the teacher and the dancers. I have to ask the school if I need to bring my own partner. For playing cards, it's my family and friends. I'll call and find out who would like to play."

"What is your answer to *How?*"

"I guess I'll have to learn how to dance the tango. As far as playing cards, I'm pretty good at it."

"Now we go to *How much?*," Starry continued. "The answer to *How much?* is the cost of the satisfying I-have you are trying to identify and collect. 'Cost' means how much money out of your financial budget, how much time out of your schedule, and how much physical, mental, and emotional energy are required to collect this I-have. What is your answer to *How much?*

"For the tango, I'll get the information from the different dance schools. For playing cards, I'll discuss it with the players."

"By the time you finish answering the questions," Starry revealed, "you usually have enough information to help you make a decision. Use your red pen to circle the answers that seem more appropriate for you and the ones that fit best with your lifestyle—location, schedule, resources, budget, and energy. Once you do, you will be amazed to see the most convenient I-have option stand out. It is often the one that looks like you, and the one that will satisfy your need for the time being.

"Once the decision is made, and once the most convenient option is chosen, you are ready to answer *D*. Setting an actual date—day, month, and year, and even the time, whenever possible—

transforms the chosen I-have option from being an idea, thought, wish, or dream inside your mind into a reality, an actual project, and an official goal. You choose the date and note it in your agenda. Your need mysteriously starts to feel satisfied, and you start feeling happy the moment you take action to try and collect the I-have—even before you actually collect it. Setting a date and writing it down is very powerful!"

"That's it!" announced Shooter. "All 5W2H-O questions are answered, your option is chosen, and the date to take action to collect the I-have is set. It is a simple yet very helpful technique."

"Wow!" I said. "Using this 5W2H-O&D is a lot easier than I thought it would be. It's actually fun. I'd like to try it for my second problem.'"

I continued, asking and answering the questions:

What?	I'm tired from always running around.
Why?	I want to satisfy my physical, mental, and emotional needs to take a break and relax.
Where?	Since I have more than one option, I'll skip this question for now.
When?	I'll also skip this question.
Who?	Skip
How?	Skip
How much?	Skip
Options?	(1) My first option is to go to a natural springs spa.

(2) My second option is to join a yoga class.

Back to *Where?*

(1) I've seen an ad for an amazing spa called Lotus Time, located about 50 miles away.

(2) I have to research and gather the information for different yoga centers around here.

Back to *When?*

(1) I'll go online or call to find the opening hours for the spa.

(2) I'll go online or call and ask about the schedule of the beginner's yoga class.

Back to *Who?*

(1) I guess it will be me, myself, and I. Oh! I'll have to ask my mother if she can watch Dunia.

(2) It will be the instructor, the people in the yoga class, and me. Maybe I'll ask Linda if she'd like to join. She's been talking about wanting to start yoga for at least two years now.

Back to *How?*

(1) I'll find out about the different services that are offered at the spa.

(2) I guess the yoga instructor will teach me different techniques.

Back to *How much?*

(1) I'll find out the spa's prices when I go online or call about the schedule. Then I'll figure out how much money and time I can afford to spend there. As

far as energy, it won't cost me any ... but
it will cost the spa *plenty*!
(2) I'll go online or call to know the
price. I think I can afford—money and
time—to go once or twice a week. Maybe
I can even go every day!

"Hey, Genius, don't get carried away and forget about your
Why? answer, which is 'to satisfy your physical, mental, and emotional needs to take a break and relax.' Don't start adding to your
schedule. *Relax!*"

"You're right, Shooter. Besides, I have to find out if they have a
child-care center where I can leave Dunia while I attend the class.
I'm sure my mom won't be able to watch her every time.

"*There!*" I concluded. "All *5W2H-O* questions are answered.
Now I get my red pen and circle the answers that fit most with my
lifestyle. Then I choose the one convenient I-have option that most
looks like me."

I thought for a moment.

"Starry, do I always have to choose one option or the other?
What about when two options look like me? Can't I choose them
both?"

"You do not always have to choose one option *or* the other.
Make sure that the *5W2H-O* answers you write down are precise,
short, and clear. Do not forget to skip a question when an answer
does not apply. Do not insist on finding an answer that does not
want to reveal itself to you, but let the answer find itself instead.

"As long as the options you choose look like you, fit with your
lifestyle, and are within your available and comfortable *How
much?*, you can choose as many options as you like. For now,

choose the one that seems to take the lead. Choose the I-have that talks to your heart the most and helps satisfy this particular need calling you for the time being. Later, you can collect and add another I-have, or replace the first I-have with the new one.

"Remember that the I-have you are choosing today is the one that satisfies your need today. Remember that, as life changes, your needs also change and so do your I-haves ... and that is okay!

"After you gather the necessary information, take your red pen and circle your chosen option. Let this option be your final choice for now, and disregard the other ones."

"Just drop them, Genius, before they drop you and take you back to your unmet need, confusion, and unhappiness. Don't think too much. Choose one option and throw away your paper. That's all! Goodbye ... *ciao* ... *adios*! Then answer D and make sure that you note the date in your agenda."

"Now," Starry suggested, "let us go to the third situation or what you feel is your problem."

I was really starting to enjoy this *5W2H-O&D* technique.

"Okay," I boldly agreed, convinced of how easy this technique seemed to be and thinking that I was already a pro at it. I took the dive.

"*What?* It's my job. *Why?* Uh ..."

I thought about it for a little while but could not come up with an answer.

"Let me help you," Shooter proposed. "Which need on the Needs chart do you want to satisfy? Is it a physical, mental, or emotional need? Is it a need to receive or to give an I-have?"

"I'm not sure ... I guess it's my need to change my job." I thought a little longer. "No, that's not it. Maybe it's my need for a new challenge ... no, that's not quite it either."

I waited, hoping that Starry would come to the rescue, but she said nothing.

"I don't know. I can't figure it out! All I *do* know is that there's something I don't want anymore but I'm not sure what it is."

I waited a little more, still hoping that Starry—or maybe even Shooter—would help me out.

"I have no clue," I mumbled. Then, I finally came up with something. "Can I call it 'my need for change' or 'to do something different'?"

"Of course you can," Starry reassured. "Remember that if your need is not listed on the Needs chart, go ahead and add it. When you are not 100% sure of what to call this need, write down the Human words that best describe it—the ones you feel interpret it as closely as possible. Even if they are sometimes limiting, Human words are very helpful and can describe, translate, and express many physical, mental, and emotional needs as well as many thoughts and emotions. No matter how little or how much Human words can express, just start from there."

"In this case," I said, "my answer to *Why?* would be 'to satisfy my need for change' because I don't want my job anymore—my whole career, that is. I *hate* what I do. I just can't stand it! It's the same thing, day after day. It's no more fun. It's boring and no longer challenging. The only thing I like about this job is the money and the benefits. I hate the place and everyone there. With my experience, maybe I can go to another company and meet new people, and I won't have to deal with those losers every day ... but who's going to hire me now? I'm too old to start over, and companies would rather hire someone younger. Besides, even if they did hire me, I'd have to start from the bottom all over again. It would just be a different place, different people, and less money ... but who knows? Maybe I'll like it better there."

I stayed quiet for a little while, absorbed in my own mind.

"*That* went well, Genius! Precise, short, and clear answers!"

Ignoring Shooter's words, I continued my lament.

"No, I don't think I'm going to like it. Actually, I'm *sure* that I won't. It's just going to be a different hell. You know, I never really liked what I do anyway. I don't even remember how I ended up doing this job in the first place. I never thought I was going to do *that* kind of job—never in my life! I always dreamed of being a designer. When I was growing up, I was sure I was going to become a designer, and my job today has nothing to do with design."

Trying to release the pressure that had built inside my chest, I inhaled deeply and then let out a long breath of despair.

"To tell you the truth, I'm not even sure that I want to be a designer anymore. That was my dream when I was young. Now, I have no *clue* what I want because what I want changes all the time. I just don't want *anything* anymore!"

Realizing that I was just rambling, I decided to keep quiet.

A complete and heavy silence filled the air.

There was a lump in my throat and tears rolled down my face. I quietly cried, just like the many times I'd hide and cry in silence so Dunia would not catch me.

Starry said nothing and I wondered if she was still there. I was afraid to look up and find out that she had bailed on me. She sounded so wise and strong, and I thought that she might not want to bother with someone like me.

Endless minutes passed before I finally dared to glance up. Starry sent me a sweet, reassuring, and comforting wink, as if to say it was okay and let me know that she was still there for me.

"I'm sorry," I whispered.

"Do you remember the blessing in disguise and the important message I told you about last night?" she quietly asked.

"Yes ..."

I wasn't sure what Starry was actually talking about but, at that point, sounding stupid on top of what just happened was not really an option.

"*Feel?*" she asked.

I said nothing.

"Green or red, Genius!"

"*Very* red," I answered with my saddest voice.

"Red means there is a blessing in disguise waiting to be discovered and a message waiting to be understood."

"I'm not sure I know what you're talking about, Starry, but one thing is for sure: Last night was a lot more fun. I think I'll let you do the rest of the talking, and let's talk about something else, *please!*"

"If you want to," she agreed, with total compassion. Then, after a little pause, she coaxed, "Do you *really* want to?"

I was now curious about the blessing in disguise and the important message. I was also glad Starry did not believe that I wanted to talk about something else.

"No," I said, truthfully. "May I start over?"

"We can try one more time. If you feel okay, we will continue; if not, we will leave it alone for now. Remember: Do not insist on finding an answer. Put the question aside for now, and let the answer find itself. Have faith that the answer will reveal itself to you when it is time for it to do so. Agreed?"

"Agreed!"

✪

"*5W2H-O&D* is a tool to help you find an I-have that satisfies your need," Starry continued. "You can use it whenever you feel confused and unhappy about a certain situation or problem concerning any aspect of your life, such as your job, your finances, your relationship, your love life, your family life, or your social life. Use it to analyze and clearly see the details, and figure out which *W* or *H* component is the guilty factor responsible for your confused, unhappy feeling.

"Let us try and find the guilty factor responsible for the confusion and unhappiness you feel about your job today."

"I don't think the guilty factor is *Where?*," I said, "because I was feeling this way at the previous company and before I started working for this one a few years ago. Actually, I'm pretty sure it's not *Where?* because the location of my work is perfect, the distance I have to commute is ideal, and the place itself is nice and comfortable.

"I also know the guilty factor is not *When?* because I really like my schedule and the hours are convenient.

"It's not *Who?* either because, despite what I said before, the truth is that my colleagues are pretty friendly, and the director and president really appreciate me.

"*How much?* is definitely not the guilty factor ... well, maybe it is. If it weren't for the money and the benefits, I would've had the courage to leave by now because *What?*, *Why?*, and *How?* are definitely not what keep me going back there every morning.   •

"For many years, my job was fun. Now, I just hate going to work. Every morning, when I get up to go there, I feel nauseated. The days seem endless. They go by so slowly and I can't wait for them to end. Yet, when I look back at all the years I've wasted feeling like this, I find that time is going by very fast and I'm there watching it. Every day is the *same* thing. I feel like I'm *stuck*. I watch life pass me by and watch myself missing out on it while I'm stuck doing this job."

"It is painful to watch time and life pass you by," Starry agreed, "and feeling stuck is scary."

"*Very* scary," I said, disappointed but somewhat comforted by Starry's apparent sympathy and understanding.

With a strange feeling of guilt suddenly starting to build inside me, I continued.

"Don't get me wrong. I used to like my job ... maybe I'm spoiled and demanding ... maybe I'm ungrateful. I should consider myself lucky that I even *have* a job, work for a big company, make good money, and have good benefits. I should appreciate the fact that the place is close to home, the hours are good, and the people are nice. I should be grateful that I have a good job and be happy about it."

Then I concluded the obvious.

"I see what you're trying to make me understand, Starry. I'm starting to feel better already. Thank you!"

"I am glad you are feeling better," she said sweetly, "and you are welcome!"

Shooter's words quickly ended my brief happiness.

"That's *not* what she's trying to do, Genius!"

"It's not?" I wondered, surprised and curiously relieved at the same time.

"Do you remember how many times you've talked yourself into 'should be grateful and happy' that you have this job?" he asked. "Do you remember how long you could fool yourself into feeling this happy, and how long this fragile happiness would last before the ghost of unhappiness started haunting you again?"

Overwhelmed by the disappointing truth that Shooter just revealed, I looked down and said nothing.

"Your job gives you the opportunity to collect many I-haves that satisfy many needs," Starry explained. "Your Needs chart will remind you of these satisfied needs and satisfying I-haves, such as money, benefits, securities, being around people, interacting, and socializing. It will remind you of the chance your job gives you to contribute and offer a satisfying I-have (a product or service) that is important to the company and the clients.

"At the same time, you feel that your job no longer satisfies a deeper need you have today, which is to do something that means more to you, something that feels more authentic and important, and that touches your heart and looks and feels more like you."

Starry's words grabbed my throat, squeezed it tightly, and slowly started to choke me. Tears welled up in my eyes and I thought, "Now *she's* the one doing the talking, and I'm still the one crying! How does she *do* that?"

"Remember," Starry continued, "many factors that belong to the life happening inside and around you, and to the story you came with and the one you came into, affect your life of Here and Now. They influence your relationship with yourself, as well as your relationship with your family, spouse, children, friends, and society around you."

"They also influence your relationship with your job or career," Shooter added.

"While the Human grows up," Starry elaborated, "they have to be the good kid. They listen to their parents and try to please them in order to get their love and approval. They study and graduate ... or maybe they do not. They drop out of school because they do not like it or because they are forced to drop out due to various reasons.

"Then they grow up, get married, raise their children, and have a successful career, money, possessions, and securities ... or maybe they do not.

"They make choices and decisions, accomplish things, fulfill responsibilities and duties, meet expectations, and reach goals, while trying to balance everything without going crazy or breaking down.

"They create a personality for themselves and try to perform their role correctly. They try to improve and prove themselves every day and everywhere. They try to do the right thing to please everyone."

"They try to do the right thing," Shooter echoed, "just like you do, Genius. You keep doing a job that pays the bills, knowing deeply inside that this job does not serve your story and does not fulfill you anymore."

"No, it does not fulfill me anymore," my choking voice confirmed, "and you *are* right, Shooter. This is not the first time I have felt this unhappiness. I have felt it many times before ... many times."

"Throughout your life," Starry continued, "you felt and identified different needs, set new goals to reach, collected satisfying I-haves, and called each one 'my I-have'—'my this,' 'my that,' 'mine,' 'I said,' 'I did,' 'I bought,' 'I got,' 'I achieved,' 'I won' ...

"Every time, you were convinced that this new goal and I-have would save you from your unhappiness and, many times, you were disappointed. Sometimes you quit before you collected the I-have and reached the goal. Other times, you did everything you could and should do, and still did not collect the I-have or reach the goal. Sometimes you worked hard, invested a lot, sacrificed and suffered, collected the I-have, reached the goal, and found happiness, only for this happiness to quickly slip away. At times you collected the I-have, reached the goal, but found that happiness was *still* not there.

"Time after time, you started to be convinced that you would spend the rest of your life chasing happiness. Dreams you once had did not come true. Your parents failed you. Your love relationship started to feel like a big mistake that you wished you never made. Your relationship partner did not turn out to be your fantasy of them. At different times, you felt that your family, friends, society, your career, your home, your body, or other I-haves failed you. Sometimes you even failed yourself.

"One deception after the other, you started to lose faith that you would ever be happy. You started to believe that, unlike other people, you do not deserve to be happy, and to be convinced that it is your fate never to be happy!"

"That's *exactly* how I feel about my job," I said. "At first, I was restless, stressed, and tense. I remember having headaches and cramps in my stomach, and sometimes my heart palpitated. Then for a while, I was angry, frustrated, and resentful. Not too long after that, I was sad and tired all the time. Now I'm just fed up. The whole time I'm there, I feel lost and bored. I feel untrue and unauthentic. I don't recognize myself anymore. I almost feel like I'm living inside someone else's body. I do things that don't look like me. I say fake things that don't sound like me. I feel like a fake, I smile fake smiles, and often I just don't smile at all!"

I stayed quiet for a moment, while my unhappiness grabbed my throat, chest, and stomach, and squeezed them tightly all over again.

"Sometimes I don't even realize where I am anymore," I continued. "*When* did I get here? *How* did I get here? What am I *doing* here? The motivation, enthusiasm, and passion I once had are completely gone. I feel like I don't care about anything or anyone anymore. Every day, I feel less and less alive. I feel numb, as if I'm just existing instead of living. I feel incomplete, unfulfilled, and unhappy. I often find myself wondering about the meaning of my life. What is the purpose of living—or should I say *existing*—like this?

"You know, Starry, living like this is starting to exhaust me. I just feel like giving up ... maybe my fate is never to be happy!"

I took a deep breath, trying to exhale unhappiness out of my body.

"I feel so empty ... a little more empty every single day. There's a hole inside of me that nothing I do at work fills and, every day, I feel more and more stuck inside this emptiness. I have no direction in my life. I have no idea what to do. I have no clue where to go from here, so I just stay where I am, stuck and empty. I *hate* this feeling. I wish it would go away so I could move on!"

"*Congratulations!*" Shooter shouted joyfully. "You're finally feeling stuck *and* empty!"

This crazy declaration stunned me.

"How can you *say* that, Shooter?"

"Cheer up, Genius! Emptiness is a wonderful place to be!"

"Are you mocking me? This is not funny!"

"Emptiness is actually the best place for you to be right now," Starry confirmed.

"It is?" I asked, confused and silently doubting Starry's wisdom about this subject.

"Do not be in a hurry to skip these empty times or move beyond them," she said. "You might miss out on something important."

"What are you *talking* about? Emptiness *hurts*, and I want to skip it as fast as I can!"

"Do you remember how your needs exist out of love for you?" she asked.

"Yes."

"Do you remember that a need is a blessing in disguise and that it has an important message for you?"

"Yes, I remember."

"In the same fashion, emptiness also comes to you out of love for you, even though it makes you feel unhappy. What it has to offer you is priceless.

"No matter how far you sometimes try to run away from it, emptiness still finds you. No matter how hard you fight it, it insists on keeping you company. It sometimes meets you at the finish line or the very top—that place you struggle to reach, thinking that ultimate fulfillment and happiness will finally be there. Instead, you find that emptiness and unhappiness are there waiting to welcome you. Emptiness sometimes comes after a disappointment, after you have fallen and lost one or more of your I-haves."

Shooter gave many examples of a lost I-have situation that leads a person to feel empty, such as a separation or divorce, or after saying a final goodbye to someone dear. He said that emptiness sometimes strikes after leaving a special place, losing a house or property, or losing a job, money, savings, possessions, securities, reputation, personality, identity, or hopes and dreams. It comes at a time of a disease, a burnout, an accident, a near-death experience, or at the time when a person gets older and fears that they are missing or have already missed out on life.

"Emptiness meets you after you have gotten angry and felt sad and numb," Starry continued, "and after you have finally accepted that it is your fate never to be happy. It haunts you after you have lost all direction and forgotten your life's purpose. It surrounds you when you feel that you have searched long enough, and you still have no clue about your reason for living.

"This is when emptiness settles in and forces you to look in the one remaining direction that has not disappointed you—the only direction where you have not yet looked, either because you forgot that it existed or because it scared you every time you saw it."

"What direction is that?"

"It is the direction that points straight to your true story, which lives deeply inside you, only to announce the close arrival of fulfillment and happiness.

"Emptiness might feel like a long, dark, cold, gloomy, spooky, and scary winter. In reality, emptiness is a blessed break where nature quietly rests before it blooms again through the fresh, splendid, and alive energy of spring.

"Emptiness takes you back to the heavenly space and divine silence that exist inside of you, and allows you to clearly see, hear, and understand what your true story is still trying to show and tell you, and let you know. Emptiness allows your true story to guide you straight to fulfillment and happiness."

✦

"My *true story?*"

"Your true story lives deeply inside you. It has never left you and will never leave. It stays loyal, like your childhood best friend. Even if you two have not spoken in a long time, you never forget about each other. It waits and finds an opportunity to speak— maybe when you feel stuck and empty. It calls you when it feels you have missed it. It speaks when it feels you have neglected it long enough. It talks to you when you feel your life is slipping away and passing you by, and you are getting older and looking less like yourself ... a little less every day.

"Your true story has been talking to you for a long time, ever since you were born—and maybe even before. Back then, its voice used to be very clear. You listened to it and knew exactly what it was telling you. You understood it well during the first few years of your life. It told you precisely what would serve and fulfill you. It told you exactly where happiness is.

"Then, slowly, it started getting lost inside the crowded and distracting I-haves, which you chased and collected—or tried to collect. Those I-haves molded your life, covered your true story, blurred its blueprint, distorted its voice, and made you drift away from your true self.

"Throughout your life, your true story talks to you. At times, it softly whispers and, at other times, it loudly screams. You often repeat what it shows and tells you, but you just forget to pay attention when you do.

"Your true story never gives up on you. No matter how long you ignore it, it is never resentful and never holds a grudge. No matter how stubborn you are, it insists on leading you to fulfillment and happiness."

"What does my true story sound like?"

"Throughout your life, your true story talks to you through signs and signals. Do you remember those times when you saw, heard, smelled, tasted, or touched and felt something that, for a brief moment, transported you to a familiar and peaceful place where you felt loved, safe, and happy?"

"Yes, I have. *Many* times!"

"Those times are the echoes of your true story's voice. Those echoes sounded so familiar that they scared you. You even wondered if you wanted to investigate them further because you thought, 'What if finding out more means giving up and losing my I-haves so I can go where this voice is telling me to go? Where will it lead and take me? At which scary or painful place would I end up?' Instead, you decided to ignore the voice and forget about it.

"The place where this voice tells you to go is where the rest of your true story is ... still waiting to be told.

"Your true story loves you. It quietly lives deeply inside you and patiently waits, no matter how old you get. It waits for the noise around and inside you to quiet down so you are able to hear it. It waits until you are ready to welcome it and listen to it. Somewhere inside this loud silence, it speaks again. From the depth of the emptiness where you feel that you are stuck, it now sounds clearer because now, it knows you can hear it ... it knows you are listening."

"... and now it will never shut up again!" Shooter yelled as he zoomed by.

"Like Shooter said," Starry laughed, "your true story 'will never shut up again.' It will help you reconnect with your forgotten passions and lost dreams, which once made you feel alive. It will remind you of your strengths, gifts, and talents. It will remind you of what you really look, sound, and feel like, of what really looks, sounds, and feels like you, and of what helps and makes you stay true to yourself. It will remind you that you are a unique Human Being with a unique story!"

"Will my true story tell me what the purpose of my life is? Will it tell me in which direction to look and which one to take? Will it tell me where to find happiness? Will it identify my satisfying I-have options and tell me which option to choose? Will it unstick me from this emptiness so I can move forward?"

"The ultimate purpose of your life is for you to be happy Here and Now, being exactly where you are, and doing exactly what you are doing— just like a star in a million!

"Your true story will tell you in which direction to look: the direction that points towards 'you.'

"It will tell you which direction to take: the direction that leads and brings you back to yourself.

"It will tell you where to find happiness: inside your true self.

"It will highlight your personal need, which is now calling you, and put the spotlight on your satisfying I-have unique option.

"Once satisfied, this need—whether it is a physical, mental, or emotional need to receive or give—will surely lead you to happiness."

✪

"I'm starting to be really curious about how my true story will talk to me."

"Your true story uses a language that it speaks beyond all Human words. It will talk to you through an emotion. For a brief moment, this emotion will get your undivided attention and touch you deeply. It will feel familiar, almost like you two have met before and you once cared for each other."

"Where can I look for this emotion? Where can I find it?"

"You do not find the emotion," Starry replied. "The emotion finds you. All you have to do is become aware of its presence and feel it. It could come to you through an image, a sound, a scent, a flavor, or someone or something you touch and feel."

Assisting Starry, Shooter showered me with endless examples. He described images, such as someone's face, smile, or gesture, or the way they walk or carry themselves. The images could be a picture from a magazine or an album, a color, a painting, a sculpture, a rock, or a jewel. They could be a street, a house, a building, a train track, a small town, or a big city. They could be a lake, a river, a beach, a desert, a mountain, a tree, a flower, or an animal. They could also be a television ad, a program, a movie scene, an event, a sentence, an article, or a book.

He described sounds, such as a word, a conversation, a story, a song, or a melody. The sounds could be someone's voice, a whisper, or a soft or loud noise. They could be background sounds, like a door slamming, a car horn honking, an airplane roaring, or a bell ringing in the distance. They could be the wind blowing, tree leaves rustling, water running, or waves slamming the shore. They could be kids playing, giggling, laughing, screaming, or crying. These sounds could be a dog barking, bees humming, birds singing, or cicadas celebrating.

He described scents, such as the scent of a flower, perfume, soap, or cream. It could be the scent of falling rain, freshly cut grass, wood burning in a fireplace, the countryside, or the ocean. It could be morning coffee, a homemade meal, cookies baking, old furniture, or hidden clothes.

He described flavors, such as baby food, a tasty fruit, a zesty meal, or a fresh drink.

He described someone or something that touches me or that I touch and feel, such as the softness of someone's hand, the tightness of their hug, the soft breeze, the strong wind, the heat of the sun, the wetness of the rain, or the cold snow.

"Whenever your true story talks to you and wherever it wants to take you," continued Starry, "go along with it. Stay with it and do not run away from it anymore. Discover what it wants to show and tell you. Watch and see it, and hear and listen well. Whenever possible, take note of what you see and hear.

"The Human brain is able to remember your true story's message for the next few seconds after your story has talked to you; then, it forgets. Try to immediately note this message and, whenever possible, take a picture of what your true story has just shown you.

"Do not worry if you cannot note the message or take the picture. An important message will insist on coming back. It will never leave you alone and will never give up on you. It will always come back. *Always!*"

⭐

"I'm not sure if *my* true story ever talks to me. I don't remember seeing or hearing any messages."

"You can take the monkey out of the jungle, Genius, but you can never take the jungle out of the monkey. Your true story talks to you all the time!"

"No it *doesn't*, Shooter! If it talked to me, I wouldn't feel so empty and stuck."

"Every Human's true story talks to them," he said, "including yours. It's just that you haven't seen or heard it in such a long time that you have forgotten what it looks and sounds like. You have forgotten the language that your true story speaks and which you used to understand. That's why you don't recognize it when it talks to you today. I guarantee it. I can prove it to you."

Still doubting Shooter's claim, I decided to take him up on his challenge.

"*Really?* Well, then, why don't you? Go ahead! *Prove* it to me!"

"Up here! *Look up here!*" he shouted.

I looked up. One more time, the sky lit up, and the million stars got busy painting something new. It was breathtaking!

⭐ ⭐ ⭐

"Look closely. Do you see anything familiar? Do you recognize anything at all?"

"Familiar? In the *sky*?"

I stared a little longer.

"Oh, my God, Shooter! Is that *me* up there? I can't *believe* what I'm seeing!"

I stared some more, completely stunned.

"That *is* me. This is amazing!"

"You were a cute kid, Genius," he said playfully.

"I was, wasn't I?" I proudly agreed.

"You are going to reunite with your true story for a little while," announced Starry, "just like you reunite with your childhood best friend whom you have not seen in a long time.

"You will go back to the story you came with, the one that looks like you and which talked to you throughout the years of your life—and still does today, no matter how many distracting I-haves try to cover it.

"You will go back to the story you came into. You will go back to each one of your life stages, which you will divide into periods of one, two, or three years at a time.

"For each period, you will go back and try to remember the person or people. You will look into their eyes, see their faces and bodies, and notice the way they moved or just sat there. You will hear their voices when they spoke or sang, and when they laughed or cried. You will smell their skin, hair, and clothes. You will feel their touch.

"You will go back and remember the event as well as the place itself where this event happened. You will clearly see the images and hear each sound that lived there. You will smell each scent that filled the air. You will remember every flavor that you tasted. You will feel what you touched and what touched you.

"You will clearly remember your thoughts at that point in time. You will remember the emotions you felt while you were seeing, hearing, smelling, tasting, and touching. Those emotions will become alive again.

"This story which you lived, witnessed, or heard, and which left an impression on you and etched its name in your mind and heart, will become alive again.

"Look up here and clearly remember your skills, talents, gifts, abilities, and strengths with which you were blessed. Remember your dreams, visions, wishes, and projects. Remember your preferences and hobbies and your favorite games and activities. Remember your passions that made you feel alive. Remember your victories as well as your losses. Remember what gave you strong sensations of joy and pleasure. Remember the sources of your fears, regrets, and deepest pain.

"Remember someone or something that made you dream and touched you deeply. Remember someone you admired and who influenced your story, one who looked like you, or one whom you wanted wanted to look like.

"For each period of your life, remember the stories that still stand out today and feel the emotions that are still alive. It does not matter whether you have or have not accepted, forgiven, or resolved these stories. Remember the stories and feel the emotions."

"I'll try," I agreed. "Where do I start?"

"Start at the beginning ... you always do! Let the memories of each period of your life reveal themselves to you, and welcome the emotions they bring with them, without analyzing or judging them."

"It's show time!" announced Shooter. "Get comfortable, sit back, relax, and watch."

I lay on the swing and contemplated in silence.

There were so many stories and emotions, ever since I was a little kid, until tonight. Curiously, though, some stories repeated and some were clearer than others were.

I lay there and continued to watch.

✪ ✪ ✪

I'm not sure how long this "show" lasted. After the stars left the stage, I quietly stared at the deep—and once again silent—sky. I closed my eyes and rested.

"Hey, Genius, are you okay? Stop scaring me every time you look up here!"

"That was *unbelievable*, Shooter. That was *my* life! *My* story!"

"... and so much more," added Starry. "Inside your story, you will find many answers to your 5W2H-O&D questions. Whenever you need to, you can celebrate a ceremony and watch your story parade in front of you.

"Just like tonight, you will choose a convenient place and time. You will comfortably sit and surround yourself with silence, or let soft music play in the background—maybe even a nostalgic tune that will awaken the memories and emotions. You can light a candle for the mood and let a familiar scent invade the place. It helps to take out a special object that might inspire you.

"Then, select a happy music record and get it ready to play once this ceremony is over. You want to visit your story and be there for a while, watch and see it, and hear and listen to it—maybe cry, if you feel like it—but you do not want to stay trapped in it. Set a time for your ceremony to start, and then set an alarm for 30 or 60 minutes later when this ceremony will end.

"Use your paper and blue pen to create a chart and take notes.

"On top of the page, write down the name of this ceremony— The True Story Shows and Tells.

"Underneath, write down your full name and date of birth.

"Divide the page into two sections. On the left side, separate your life stages into periods of one, two, or three years. On the right side, and for each period, write down the memories that stand out and the emotions that are still alive today.

"Close your eyes.

"Take three deep breaths.

"Invite the noise around and inside you to leave.

"Let yourself go and travel deeply into your story.

"Make space for this story ... make room for it.

"Let the people, places, and events show and tell you.

"Watch, listen, and remember without analyzing or judging, and take notes.

"When this ceremony and the visit with your story are over, and when the alarm goes off, play the happy music record you selected and *come back to Here and Now.*

"Get up. If you have cried, wipe your tears. Shake your hands to lighten and release the possibly heavy energy of this ceremony. Move your body, stretch a little, and go on with your day.

"You may need to celebrate this ceremony a few times before you are able to fill out the chart. Whenever possible, it helps to ask someone you trust to accompany you while you visit your story and create this chart. It could be someone who knew you well during your childhood and still remembers, such as a caregiver, parent, relative, neighbor, family friend, or teacher. It could also be a therapist or a mentor.

"Do not forget to keep the chart in your Precious Box where you can easily refer to it when you need its help."

"How will this chart help me?"

"Your true story acts like a matrix for many answers to your *5W2H-O&D* questions, and many satisfying I-have options. With your red pen, circle those answers and options on the chart. Your true story holds many messages for you. These messages are inside your past. Others are inside your present."

"When will the messages of my present find me? When will they come to me?"

"They will find you when they have an opportunity to get your attention. They may come as a dream while you sleep, or as a thought, an idea, a daydream, an imagination, a fantasy, a vision, an interest, or a desire while you are awake.

"They sometimes come from a deep and mysterious place inside you, which you refer to as your sixth sense, gut feeling, impression, inspiration, intuition, calling, or revelation.

"They could show up during a conversation or meeting that you are having, or a course you are taking. They might come as an occasion, an event, an opportunity, a job offer, an invitation, a visit, or an encounter.

"Messages could come in the midst of what feels like an unhappy time that belongs to your own or to someone else's story, one you are witnessing or hearing, even when it is then more difficult for you to see or hear these messages. They could come at a time of an unmet need, a time of emptiness, an incident, a difficulty, a resistance, an obstacle, a challenge, a mistake, a problem, an accident, a disease, a loss, a burnout, a breakup, or a separation from a loved one.

"When the messages come, you might recognize them because you have seen and heard them many times before; however, some might be visiting you for the first time. Some messages may be unique, sudden, unexpected, or unusual. They can happen at a weird place and time, and in a weird way.

"Take note of the messages as soon as they appear, and as soon as you feel that they have shown or told you something important.

"Messages are best seen and heard where silence is loudest, after the noise outside and inside you has quieted down, such as during breaks, times of retreat, meditation, or prayer. They often look and sound clearer very early in the morning, or after you have gone to bed at night."

Shooter said that messages are also inspired to come to me when I'm surrounded with nature, sitting in the park, or hiking in the countryside or mountains. They could come to me when I'm close to water, such as near a fountain, a waterfall, a river, a lake, or an ocean. They could also come to me when I'm in my backyard, under the moon and the bright sky, and while talking to a star.

"Will these messages *unstick* me from my emptiness so I can move forward?"

"Do not be in a hurry!" Starry reminded me. "Give emptiness space and time. Let your true story talk to you wherever and whenever it wants. Let it show and tell you for as long as it needs.

You have ignored it for too long; it has pulled itself back deeply inside of you. Give it a chance to resurface. Trust it. Do not give up on it, just like it does not give up on you.

"Have faith that the emotions, the signs and signals, and the answers and messages will come to you. When they do, feel, watch, and listen, but be careful not to force them to show or tell you. Do not chase them for they might mislead you.

"Allow your life to flow and just flow with it. Enjoy your time of emptiness, this necessary break and blessed stop area that life created especially for you, out of love for you, so you temporarily stop, rest, and recharge, just like nature patiently rests and silently recharges during winter."

"While I'm patiently resting and silently recharging, what else can I do to better understand these messages?"

"I suggest you go see a fortune teller like you usually do, Genius!"

"Make a note of what you have no more passion for," Starry said, "and what no longer looks or feels like you or serves you, whether the situation concerns your personal life, your love life, your family life, your social life, or your health, career, hobbies, or lifestyle.

"Go back to your Needs chart, read it again, and ask yourself, 'Which one of my needs keeps coming back? Which one did I neglect and leave behind?'

"Through your happy or unhappy feeling, try to identify which unmet need is calling you. If this need is not listed—whether it is one to receive or to give—add it to the chart.

"Fill out The True Story Shows and Tells chart, and circle the memories and the emotions that stand out.

"Write down the signs, signals, answers, and messages. Write down your new or recurrent dreams, thoughts, ideas, and events that touch you. Collect the pictures that talk to you. Keep the articles that get your attention.

"Inside the information you have gathered, you will find at least one I-have that could satisfy this neglected need and serve your story. Use this need and this I-have as pieces of a puzzle. Collect the pieces, and then put them together so you can get a full and clear picture. Do not forget to ask someone whom you trust to help you build this puzzle.

"Today, you are here. Today, this is your unmet need and this is the I-have that would satisfy it. Collecting this I-have becomes your new goal.

"With the help of 5W2H-O&D, you will answer *What?*, *Why?*, *Where?*, *When?*, *Who?*, *How?*, *How much?*, and *Options?* You will choose only one option, answer *D*, take action, collect the I-have, and reach your goal.

"Wherever you are, start Here and start Now ... one step at a time.

"Today, you are thankful for the I-have that you feel no longer serves you. You are grateful for what it has offered you until now. Today, you release it. You make room for the new I-have that will satisfy your new need, and allow you to feel happy."

Shooter offered a list of questions to ask myself out loud:

- Am I feeling someone else's need or my own?

- Am I watching and listening to someone else's story or my true story?

- Is this situation convenient for me? Does it serve my true story? Does it make me happy and put a smile on my face?
- What do I not want to do or be anymore?
- What does not serve me anymore?
- What price do I not want to pay anymore?
- What is something that I cannot imagine myself doing or being anymore?
- What is something that I cannot imagine myself not already doing or being?
- Do I still want to do what I do not want to do anymore?
- Do I still want to be whom, what, or where I no longer want to be?
- What is something that I know I will one day regret not having done or been?

Once the questions were answered, Shooter invited me to make these conclusions and repeat them out loud:

- Today, I say *enough*!
- Today, I say enough to what no longer serves my story and me.
- Today, I see what my true story shows me, listen to what it tells me, and try to understand its messages.
- Today, I live the life I want to live—and not the life I *have* to live.
- Today, I look forward to waking up, getting out of bed, and starting my day.
- Today, I stay true to my dreams and passions.

- Today, I stay true to my story.

✦

Even though I trusted Starry's wisdom and Shooter's instructions by now, I still found myself debating in my head, "Easier said than done!"

"There will come a time when your emptiness has lasted long enough," Starry announced, "when you have rested long enough, and when your need starts expressing itself clearly. The time for spring *will* come. When it does, your needs and I-haves will reorganize themselves to gracefully make room for the new, unmet need that is now calling you. Your priority list will mysteriously rearrange itself. It always does!"

Shooter said that, all of a sudden, a person is ready to give up a relationship with someone or something—whether partially or totally, and whether temporarily or permanently—so they can start a new one.

They are ready to let go of a love relationship so they can create a new one with themselves and a new partner.

They are ready to give up their professional success, plans, and ambitions so they can start a family.

They are ready to cut down their work hours—or maybe even quit their current job—so they can take that class, assist, or volunteer, or even expand a hobby that, once mastered, could possibly become their new career.

They find the courage to start that business they have been planning for a while.

They are ready to start a new project or help with a cause that means a great deal to them.

They are ready to reorganize their budget or work extra hours so they can afford to buy the new car they want or go on that trip, which they have been putting off for many years.

They now dare to leave their home, and move to a new place they have been dreaming about for a long time.

They find the courage to let go of some of their old I-haves in order to collect a new I-have that satisfies a need closer to their heart.

"Your emptiness is a blank page where your true story is waiting to be written," Starry continued.

"Write that first letter," Shooter added. "Write that first word. Take that first step!"

"Taking the first step is the hardest part for me," I complained.

"By watching your true story and listening to it," Starry explained, "you have already taken the first step. After that, there is nowhere else to go but to the next.

"Take that first step and stay with it. The first step always leads you to the next one, and so on, until you reach your destination, and until you make that forgotten dream, which you put on hold and ignored for so long, come true ... one step at a time!"

"By the way, Genius, rest assured that, when it's time for you to take that first step, ready or not, life will take charge. It will take care of your first step, your second, and every step along the way.

"Talk to that person *now!* Make that phone call, send that e-mail, set up that appointment, attend that meeting, visit that place, take that course, reorganize your budget, get that loan ..."

Shooter had more words for me to repeat out loud:

- Today, I say *enough!*
- Today, I stop complaining about someone or dwelling on something.
- Today, I get up and I do something about it.
- Today, I make a decision, choose one option, and set a date to take action.
- Today, I take the first step on the path that leads me back to my true story.

"Taking a step is scary because it always ends up costing me at least one I-have out of my source of love, safety, and happiness."

"You will always have love, safety, and happiness!" Starry reassured me. "Look around you. Every I-have you once collected exists Here and Now because one day, despite your fear of losing love, safety, and happiness, you had the courage to take that first step, which eventually turned your need—thought, idea, or dream—into an action plan and project, and helped you collect the satisfying I-have.

"This happened because your new, unmet need had become a priority, sometimes even a passion. This priority and passion gave you courage, and your courage became bigger than your fear to lose any I-have or to step outside your comfort zone to which you were accustomed.

"Every Human has their own stories of achievements, successes, and I-haves they once collected to satisfy their needs that had, at one point, become a priority in their life ... and so do you.

"Until you identify your unmet need that is calling you, and until you collect the I-have that satisfies it, keep enjoying this break that emptiness is offering you, and this stop area necessary for you to rest, recharge, re-energize, and get ready for your next step.

"Be patient, enjoy winter, and have faith that spring will be back. Spring *always* comes back. It is the cycle of nature. It is also the natural cycle of your story."

"It's the natural cycle of *every* Human Being's story," added Shooter.

"Shooter, it is almost morning," Starry said. "We have to go soon."

"You're leaving *already*?" I asked. "You must be tired. I'm tired, too. My Human Being's need to sleep has now become a priority," I concluded, amused, as I yawned and stretched my arms.

"Every Human needs sleep. The Being never does, Genius!"

"What did you say?"

"It's your *Human* that needs sleep," Shooter repeated. "The *Being* does not."

"I don't understand!"

"Do you remember your Needs chart?" Starry asked.

"Yes, you've been talking to me about it for two nights: my needs, my I-haves, my story, the emptiness, the messages ... of course, I remember."

"Do you remember the first question you asked last night before we started our conversation?"

"I was wondering about who I was, and you said that I was a great Human Being. I thought that's what you've been explaining to me this whole time. Isn't it?"

"Until now, Starry has mostly been talking about your Human," Shooter answered.

"You mean there's *more*?"

"There is also the Being," he said.

"Now I'm *really* confused!"

"You are the Human and you are the Being," Starry declared.

At that point, I started to feel exasperated.

"I thought that I was a unique Human Being with a unique story, and physical, mental, and emotional needs to receive and give. I thought that I had a true story that looks like me and from which I was distracted. I was finally starting to understand that my life's purpose was to feel and identify my unmet needs, and then collect the I-haves that would satisfy them. Are you now saying that it's *not*? Taking the first step and fulfilling that purpose was finally going to unstick me from my emptiness and lead me to happiness. Are you now saying that it *won't*?"

I felt worried and desperate, and hoped that Starry would confirm that what I just said was true and reassure me that I have finally found the answers that would save me from my ongoing deceptions, emptiness, and endless unhappiness.

"I don't understand. Just a minute ago, I was sure that I was so close to finding happiness. I was sure that I finally discovered the winning recipe."

I took a long, deep breath of disappointment, confusion, and frustration.

"I *knew* it! I'll *never* be happy. What more *is* there? What more can I *do*? What more do I have to do to be *happy*?"

"The Human needs many satisfying I-haves to be happy," Starry said, "while the Being only needs to be: I-am.

"The Human has a unique story with endless personal needs and I-haves, while the Being is one—universal and common to all Humans. The Being is beyond all stories, all needs, and all I-haves.

"The Human life is temporary and lasts for the time when the Human body lives on Earth. The Being is eternal, existed before the Human life on Earth began, and will exist way after the Human life has ended.

"The Human has a name and a physical shape. The Human sees, hears, breathes, smells, tastes, thinks, feels, needs, speaks, laughs, cries, and acts. The Human grows old and changes all the time. The Human story is relative and affected by the life happening inside and around the Human, and depends on many needs and I-haves.

"The Being has no name, shape, body, mind, or emotions, and has no age and never changes. The Being is not relative or affected by the life happening inside or around the Human, and does not depend on any needs or I-haves.

"The satisfaction that the Human life gives is temporary. It is never good enough, never perfect, and never gives complete fulfillment or lasting happiness. The satisfaction that the Being gives is permanent. It is the ultimate perfection. The Being gives complete fulfillment and true happiness.

"The Human life sometimes gets crowded, loud, and noisy. The Being is pure and constantly remains calm, serene, peaceful, and still.

"The Human has a shallow, fragile, and temporary connection with needs and I-haves. The Being has a deep, solid, and eternal connection with God."

✫

"So where can I find the Being?"
"You find the Being wherever you are. Just close your eyes and look deeply inside yourself. Close them so you no longer see your Human life happening around you—your story, your name, your age, your body, other people, creatures, things, needs, or I-haves. Close them so you no longer see your Human life happening inside you—your thoughts, emotions and feelings, dreams, pleasures, hopes, deceptions, fears, or pains. Close them and turn them towards yourself. *There* is where the Being resides.

"You find the Being inside of you and inside every Human—and every creature—when you look deeply into them. The Being is the pure 'you,' sometimes called soul, spirit, or essence.

"The Being is how little children see you, and how God sees you—naked from all needs and I-haves."

✫

"What purpose does the Being have?"
"The only purpose the Being has is to give you complete fulfillment and true happiness."
"Then the Being is more important than my Human."
"Both your Human and the Being are equally important. They work together, and complete and exist through each other during your life on Earth.

"Your Human shelters and gives the Being the physical, mental, and emotional tools to express Itself through what your Human sees, hears, smells, tastes, and touches and feels. Your Human helps the Being manifest Itself, shine, and glow through your Human words, gestures, and actions.

"Your Human allows the Being inside you to have a relationship and interconnect with the Being inside every Human."

✦

"How does my Human exist through the Being?"

"The Being preciously takes care of your Human," Starry said. "The Being gives you complete fulfillment and true happiness."

"Guess what else?" Shooter added. "The Being unsticks you from your emptiness!"

My eyes opened wide and my breath was taken away. I had been waiting for these magic words all night!

"Did you say 'unstick me from my emptiness'? How? Tell me! *How?*"

"I thought you'd never ask, Genius!"

"The Being helps you discover the blessings in disguise," Starry revealed, "learn the language spoken beyond all Human words, and understand the messages.

"The Being keeps you in constant connection with the life happening inside and around you Here and Now.

"The Being helps you become aware that Here and Now is an opportunity for you to grow and glow a little more every day!"

"Is that when I will be completely fulfilled and truly happy?" I asked excitedly.

Without waiting for an answer, I continued.

"Then tell me: How do I *do* that? How do I discover the blessings in disguise? How do I learn the language spoken beyond all Human words? How do I understand the messages? How do I stay in constant connection with the life happening inside and around me Here and Now? How do I grow and glow a little more every day? *Tell* me!"

Starry said nothing. Shooter made no comment either.

I looked up.

Morning had come and, once again, Starry and Shooter were gone.

CHAPTER THREE

The Thought

I snuck into bed even though I knew that Dunia would be waking up soon.

Throughout the day, my body felt energized, despite the fact that I had not slept a wink all night. I felt the joy of someone who had just discovered a treasure ... someone who had won something big. I was excited and very happy!

The day seemed as if it would never end. Night finally came and, one more time, I tucked Dunia in bed, went outside, sat on the swing, and waited for Starry to come to the rendezvous.

I waited.

I waited some more.

"Did she *forget*?" I wondered, and then reassured myself. "She's probably just late. She'll be here soon, I'm sure."

Still, no Starry.

"Maybe I said something to upset her. Maybe she doesn't think I'm smart enough to understand what she's been telling me. Maybe she decided to move on and talk to someone else who's more worthy of her time. Maybe there's something wrong with her or Shooter. Maybe she just has nothing more to say, and I'm supposed to figure out the rest on my own. How am I going to do that? I *can't* do that! I'll *never* be able to figure out the rest alone!"

I lay down on the swing and comforted myself.

"It's late, but she'll be here soon."

Soon never came that night.

"Wake up!" whispered the morning breeze.

"It's a brand new day!" chirped the birds' melodies. In a language spoken beyond all Human words, crazy notes from excited birds meant that they were happy, simply because it was a brand new day.

The sun peeked above the horizon, its warmth and shy colors welcoming the new day.

"I can't believe I slept out here all night!" I thought.

I got up from the swing and went in the house. I had to get myself ready, get Dunia ready, drop her off at my parents' house, and meet Susan to work on our project of establishing a small community center. In Needs chart terms, I guess we were trying to satisfy our "emotional need to contribute and give back."

I took a shower, dried and fixed my hair, and put on my makeup—all *five* of my creams, my eyeliner, and my lipstick. I opened the closet door, and picked out my light blue shirt (the one with three daisies across the left shoulder) and my dark blue skirt (the one that barely hides my knees).

I got dressed, stood in front of the mirror, and tucked my shirt inside my skirt.

"No, no, *no!*" I thought. "Are you *crazy?* Look at how your stomach is sticking out! This looks *ugly!* Just leave the shirt out!"

I pulled my shirt back out and thought of another idea.

"Maybe I'll put on the nice belt I bought last week."

I got the belt, put it around my waist, and resumed my thoughts.

"You look so *short* with the belt and skirt like that. Why are you wearing *this* skirt? Isn't it kind of short for *your* age?"

I looked at myself again.

"Wait a minute! What's that on your *legs?*"

I moved closer to the mirror ... closer ... I turned to the left and then to the right.

"Are these *veins?* Oh, my God! They *are!* I can't *believe* this! Where did all these veins come from? Since when do I have so *many?*"

I turned around, trying to see the backs of my legs.

"You can see these from a mile away! Your legs look *horrible!* These veins look like you have a map tattooed back there. You need to get these taken care of ... and what shoes are you going to wear? The black sandals with the heels? No, not *those!* Don't you remember how your knee was killing you after you wore them last week?"

I sighed, discouraged and frustrated, and continued to think.

"I'm so stupid and lazy! Why do I let myself *go* like this? I'm so out of shape. I need to lose weight. I need to go back to the gym. My legs look horrible ... *I* look horrible!"

✪

"Horrible. *I look horrible!*" I said out loud.

"You don't look horrible, Mommy. You just look like you."

I stood there, caught by surprise, and said nothing.

"You look like *you*," repeated Dunia with her tiny voice.

For a frozen moment, I swear that I could hear Starry's words: "The Being is how little children see you and how God sees you."

"Mommy, is your head talking to you again?" she asked.

I turned around.

Dunia was standing at my bedroom door, staring at me with confused eyes. Her hair was wild, her pajamas were messy, and she was barefoot, proving that she just woke up.

"Good morning, baby!"

I put on a big smile and opened my arms to greet her. She ran to me and gave me the biggest, tightest hug in the world. I wondered if I was speaking out loud. I wondered how long she had been standing there and how much she had heard.

"Did you wake up a long time ago?" I cautiously asked.

"Nope!" she answered, and then comforted me with another big hug and innocently said, "Who cares if you look horrible, Mommy? I love you anyways."

"I love you, too, baby! I was talking about the skirt. The *skirt* looks horrible. I need to buy a new one."

She stared at me for a few seconds and then, out of nowhere, asked, "Can I have some chocolate milk?"

"Ah, well," I thought, relieved, "I guess Dunia doesn't really care about my skirt story after all, and she doesn't think I look horrible either. All I need is for *my* daughter to say that I look horrible!"

✪

"You were doing a fine job shooting yourself down on your own. You don't really need Dunia's help."

"Shooter? Is that you?"

"Yep, it's me, the 'Shooter.' I shoot up and across, but I never shoot down because you don't really need anybody's help to do *that*, Genius."

"Be nice, Shooter!" warned Starry.

"If I'm nice, can I also have some chocolate milk?" he joked.

I was both surprised and excited to hear Starry's and Shooter's voice again.

"Wow! You can see and hear *everything*? Night *and* day?" I asked.

"You cannot be left alone, Genius. Look at what happens when you are. That's why I need my chocolate milk. I need all the energy I can get to keep up with you!"

I laughed. I was happy that they were both here, like the joy of reuniting with dear friends.

"By the way, I waited for you last night. Where *were* you?" I teased. "I am now getting ready to meet my friend Susan for a few hours. Will you still be here when I come back? Will you wait for me? If not, I can cancel my appointment and stay here so we can talk some more."

"Go ahead with your appointment and your day. We will talk along the way."

I wasn't exactly sure what Starry meant, but I finished getting ready and helped Dunia get dressed. We sat at the kitchen table and had breakfast, including her chocolate milk.

I wondered if Shooter had his!

✬

We left the house. I put Dunia in the back seat of the car and we were on our way. I was meeting Susan at her place, which was about half an hour away, but I had to drive Dunia to my parents' house first. My mom was then going to take her to Aunt Maryam's house to spend the day. I hadn't seen my aunt in almost three months, ever since she got mad at me for not trying to get her daughter a job at the company where I work.

"Aunt Maryam is crazy," I thought as I drove. "As far as I'm concerned, her daughter is irresponsible. In fact, *she* is also crazy. Lucky for me, her house has a pool and, as long as Dunia has fun there, I'll humor her. In reality, I don't care if I don't talk to her for a whole year! I wouldn't want to see her daughter's face every day anyway.

"Hey," I continued, lost in my own head, "maybe I have time to swing by the bank and see what's happening with the credit they owe me. Why do banks hire incompetent people anyway? This girl has screwed up my statement *three* times already! Why is she still *there*? She's a real idiot, but I have to admit that she's *gorgeous*. I wonder if Paul is having an affair with her. I'll bet he is. I mean, why not? I don't think he'll be married for a long time anyway, because Carol ..."

"Are we going straight to Grandma's?"

Dunia's question interrupted my thoughts.

"Yes, we are. Grandma is taking you to Aunt Maryam's house. Cousins Lisa and John will be there. I brought your bathing suit, so you can swim if you want."

"*Yeah!*" she cheered. "Can I sleep over if Lisa and John are sleeping there, too?"

"We'll have to ask Grandma and Aunt Maryam if it's okay with them."

"Mommy, can you play the 'raindrops' song you played for me yesterday?"

"Of course I can, sweetheart."

I selected the requested song. As the "raindrops" song played, I looked at Dunia through the rearview mirror. Her beautiful and satisfied smile lit up her face.

"An emotional need to listen to a pretty song is identified and expressed," I silently thought. "A satisfying I-have is collected and the need is satisfied. Mission accomplished! We move on, from one need to the next ..."

My thoughts continued.

"Anyway, Carol is not ..."

"Carol, the mistress?" asked Shooter.

"Carol is Paul's wife. Paul is the branch director. *Sharon* is the girl he's having the affair with. She doesn't really deserve him."

"*Sharon?*" he asked, confused.

"No, *Carol*! I mean she's nice and everything, but ..."

"Who's telling you all this?" he interrupted.

"*Everyone* knows!"

"I mean, who's talking to you?"

"What do you mean, Shooter?"

"*Who* is talking to you?"

"Right *now*?"

"Yes. Who's talking to you *now*?"

I hesitated for a moment and then answered, "Dunia! Dunia was just talking to me."

"Besides Dunia, who was talking to you for the past few minutes, before she asked and after you played her song? Who's been talking to you since this morning, when you were getting dressed in front of your bedroom mirror? Who was talking to you last night when you were waiting for Starry and me?"

"I don't understand your question."

"Who was telling you the stories about Carol, the branch director's wife, and Sharon, the gorgeous idiot he's having the affair with? Who was telling you about your crazy Aunt Maryam and her crazy daughter? Who was telling you about how stupid, out of shape, and horrible you look? Who was telling you that Starry doesn't think you're smart enough or worthy of her time?"

I searched in my head.

"Nobody ... nobody really. I was just thinking to myself."

"So Dunia was right! Your head *was* talking to you."

"I never really thought of it this way, but I guess you can say that. My head was talking to me," I confirmed, laughing.

"You know that your head often does that, Genius. Not only does it talk to you, but you sometimes talk back to it."

I said nothing.

"... and out *loud*! Your head never shuts up with endless conversations ... monologues ... dialogues. Hey, Genius, have you ever noticed what language your head speaks when it talks to you?"

"No, not really," I answered. "I never really paid attention. What language *does* my head speak?"

"Your head, or rather the thought," explained Starry, "uses any language that your Human can speak or understand, and sometimes it uses no words at all. Its voice has no real tone and sounds like nothing in particular. It talks to you through words and full sentences that only *you* can hear, no matter how softly it whispers or how loudly it screams. It shows you images and scenes—even full movies—that you, and only *you*, can see.

"Whenever it feels like it, the thought ..."

"*Old Teller*," Shooter interrupted.

"Who?" I asked.

"Old Teller," he repeated. "It's the storyteller that lives inside your head."

"The thought," Starry continued, "or Old Teller, invites itself to speak and tell you stories."

"*O'stories*," added Shooter. "Old Teller's story—the story or the scene itself, the words and the images—is called an O'story."

"Old Teller presents its monologue," Starry explained. "It could talk for hours and hours, almost nonstop. It talks *to* you and addresses you as 'you,' such as 'Are *you* crazy ... *your* stomach ... *you* look short ... *your* age ... *you* can ... *your* legs ... *you* have ... *you* need ... *you* remember ... *your* knee.'

"Sometimes it pretends to *be* you and speaks on your behalf, such as '*I'm* smart ... *I'm* supposed to ... *I'll* never ... *I'm* so stupid and lazy ... *I* let *myself* ... *I'm* so out of shape ... *I* need ... *my* legs ... *I* look.'"

"Old Teller could even trick you into having complete conversations with it, Genius!"

"At times," Starry continued, "Old Teller puts on its Happy face and tells you a happy O'story. At other times, it puts on its Unhappy face and tells you an unhappy O'story.

"Old Teller puts on an Unhappy Past face, such as its I-am-the-Victim face, asks why your happy past is gone and lost, and wishes it would come back. It reminds you of your sad past and asks why this sad past happened and how it could have happened to you. It wants you to feel sorry for yourself, and wants everyone else to feel sorry for you. It tells you O'stories that keep you stuck in a prison you build around yourself out of this past of yours, and prevent you from moving on.

"Old Teller puts on an Unhappy Present face, such as its Worry face, and tells you to worry about yourself and your loved ones, and about what you have to do and whom you have to be.

"It puts on a different Unhappy face and critiques your present. It criticizes you, and everyone and everything around you. It judges, labels, compares, and complains, and puts you and other people down. It lowers your self-confidence and your trust in yourself and in others. It reduces and even eliminates your self-esteem, self-compassion, and self-love.

"Old Teller puts on a Happy Future face, such as its Future Promise and Salvation face, and tells you O'stories about a future that is full of hope, dreams, and promise, which will save you from your present that you resent and judge as unhappy, making this present of yours feel even unhappier.

"Old Teller puts on an Unhappy Future face, such as its Fear face, and tells you O'stories about a dramatic and scary future— *your* scary future. The O'stories describe huge obstacles that you will encounter, terrible outcomes, misfortunes and losses that you will have, and deceptions, pain, and unhappiness that you will feel. They convince you that you will never get what you want, never make it, and never be happy. The O'stories can scare, discourage, and even paralyze you. They lead you to build a prison around yourself out of this future of yours, and prevent you from moving forward.

The Thought

"Old Teller sometimes puts on many Unhappy faces at the same time, dwells on one O'story and repeats it, playing it like an old record or a movie. It sometimes repeats the same O'story, while other times, it jumps from one O'story to the next one. The O'story may belong to you or to someone you may or may not know. It may not even belong to anyone at all! It could be the work of Old Teller's pure and complete imagination. Some O'stories make sense, and some make no sense at all.

"These O'stories—words and images—can become so crowded, noisy, and confusing that they absorb you deeply. They transport you from where you are—where your body is—into your mind, preventing you from having a true relationship with the life happening inside and around you.

"Your eyes look at the images and your ears capture the sounds around you, but you do not see or hear anything. You completely forget where you are and what you are doing at the present moment."

Shooter reminded me of many experiences when one detail, such as an idea, an image, a sound, a scent, a flavor, a touch, a word, a gesture, or an action lead Old Teller to speak and an O'story to play.

For example, I'd be having a conversation with someone or watching a movie, and one detail would wake up a memory from the past or project me into a promising or scary future. Then, I'd soon realize that I had missed a part of that conversation or movie, even though my eyes were wide open, looking at the person or movie screen, and my ears had captured every sound and word.

Shooter also reminded me of the numerous times when I'd be driving, and Old Teller would divert my attention to an O'story. My eyes would be looking at the road straight ahead and the details around me, but I would not see the road or the details. My ears would capture the sounds around me, maybe even my favorite song on the radio, but the song would be over and I would've missed every lyric and note. I'd forget that I was driving and, by the time I'd realize it, I would've already reached my destination.

I smiled and nodded, agreeing with Shooter, as I pulled into my parents' driveway.

"We're here, Dunia!"

My mother was already standing at the front door. I waved and helped Dunia out of the car.

"Good morning, Mom!"

"Look who's *here!*" my mother cheered.

"*Grandma!*"

Dunia ran into her welcoming arms.

"How's my baby?"

I think my mother kissed Dunia 20 times, as if she had not seen her in over ... a week. Then she remembered to kiss me ... once!

"Why don't you come with us to visit your aunt?" she asked.

"I'm going to meet Susan."

"You're not busy then. Maybe you should come with us to see your aunt. Did you call her yet? You should call her. You should talk to her. *Call* her already! You haven't talked to her since Christmas. You should call her ..."

"*Christmas?*" I thought, surprised at my mother's poor memory and, at that point, annoyed with her attitude and nagging.

"Bye, Mom. I'll see you later. Have fun today!"

I figured that ignoring her comment was the best way to avoid a confrontation. I kissed Dunia goodbye, got back in the car, and drove away.

✫

"This woman nags all the time! Why does she have to *nag* so much? Does she have to talk about this *every* time I see her? Why does she care if I call my aunt or not? Why should *I* be the one who calls first anyway? I did nothing wrong! My dear aunt shouldn't have asked me to get her daughter a job in the first place. Besides, I don't want to see that girl's face every day. It's better this way."

I stewed with my thoughts.

"'You're not busy then ...' What's *that* supposed to mean? Yes, I *am* busy and I *am* going to meet Susan, and I'm *not* going to visit or call my stupid aunt. Why does this woman *do* this? Why doesn't she just drop it? What does she *want* from me? Why does she have to piss me off all the time? What's in it for her?"

"What's in it for *you*, Genius?"

"What's in it for me to call my aunt? Nothing!"

"What's in it for you to listen to Old Teller? Right now, your mother is no longer talking to you or asking you to call your aunt. She's not even here anymore, for God's sake, and your aunt is certainly not here either."

I said nothing. I had not even realized that Old Teller had started speaking again. I had been back in the car for less than two minutes!

"If you allow it," Starry said, "Old Teller will speak day and night."

"It will never shut up," Shooter added.

85

"It will dwell on what just happened," Starry continued, "on what you just saw or heard, and on what someone just said or did. It will dwell for a minute, an hour, a month, or a whole year ... it can even dwell for a lifetime! It will stress and exhaust you. The O'stories it tells you have the ability to absorb you deeply. They have the power to wake up your emotions and make your body react."

"You should've seen your face a few minutes ago when Old Teller was talking to you, Genius!"

"What about my face?"

"Let's say that you've looked better," he chided. "Your forehead was stiff, your eyebrows were frowning, your eyes looked both frozen and empty, and your nose was breathing fast and heavy. The muscles of your jaw looked like they were bouncing, and at one point you even said something!"

I thought for a moment.

"I *did*?"

"Old Teller speaks loudly right after an event," Starry explained. "It also speaks after the outside noise has quieted down, especially when you are alone—driving in your car, for example, or at night after you have gone to bed.

"The O'stories of your mind can go wild while everything around you is quiet. One O'story can sometimes get so intense that it starts to feel real, as if it were happening Here and Now, and you actually start to feel happy or unhappy, depending on what the O'story is describing. Your body then expresses this happiness and unhappiness with a physical reaction."

"Hey, Genius! When you start conversing with Old Teller, it gets more interesting. You sometimes shrug your shoulders, make weird hand gestures, nod or shake your head, make funny faces, and your lips actually mumble."

86

"Don't be silly, Shooter. I don't do *that*!"

"You sometimes even speak out loud and tell yourself how horrible you look!"

I pondered for a moment, and then admitted this fact.

"Touché! I hope I don't do that very often ... *do* I?"

"Like I said, Genius, Old Teller never shuts up!"

"Is there a way to keep Old Teller quiet or make it go away ... or at least make it tell me only happy O'stories?"

"First," Starry answered, "start by becoming aware that Old Teller is now talking to you and an O'story is playing inside your mind."

"How do I do that?"

"*Feel?*" she reminded me. "It's either happy-green (move on and the coast is clear) or unhappy-red (stop, watch and see, listen, and understand).

"While you are listening to Old Teller and watching an unhappy O'story, your body reacts, just like it does when you read an unmet need on the Needs chart. The first sign of an unhappy-red feeling is usually a subtle change in your breathing and heartbeat. Your breathing becomes rapid, short, and heavy, and your heart beats faster than usual. Either simultaneously or shortly after that, a knot—a small muscle tension or tightness—could build up in different parts of your body. Most Humans feel this knot in their throat, chest, or stomach.

"As the O'story plays on, your body's reaction increases. Your breathing becomes more rapid, shorter, and heavier. Your heart beats even faster, and the knot goes from discreet to obvious."

I recapitulated.

"When I feel unhappy-red, my breathing and heartbeat change and a knot appears. This means that I'm listening to Old Teller and watching an unhappy O'story.

"You know, it's not always easy for me to pay attention to how I'm feeling. Often, my unhappiness just takes over."

"Your body's reaction is your expression of your happy or unhappy feeling that, in its turn, is your reaction to Old Teller and the O'story.

"At first, you will probably breathe rapidly with short and heavy breaths, your heart will beat fast, the knot will be obvious, and you will feel unhappy-red for a while—all before you remember to ask yourself *Feel?*

"Soon, the unhappy-red feeling will not last as long before you notice it. Eventually, you will become aware of this feeling as soon as it arises. You will become aware of the change in your breathing and heartbeat, as well as the presence of the knot, as soon as they happen.

"At the beginning, becoming aware of your unhappy-red feeling will require your conscious attention and effort. Slowly, with time, patience, and practice, you will become aware and able to catch the unhappy-red feeling, Old Teller, and the O'story more frequently, quickly, and easily."

"How do I do that? How do I catch Old Teller and the O'story?"

"Pull over into the parking lot of that mall."

"Pull *over*? Did you say *the mall*?"

"The mall on the right, Genius! Do you see it? Just slow down and make a right."

I pulled into the parking lot as Starry requested.

"Now what?"

"Park somewhere," she said.

I chose a parking space and stopped my car.

"Is here okay?"

"Here is perfect. I want you to look around and name 10 things that you see."

I had no clue what kind of a game this was but, at that point, my trust in Starry was beyond any doubt.

"Well, I see a lot of parked cars—more than 10," I joked.

"Nice try, Genius! The cars will count for *one* thing. What else do you see?"

"I see the mall. I see the sidewalk. I see a tree. I see a stop sign. I see a no-parking sign. I see ... uh ... the white lines of the parking spaces. I see a police car driving by. I see ... uh ... how many things do I have already?"

"Eight," Shooter answered. You need to name two more."

"The motorcycle and the construction truck over there. That's 10!"

"Perfect!" Starry said. "Where do all these things that you see exist?"

I thought for a minute, and then came up with an answer.

"In the city."

"Genius!"

"Wrong answer, I guess," I humbly concluded, and tried again. "They exist ... uh ..."

"Inside a space," prompted Starry.

"I knew that! That's what I was *about* to say."

"Of course it was, Genius."

"Watch closely and see the space that exists around each thing and between all these things," Starry continued. "Can you see the space?"

I observed for a while, and then answered in a hesitant voice. "I think I can."

"Try to imagine the empty space without these things in it," she said. "Can you?"

"You mean as if all these things were not here?"

"Yes, only the space is here."

"I guess I can," I answered, weakly.

"Become aware of the limited space that each one of these things occupies within the big space. Space is the matrix where all things exist. It is the blank around each thing and between all things. It is where no thing exists. Can you see the empty space?"

"Yes, Starry. Yes I *can!*" I answered with more assurance. "I can clearly see it!"

"Now, name five sounds that you hear."

Starry was not giving me a break.

"What is the point of these games?" I thought.

"Play along, Genius. Just *do* it!"

"I hear the sound of cars driving by. I hear people walking by and talking. I hear music at the entrance of the mall. I hear the sound of the construction truck ... uh ... I hear birds singing!"

"Where do these sounds exist?" Starry asked.

"In the city!" Shooter rushed to answer, quite amused.

We all laughed. I had to admit that his comeback was funny!

"Good one, Shooter!" I said. "I bet the answer is 'in the background.'"

"These sounds exist inside silence," Starry said. "Just like space is to things, silence is the matrix where all sounds exist. Each sound occupies a limited space inside this silence. Silence is the blank around each sound and between all sounds. It is where no sound exists. Listen carefully ... Can you hear the silence?"

"I can! Yes, I *can*!" I answered, surprised and proud at the same time.

"See the empty space and hear the loud silence!"

After these words, Starry said nothing for a little while, giving me a chance to see the space and hear the silence.

"Now," Starry continued, "let us go inside your mind."

"Inside *where*?"

"Your head, Genius! You know, that part of your body that you use every once in a while!"

"Just like space and silence are the matrix for the things and sounds," Starry elaborated, "your mind is the matrix for the O'stories. Each O'story occupies a limited space inside your mind. The endless space and ultimate silence where no O'story exists is the stillness of your mind. Stillness is the blank around each O'story and between all O'stories. It is where no O'story exists. Can you feel the stillness?"

"I think so, Starry ... but I'm not really sure."

"Imagine yourself sitting in your mind, just like you are now sitting in this parking lot. You can compare the O'stories that are playing—every scene and image you see, and every sentence, word, and sound you hear—to the things and sounds in this parking lot.

"Watch closely and see the space, and listen carefully and hear the silence around each O'story and between all O'stories, but do not get involved with them.

"Do not get involved with the O'stories and do not become one with them. Do not become one with the images or sounds, just like you do not become one with the things you see and the sounds you hear in this parking lot. Sit there and watch ... Do you feel it? Do you feel the stillness of your mind?"

"I do, Starry. Well, I *think* I do ..."

"Haven't you ever watched a movie scene in the making?" Shooter asked. "Haven't you seen how the director sits in a chair, rises, and watches from above, without getting involved with the actors or the scene itself? The director just stays up there and watches.

"You are the director inside your mind, Genius. Sit up there and watch from above. Watch the O'stories the same way the movie director watches the actors and the scene."

"Old Teller and the O'stories exist inside your mind," continued Starry. "They are not your mind and they are not you. Since your happy or unhappy feeling is your reaction to Old Teller and the O'story, your feeling is not you. Since your feeling is the translation of your emotion, your emotion is not you either.

"Do not become one with the feeling. Do not become the emotion itself.

"Sit up there and watch."

✦

The Thought

"You make it sound so simple. It's not that easy, you know. It's not easy for me to *not* get involved, to sit up there and watch, especially when I'm feeling unhappy-red."

"You are right," Starry agreed compassionately. "It is not easy, but it is certainly not impossible! With time, patience, and practice, you will be able to sit up there, watch, and not get involved."

"Did you say *practice*?"

"With practice," she answered, "it is possible to become aware of your thoughts and feelings. You will choose one day of the week and practice to 'sit up there and watch.'"

"Refer to *5W2H-O&D*, answer *D*, and set a date to practice," said Shooter. "What day of the week will that be?"

"First, let me see what this practice is all about."

"It doesn't really matter, Genius, because when you have felt unhappy-red long enough, and if you haven't chosen it yet, that day will choose *you!*"

"At first," continued Starry, "you can use the help of an alarm. Once an hour, no matter where you are and what you are doing, this alarm will remind you to stop for a moment and ask yourself *Feel?*

"Then, go into your body and answer happy-green or unhappy-red. When you feel happy-green, smile and move on. When you feel unhappy-red, become aware of the change in your breathing or heartbeat, and feel the knot. An unhappy feeling is a reaction to Old Teller and the O'story—unless, of course, it is a reaction to a real and dangerous situation happening Here and Now.

"Go into your mind and catch Old Teller and the O'story. Sit in your movie director's chair, rise up, watch the images and hear the words, stay above them, and do not become one with them.

"Observe Old Teller and the O'story for just a moment. Then, turn the stage spotlight off, come down from your chair, and walk away. Leave the actors and the play, and leave the scene.

"Go back to the empty space, the loud silence, and the deep stillness of your mind. Stay there for a moment. Then come back to where you are and to what you are doing. Come back to Here and Now."

"It's going to take me a lot longer than just one day to practice all *that*."

"Then let it take longer, Genius."

"Time and patience," reminded Starry. "You are blessed with as much of that as you need. Repeat this practice a few times a week, gradually reducing the frequency of your alarm to once every two hours, then four, and so on, until you no longer need its assistance. Eventually, and without the help of any reminder, you will more often remember to ask yourself *Feel?* and catch the unhappy-red feeling, catch Old Teller and the O'story, and watch without getting involved."

"Then you get up and leave!" Shooter concluded. He paused for a moment, and then repeated, "Get up and leave!"

"Susan is waiting," Starry said. "*Go!*"

"Remember: You are the movie director," shouted Shooter as he flew by. "Stay in your chair and watch from *up there!*"

I drove off to meet Susan. We spent the rest of the morning researching locations, numbers, sponsors, and donations for our community center, and then went for lunch. At least once a month, Susan and I ate at Nonna's place.

The Thought

"Nonna" means "Grandma" in Italian. Nonna Serafina is the chef. She was born in Italy where she married and raised her five children. Massimo, her oldest, moved here about 20 years ago, and his brothers and sisters followed a couple of years later. The family owns and runs "the best Italian bakery in the whole world," according to Susan.

After her husband passed away, Nonna Fina—as everyone calls her—came to join her kids and has been here for about five years. Shortly after she arrived, her kids thought it would keep her busy and entertained if she came and hung out with them at the bakery. Have you ever heard of an Italian Nonna *just* hanging out?

Soon enough, Nonna got busy. She made her first panini for the bakery. Next came the antipasto and then, needless to say, her famous pasta. Everything there is homemade with Nonna's oldest, most authentic recipes. All the food is beyond delicious, and her hands are blessed by the kitchen gods! In the bakery, there is now a reserved section—"Nonna's place"—for her specialties. They kept it small ... just enough for her to keep busy and hang out.

Nonna often comes out of her kitchen to talk to her customers, who are now part of her big family.

"Buongiorno! Tutto bene?"

Even though she's greeting you and asking if you're okay, she doesn't really wait for an answer. I think she got busy too quickly and never took the time to learn English. When someone talks to her, she pretends to understand, nods her head, and smiles.

"Sì, sì, bene, bene!"

If anyone dares to ask for her *ricetta segreta*—her secret recipe—she answers in her native tongue.

"La ricetta? Vuoi la ricetta segreta? Va bene: pasta, pomodori, origano ... in più, un po' di sale ..."

95

Then she pauses and proudly smiles, amused by her famous punch line.

"E il mio segreto: molto amore!"

Susan had the linguine. After my morning's "horrible" scene in front of my bedroom mirror, I obviously had the antipasto salad.

My mother called to let me know that it was okay for Dunia to sleep over at Aunt Maryam's house. I wasn't thrilled with the idea, but then I thought better of it.

"Maybe my soirée with Starry could start earlier tonight."

I waited for the rest of the day and all evening for Starry to come back. I went outside and waited until past midnight. Then it started to get quite cool in the backyard, so I decided to go inside. I had to wake up early the next morning ... I had a million things to do.

Tomorrow was another day!

CHAPTER FOUR

The Past

"Hello?"

"Are you ready?"

"Who's this?"

"It's me, Susan. I'll be there in 10 minutes."

"You'll be *where*?"

"At your house to pick you up! We have an appointment with Ron in half an hour ... are you still sleeping?"

"*Oh, no!*" I shouted as I jumped out of bed.

"I *knew* it. I should've called you earlier!"

"I can't believe I did not wake up. Why didn't my alarm go off?"

I looked over to see what time it was and try to figure out why the alarm did not go off.

"Oh, man, I snoozed it! I can't believe this ... I *snoozed* it!"

"Listen, I'm going to call Ron and tell him that we're going to be half an hour late."

"Okay. I'll get ready as fast as I can ... no wait ... I *can't*! I have another appointment at 10. I booked it six months ago and I can't reschedule. I'm really sorry, Susan. Do you mind meeting with Ron alone? Maybe you can call and tell him that we'll meet tomorrow."

"No, you call him. I've already postponed our meeting with him twice. He's going to think I'm not serious about this. *You* call him!"

"Okay, I will. Are you still coming over?"

Susan said nothing. I knew that she was upset with me and maybe even hated me.

"Susan, I'm *really* sorry."

"You know what? Let me go ahead and meet with Ron. I'll call you later."

"Okay."

"Okay, bye."

"Bye."

I hung up the phone.

"*Ahhhhh!*" I screamed. "I can't *believe* I did not wake up. I'm so *stupid*! Why did I snooze? Why do I even have an alarm clock with a snooze button? I can't believe I'm missing my appointment with Ron. He's going to think I'm irresponsible, and now Susan hates me. *Damn it*! She's probably thinking of finding someone else, someone more serious and more reliable for this project. Well, I can't even blame her if she wants to find a new friend!"

★

"*Feel?*"

"Shooter, is that you?"

"Good morning!"

"Maybe to *you* it is. My morning's off to a bad start already. I have a million things to do today, I'm late, I missed an important meeting, and my best friend *hates* me."

"*Feel?*"

"Did you hear what I just said? Don't you *care?*"

"Of course I do, Genius. That's why I'm asking you how you feel."

"I feel *horrible!* How do you *want* me to feel? I feel badly that I disappointed my best friend. I feel awful that I missed an important meeting for an important project. I'm irresponsible and stupid. I'm angry with myself. I'm ..."

"Do not become one with the feeling," interrupted Starry. "Do not become the emotion itself."

"Just say happy-green or unhappy-red, Genius."

"*Very* unhappy ... *very* red," I said angrily.

"When you feel unhappy-red, it means that Old Teller is telling you an unhappy O'story, remember?"

"Old Teller is not telling me *anything*, Shooter! The story happened, right here, outside my mind, inside my bedroom. It really happened ... in real life, I mean. You just missed it."

"I did not miss it. Starry and I were right here. We saw and heard it all but, right now, we don't see or hear anything anymore, while you still do. Old Teller is still repeating what just happened. It's also telling you that Susan hates you and wants to replace you with a new partner and a new friend. Did Susan *really* say that?"

I thought for a moment.

"No."

"Old Teller is also telling you that Ron thinks you're irresponsible. Ron did not say that either, did he?"

"No," I mumbled, and then thought to myself, "Shooter is right. Ron doesn't even have a clue about what just happened."

"The thought, or Old Teller," Starry continued, "is telling you that you are stupid, and I do not think you are stupid at all. I do not think you really believe that, do you?"

"Now wait a minute," Shooter chimed in. "Old Teller *might* have a point there."

"Be nice, Shooter!" Starry warned.

"What? She calls *herself* stupid and that's okay, but if someone *else* calls her that, she gets upset. Now how 'not stupid' is that?"

"Do not become one with Old Teller or the O'story," continued Starry. "Ask yourself *Feel?* Then answer happy-green or unhappy-red. Become aware of the change in your breathing and heartbeat as well as the knot in your throat, chest, or stomach.

"Go back to the matrix of your mind. Become the movie director, sit in your chair, rise up, and watch the scene from above. Catch Old Teller and the O'story. Stay above them, and watch without getting involved.

"See the empty space, hear the loud silence, and feel the stillness."

"Use an alarm as a reminder to ask yourself *Feel?*" Shooter added, "and make sure you do not *snooze!*"

I sat on my bed for a few minutes, absorbed in my mind, trying to become the movie director and watch the scene from above.

Then I got up, got ready, and left the house, off to do the million things that were awaiting me.

Throughout the day, I tried to *feel* green or red. I tried to become aware of the change in my breathing and heartbeat as well as the knot—signs of my unhappy-red feeling. I tried to catch Old Teller and the O'stories and watch without getting involved.

Susan called me later to tell me that she spent most of the day with Ron. She was actually glad that I did not make it to the meeting. It turned out to be more than just a business interest between them. I asked if she hated me and she said no. She even thanked me and said that she loved me.

I picked up Dunia after dinner, and my mother told me—one more time—that I should've gone to see Aunt Maryam with them and that I should call her soon.

Dunia and I had a tea party before she went to bed. She told me about cousins Lisa and John, and proudly described how she can now swim "like a mermaid"!

After she went to sleep, I stepped back outside. I wasn't sure if Starry was going to show up, but I was hoping she would, very soon. I wanted to tell her about Susan and Ron, even though I suspected that she already knew. I wanted to ask her what to do after I've tried to rise up and watch from above even if, throughout the day, most of my attempts were not very successful, and after I've tried to go back to the stillness of my mind—with not much success there either.

I wanted to ask her many questions: "What do I do when Old Teller won't shut up? What do I do when it becomes so loud that I can no longer hear the loud silence? What do I do when the O'stories become so crowded that I can no longer find my director's chair or see the empty space? What do I do when I no longer feel the stillness?"

I wanted to know why some stories about what already happened and what was no longer happening kept coming back. I wanted to know why this morning's story with Susan kept playing in my mind and why I still felt badly about it, and why my mother's nagging about calling my aunt annoyed me so much. I wanted to know why these past stories come back.

✦

"Because they love you."

"I know they love me."

"I'm not talking about Susan, your mom, *or* your aunt, Genius!"

"You're *not*? Whom are you talking about then? *Who* loves me?"

"The past stories that come back ... they love you and come back to tell you that they do."

"Every day," Starry explained, "you get busy trying to collect different I-haves to satisfy your needs. While you do, you meet different people, deal with different situations, live different experiences, witness different events, and hear different comments.

"Every day, many stories are born. You judge some of them as pleasant and you feel happy, and some as unpleasant and you feel unhappy.

The Past

"A story is born and happens Here and Now. Then, it becomes part of your past. First, it becomes the past that just happened. After, it becomes the past that happened recently. Later, it becomes the past that happened a while back. Much later, it becomes the past that happened a long time ago.

"Regardless of when the true story happened, it is now part of your past. Whether they make you feel happy or unhappy, many of these stories are gathered and stored in your mind as memories (like Human words call them) or as O'stories (Old Teller's version of the original stories), which are part of Old Teller's repertoire.

"The stories that come back love you, and their memories stay dear to you, no matter how long ago they happened."

"Many happy stories feel light and pleasant. When I remember them, I feel happy."

"... and I can tell when you do, Genius! Your face relaxes and lights up, and sometimes, believe it or not, you actually even smile."

"I can see how such stories love me," I said. "There are some happy stories, though, that make me feel unhappy when they come back. How can a *happy* story make me feel *unhappy*? How can it love me?"

"What makes you feel unhappy," Starry explained, "is the fact that this happy story is lost and no longer here, while your heart refuses to believe this sad reality and resists this painful loss. You keep fighting the absence of a certain I-have out of your source of love, safety, and happiness, which once was yours. Your happy past that is now gone is what Human words refer to as the 'good old days.'"

"Up here! *Look up here!*" Shooter yelled.

I looked up. The million stars once again illuminated the sky, presenting another spectacle—My Good Old Days.

✦ ✦ ✦

My Good Old Days

"Look at your good old days!" Starry said. "Your innocent childhood—the special time in your life when you worried about nothing. Look at how peaceful you felt within the comfort of your family, surrounded by ultimate love, unquestionable safety, and true happiness."

"Look at you on Sunday mornings," Shooter took over, "cuddling with your parents, jumping on the bed, and having pillow fights with your brothers and sisters.

"Look at you riding your bike in the afternoons, going to the park, playing on the swings, and building castles with nothing but sand and dirt.

"Look at the games, the fighting, and the telling on each other.

"Look at the birthday parties, family barbecues, picnics, getaways, and holidays with your grandparents, aunts, uncles, cousins, and friends.

"Look at the road trips and how you'd fall asleep in the back seat of the car on the way home. Hey, Genius! Watch how many times you faked being deeply asleep just so your dad would pick you up in his arms and take you into the house!"

"He'd carry me straight to my room and put me in bed ... I used to *love* it!"

I reminisced and sighed loudly.

"*Ahhhhh* ! My home, my bedroom ... home, sweet home!"

"Look at your bedroom and your toys," Shooter continued. "Look at you here in the kitchen, watching your mother and helping her cook your favorite meals, bake your favorite cookies, and then let you lick the leftover dough off the big spoon. Look at you standing on the stool so you can reach the sink and help wash the dishes.

"Look at you in the living room, watching your favorite shows and movies, dreaming, fantasizing, and imitating your heroes.

"Look at you in the backyard playing with your dog. She was such a nice dog! What was her name again?"

"Daisy. I miss her so much!"

Shooter allowed me a minute to watch Daisy before he continued scrolling through my good old days.

"Look at the driveway, alleys, streets, neighborhood, and neighbors. Look at the local store where you secretly bought all the candy, and those multicolored tiny chewing gums that used to pop. Do you remember the gooey, yucky ones you could not even fit in your mouth, Genius?"

"Yes," I laughed. "Those were *awesome* good old days!"

"Look at your school, and the yard where you drew on the ground, threw the ball, and ran and played catch with your friends.

"Look at your classrooms and teachers—those who were your idols and those you hated—and the lessons, the homework, and the exams."

"I'm not sure how good *those* old days were, Shooter, but the school activities, the dances, the outings, the day trips, the get-togethers, and the pajama parties ... now *those* were good!"

"Look here! It's your high school prom night. Do you remember Jason? You had a crush on him. He was your first official date. Look at you dancing with him. This was your first slow dance ... and *this* here, was your first kiss. *Ahhhhh*, Genius. I was so jealous! *There* is one advantage you Humans have over me!"

Shooter paused and, this time, allowed himself more than just one minute to watch *that* scene.

"Look at you during your freshman years," he continued. "The energy you had to attend your classes, have a part-time job, study hard, and *still* be able to go out late and party even harder. The crazy things you did, without worrying about anything or caring about any consequences. You weren't even tired! What were you *made* of, Genius?"

"I know what you mean, Shooter," I laughed. "Those were good old days indeed!"

"The good old days," he added, "when you were full of ambition and had big dreams, ideas, and plans to find a secure job, work hard, make a lot of money—maybe even a fortune—and have abundant possessions and a luxurious lifestyle, and travel and see the world. You were full of dreams to succeed socially, build a prestigious status and reputation, maybe become famous, impress everyone, earn people's respect, and deserve their admiration and love. You were full of dreams to become socially active, help others, and give back.

"Look at *these* good old days. You were so much in love! Look how *beautiful* you were on your wedding day! Look here when Dunia came into this world and into your life. You were so *happy*!

106

You could not stop looking at her. You could not get enough of touching, holding, squeezing, smelling, and kissing her.

"Look at you here, when you heard her call out 'Mom' for the first time; I still remember how happy you were. Look when *she* took her first step and *you* danced with joy! Look here—just last week—when you cheered for the first tooth she lost and became the tooth fairy."

The million stars glowed in the sky until the last shining star exited the stage and my good old days disappeared ...

✮ ✮ ✮

"The good old days are no longer here," Starry explained. "You miss them, regret their absence, and wish they would come back, especially the ones that were suddenly interrupted—those you were not ready or expecting to end so soon. You wish they would come back and bring back your youth, as well as the dear people you lost—those whom you love, the ones who have changed, or those who may never be coming back. You wish they would come back and return what you lost—the priceless times, the special places, and the precious things."

"... and *this* is why you feel unhappy when you remember the happy stories from your good old days," concluded Shooter.

He then described more good days that would eventually become old, and which I will miss one day:

I will look back at the good old days when I used to have tea parties with Dunia before she went to sleep, and I'd step outside to talk to a star.

I will look back at Dunia's first day of school when I stood there and encouraged her to get on that school bus like a big girl, while my heart was breaking, and I was trying to hold back the tears and look strong in front of her.

I will look back at when I—the "chauffeur"—would drive her around. She would still listen to me, do as I say, and not answer back. I would still be able to sleep at night because I did not worry about her being out so late. She was still living at home, making a mess, and filling it with noise and loud music ... before this nest became empty and painful.

I will look back at the good old days when I still had a job, and was still active, and felt useful, appreciated, and admired.

I will look back at the good old days when my close friends were still around and my parents were still alive.

I will look back at the good old days when my body was still healthy and pain free, and I still moved freely and functioned without limitation. I could still see well and hear clearly. My hands did not shake. My joints did not hurt or crack. My knee or back did not lock. I could still bend, go up and down stairs, and stand up and walk. My mind was still sharp and I could still focus and remember. I was still physically and mentally independent.

I pondered what Starry explained and what Shooter described, and realized how the happy stories from my good old days—or rather the fact that these days and stories are no longer here—can indeed make me feel unhappy.

"Your good old days love you in their own way," Starry continued. "Every time you run to them, they are happy to see you and anxious for you to watch and listen to them again. They keep you company, and entertain and comfort you every time you feel lonely, unloved, unfulfilled, and unhappy. They are your temporary refuge, and an oasis of love, safety, and happiness."

"... and *this* is how the past stories that come back love you," concluded Shooter.

✡

"What about *unhappy* stories of my past that make me feel *unhappy*? How do *these* stories love me?"

"One Human's unhappy story of their past could have been the loss of their good old days, such as the loss of a special place—their home, school, neighborhood, land, city, or country. It could have been saying goodbye and leaving loved ones behind, or staying behind after loved ones left. It could have been a story of feeling lonely and abandoned after a separation, like the divorce of their parents or one's own divorce, living in an empty nest after the children have left, or after the death of a loved one.

"One unhappy story of their past could have been the absence of a certain I-have out of their source of love, safety, and happiness, such as the care of one or both parents, or the absence of basic resources, money, stability, or security.

"One Human's unhappy story of their past could have been tough times while trying to survive, or an experience of fear, pain, and suffering. It could have been struggling with an addiction, or enduring physical, mental, or emotional violence, aggression, or abuse. It could have been the loss of health due to a disease or an accident. It could have been the loss of hopes and dreams.

"One or more of these stories of loss of good old days, or of absence of love, safety, and happiness, might have belonged to your own past. When you remember them, you feel unhappy. They might have belonged to the past of a loved one, or maybe to someone you do not even know. They might have been stories you witnessed or just heard about; yet, when you remember them, you also find yourself feeling unhappy."

"Yes, I do," I agreed.

I thought for a moment, and wondered about another kind of story that makes me feel unhappy.

"There are stories about which I cannot seem to remember *anything* bad, but they also make me feel *unhappy*. Why is that? How do *these* stories love me?"

"Some stories of the past are very tricky," Starry explained. "They seem harmless, and look and sound innocent, yet they are painful and make you feel unhappy. Their hurtful details hide in the deepest place of your mind—so deeply that you sometimes forget them.

"The sleeping pain with which these stories are charged exists because one day—sometimes even a long time ago—someone dear to you unconsciously hurt you. It could have been your mother or father, a relative, or a teacher—someone you considered to be your reliable, solid, sacred, unquestionable, and untouchable source of love, safety, and happiness. They might have said or done something out of love and concern and with the purpose of protecting you, raising you properly, and teaching you right. What they said or did might have also been with the purpose of satisfying *their* needs and with no intention to harm you.

"The hurtful detail of the story might have been an innocent word or just a certain tone of voice that was used. It might have been the absence of words of recognition, approval, admiration, encouragement, affection, or love, which you expected but did not hear from them. It might have been a gesture or an action that hurt you. It might have been a nice gesture or an action that you expected and which you did not receive, such as a glance or a touch to show that they cared about you and loved you.

"The story happened. The O'story was born and, along with it, emotional insecurities about yourself—your looks, intelligence, strengths, skills, and talents, and how important and loved you are."

Shooter described some emotions that are born with the O'stories, such as being hurt, accused, judged, insulted, belittled, ridiculed, or embarrassed. They are emotions of not being recognized, approved of, accepted, or loved.

He explained that the emotional insecurities existed, and still exist today, because Old Teller translated these words, gestures, and actions that I received—as well as ones I expected but did not receive—into this: "I'm not pretty, attractive, or desired enough. I'm not smart enough. I'm not strong enough. I'm not nice enough. What I think, feel, say, or do is not important. I'm not important. I'm not good enough—or as good as the others. I'm not worthy of being loved. I don't deserve to be loved. I'm not loved."

I heard a loud silence around and inside me. It was a profound silence necessary to keep Old Teller quiet, and numb the emotions that Shooter described before these emotions started to win me over ... and God knows they would!

"Every time a story of lost good old days," continued Starry, "an unhappy story of absence of love, safety, and happiness, or an apparently innocent but hurtful story of your past tries to speak, Old Teller is alert and wants to protect you in its own way. It puts on its I-am-the-Victim face, pulls an O'story out of its repertoire, and starts dwelling. It repeats this O'story of loss, pain, and unhappiness, giving you a sense of self-pity that often feels like a comforting kind of self-love, and you believe that you are loved.

"Old Teller sometimes asks you to dwell, and assists you while you do. You start repeating the O'story out loud to other people, and this gives you a curious sense of satisfaction because you think that others are listening to you and feel that they are interested in you. You confuse their interest in the O'story with the idea of 'someone is interested in me.'

"You sometimes become the hero because you are the victim. You feel important because you now have someone's attention, compassion, or sympathy. You believe that you have their recognition, approval, and maybe even their admiration. You think that you now deserve their love and you are loved.

"Old Teller sometimes helps you repeat this O'story to God, asking Him why He let the good days end, why this unhappy story of absence of love, safety, and happiness, or the apparently innocent but hurtful story, happened to you and how He allowed it to happen. You hope for a miracle while sustaining yourself in God's mercy, and you feel loved."

"... and *this* is how the past stories that come back love you, Genius!"

"Sometimes," Starry continued, "when the original story of your past is too painful, Old Teller twists its O'story to your advantage. It plays back your forever-gone good old days. You go back to that place that is no longer here, and spend as much time as you want there. You go back to win what was lost. You then feel victorious, satisfied, and happy.

"You bring back that person who left you or who you feel does not love you anymore, and win back their love. You even bring back a loved one who is probably no longer alive. You touch and hold them, and they touch and hold you for as long as you please. You win back their presence and love all over again, and you live happily ever after. You then feel loved, safe, and happy.

"Old Teller plays back your past's unhappy stories but, this time, the absence of a certain I-have and the pain, suffering, and unhappiness are not present. Instead, the O'story is full of abundant I-haves, safety, love, and happiness.

"Old Teller plays back your apparently innocent but hurtful past but, this time, the O'story convinces you that you are important, you are good enough, you are worthy of being loved, you deserve to be loved, and you are loved."

"... and *this* is how the past stories that come back love you, Genius!"

"The stories of your past hang on to you," continued Starry, "and you hang on to them. They do not let go of you, and you do not let go of them. You do not want to let go of them because, somewhere inside of you, you believe that losing them could mean losing a part of yourself. You are convinced that this loss will leave a void, and you confuse this void with a painful emptiness and scary loneliness. You are afraid that this emptiness and loneliness will hurt you more than the pain and unhappiness caused by the memories themselves.

"Keeping you entertained, giving you comfort and compassion, and making you feel safe, welcome, wanted, important, and loved, in their own way, are some ways in which the past stories that come back love you."

"*Some* ways? You mean there are *more*?"

"Just like Human needs and emptiness, each story of your past is also a blessing in disguise. Each one holds an important message for you.

"As long as the story serves you, you do not let go of it. As long as you have not discovered the blessing and understood the message, it stays unresolved and does not let go of you. It remains deeply inside your mind. It hides and patiently waits."

"What does it wait for?"

"A chance to speak. The story waits for a trigger to help it resurface to a place where it gets an opportunity to express itself, show you what it wants you to see, tell you what it needs you to hear, and deliver its message. As long as you do not get the message, the story goes back and hides again. It waits for another trigger and for another chance to speak.

"The story does not give up on you. It keeps coming back and tries to talk to you, out of love for you. It talks to you and, if it has to, sometimes even screams. When it does, the pain it holds inside vividly wakes up, sometimes erupting like an apparently dormant volcano that has been brewing for a long time. The pain—sadness, anger, or resentment—explodes and hurts you.

"Each story keeps coming back until the day you see what it is trying to show you, listen to what it is trying to tell you, and finally understand its message that will help you grow and glow.

"Once you understand this message, the story becomes resolved and released. It no longer needs to speak. It no longer needs the assistance of any trigger. It may come back but, every time it does, it will feel lighter and carry less pain and unhappiness, until it is eventually free of them.

"One day, it will visit you for a little while and put happiness in your heart and a smile on your face. After it is gone, it leaves a sweet yet powerful, happy, and blessed energy that pushes you forward on your path of growth."

"What does a trigger look like?"

"I have no clue," Starry answered.

"You *don't*?"

"What do you *mean* you have no clue?" Shooter intervened. "If a trigger is able to awaken pain, it must be scary looking. It must be bad! How can you have no clue? You're Starry! You're supposed to know *everything*!"

Starry laughed.

"I do not know what a trigger looks like. I do not know where or when it shows up. A trigger is not good or bad. A trigger is neutral."

"Starry, if *you* don't even know what a trigger looks like, then how am *I* supposed to recognize it?" I asked.

"You recognize a trigger by what it does. A trigger could come to you from anyone or anything, and it could happen anywhere. It could be an image, a sound, a scent, or a flavor. It could be someone or something you touch or that touches you. It could be a situation or an incident that you witness. It could even be an O'story of your mind.

"A trigger can sometimes be an offensive word, gesture, or action. It can be an innocent word that someone says to you, a personal opinion they give you, an objective observation, or a neutral comment—one that is not good or bad. It could also be the absence of a pleasant word that you expected to hear.

"A trigger could be a certain tone of voice that someone uses while talking to you, an otherwise meaningless gesture or action that they do, or the absence of a nice gesture or action you expected to receive."

"Great!" I said. "Now I'm *sure* it will be impossible for me to recognize a trigger! How am I supposed to recognize it if it can be *anything*? How do I know it's there if it can happen *anywhere*?"

"You recognize a trigger by what it does," Starry repeated. "Your life is a collection of past stories. When a story is resolved and released, its memory becomes light and pleasant and makes you feel happy. As long as the story is unresolved, it remains charged with a deep pain, and makes you feel unhappy.

"It could be the pain of your forever-gone good old days, or the pain of the absence of love, safety, or happiness, which once hurt you and still hurts you today. It could be the pain of an apparently innocent but hurtful detail, which still tells you that you are not important, not good enough, not worthy of being loved, you do not deserve to be loved, and you are not loved.

"Such past stories feel like roadblocks that prevent your life from freely flowing. A trigger gives an unresolved past story an opportunity to speak and express itself, so it gets released and the roadblock is removed, allowing your life to freely flow Here and Now."

"How does a trigger do that?"

"Throughout your life, you were blessed with many I-haves, while you made efforts to collect many more, hoping they would satisfy your different physical, mental, and emotional needs. You gathered these I-haves and created—or tried to create—your comfort zone.

"Different I-haves were collected to assure your survival, to give you safety and security, or to please and indulge your senses. Some were collected and used to build a protective shield, which covers the unresolved stories of your past and hides and numbs the pain that resides in there.

"The stories were covered and the pain was hidden and numbed so well that you sometimes forgot about them, or thought that these stories were already resolved. Sometimes you tried to resolve them but, for some reason, you gave up and bailed instead.

Sometimes you avoided facing them because, deep inside, you knew that the pain that could wake up would be overwhelming.

"You ran away from the stories and the pain. You ignored them, pretending as if they were not there. Sometimes, when a story tried to talk to you, you got busy collecting different and more I-haves to make the cover-up shield thicker, hoping it would do the job—cover the story and hide the pain even deeper in your mind.

"You wanted the story and pain to go away and convinced yourself that your collection of I-haves is your true source of love, safety, and happiness, and these I-haves are the ones on which you depend. They are the ones you need, hang on to, and protect because you believe that they protect you and make you happy.

"Time after time, you played this cover-up and hiding game and, over the years, you got very good at it. You played it so well that you fooled everyone around you—even yourself. You started confusing your pure I-am (your true source of love, safety, and happiness) with your I-haves and, instead of *having* an I-have, you started *being* the I-have."

Shooter gave many examples of I-haves out of which people, including myself, sometimes build the cover-up shield. He said that, instead of *having* a Human identity, such as a name, background, ethnicity, race, history, language, or religion, and instead of having a personality, many people *become* their identity and personality.

Instead of having physical good looks, intelligence, strengths, and talents, they become beautiful, desired, intelligent, strong, and talented.

Instead of having a social role, they start being their social role.

Instead of having an education, a degree, a job, a position, and a title, they become the degree, job, position, and title.

Instead of achieving success, they become an achiever and successful.

Instead of having a social image, they become recognized, respected, popular, and admired.

Instead of having money and possessions, they identify themselves with their bank account and possessions, such as their clothes, car, or house.

Shooter said that I, like those people, became so confused that I started interacting with others, confusing their I-am with their I-haves: identity and personality, social role, job, position, and title. I confused their I-am with their achievements and successes—and even their failures: money, possessions, clothes, car, and house. People became employees, clients, cases, files, numbers, contracts, projects, investments, connections, sources of opportunities and income.

I became so confused that I identified the love that I have, and the love that I receive and give, with those I-haves that offer me comfort, stability, and security; the ones that represent my identity and personality; protect my rights, reputation, integrity, and dignity; and assure my self-worth, self-esteem, self-respect, and self-love as well as others' respect and love for me.

"You forgot that your I-haves, along with the love, safety, and happiness they give you, come and go," Starry continued, "but your I-am, your source of true love, safety, and happiness, always stays. You forgot that if you lose one I-have, you can replace it with another one, while your I-am is irreplaceable. You forgot that, even if you lose all your I-haves, your I-am remains untouchable.

"You started feeling that your love, safety, and happiness depend on your I-haves, and you became attached to these I-haves. This is why losing one of them, even the fear of that loss, now becomes a great source of pain and unhappiness because it feels as if you are losing your I-am."

"So what does a trigger have to do with all that?" I asked.

"When a trigger happens," Starry answered, "whether it is an image, a sound, a scent, a flavor, a touch, a word, a gesture, or an action, it sometimes feels like a true danger trying to hurt you by claiming an I-have of yours and jeopardizing your source of love, safety, and happiness.

"When the trigger is someone's words, gesture, or action, and when the threatened I-have is part of your cover-up protective shield, the trigger goes beyond this particular I-have, right through the protective shield, straight to the unresolved past story hiding underneath, and pokes this story.

"The pain that resides inside the story instantly wakes up. When it is intense, this pain explodes, hurting you and the person-trigger—the person whom you consider to be the source of the trigger or maybe even the trigger itself—and probably innocent people around you along the way."

"When the pain explodes," Shooter said, "the alarm of danger goes off, and guess who comes to the rescue?"

"Who?"

"Old Teller!" he announced. "Old Teller loves you. It is your guardian ... well, it believes itself to be."

"When the trigger threatens your I-have," Starry explained, "Old Teller becomes alert. It starts to speak and warn you about the risk of losing this now threatened I-have, and the pain you will feel in case you lost it. It wants to make sure that, regardless of the situation, you stay powerful and in control, and do whatever it takes to protect this I-have.

"At the same time, somewhere in the background, and from under the protective cover-up shield, your unresolved past story is also trying to speak.

"Remember that the true role of a trigger is to give the unresolved story an opportunity to express itself. Once it has helped the story resurface, and once it has put it on the table, this trigger no longer needs to stick around. Mission accomplished. It can now leave.

"However, it often does not leave because a trigger likes the attention it gets from you and the challenging power that it receives from Old Teller. It would rather stick around, flaunting itself and putting on a show. It acts as if it is the highlight of the situation when, in reality, it is not.

"When the source of the trigger is a person, this trigger immediately goes from being an ordinary word, gesture, or action to being the star of the show. It takes center stage where the scene is happening. It traps you, keeping you uselessly stuck, going round and round inside the fear of the pain—and the pain of the fear—of losing the now threatened I-have, and inside the greater pain of the unresolved story.

"Old Teller convinces you that the person-trigger is truly threatening you, and they are indeed the true source and cause of your unhappiness. This becomes especially true when this person is one of your closest loved ones, namely your parents, caregivers, siblings, spouse, children, or best friend."

"Why is that, Starry?" I asked.

"It is because you have baptized your closest loved ones as your most reliable source of love, safety, and happiness. They are the ones you always run to when other I-haves fail you. You give them this role and expect them to fulfill it by answering your requests and satisfying your needs, every time you turn to them.

"When they—your source of love, safety, and happiness— suddenly *become* the trigger that is threatening your I-have, which is also your source of love, safety, and happiness, you become confused, sad, scared, and angry, and feel betrayed and unhappy. Your main source of help, support, love, safety, and happiness has now turned on you. This could be the ultimate disappointment and cause you great pain."

"The trigger can do all *that*?"

"Yes, it can, almost instantly, leading you to miss its real purpose, which is to give your unresolved story an opportunity to express itself and deliver its message to you.

"Old Teller speaks out of love. After the trigger has threatened your I-have and poked the painful, unresolved story, and after Old Teller has warned you about the presence of the danger, the next thing Old Teller wants to do is help you protect yourself against the person-trigger. It puts on a loving face that Human words call 'ego,' and speaks with you."

"What are you *talking* about, Starry?" Shooter rebelled. "You said that needs talk out of love, and Genius and I agreed. You said that emptiness exists out of love, and we listened. You said that unhappy stories of the past come back out of love, and that's fine. Now you're saying that ego speaks out of *love*?"

Confused by what just sounded like a crazy statement, and teaming up with Shooter, I asked my own questions.

"Ego has a *loving* intention? Are you saying that ego is *good*?"

"This is *ridiculous*!" continued Shooter. "Ego is not good. Ego is bad. It is *very* bad ... *everyone* knows that! Ego O'stories are full of anger, bitterness, resentment, and sometimes even a desire for revenge!"

"Ego O'stories are full of fear of losing love, safety, and happiness," Starry calmly announced. "Old Teller tells you to react in order to protect yourself: either run and hide, or put up a fight by saying or doing something to try to stop the trigger—the danger you feel it is—before it hurts you.

"Old Teller tells you to react by asking the person-trigger to stop. It tells you to judge and criticize what they just said or did, and sometimes even criticize their whole person. It pushes you to humiliate them, ridicule and belittle their looks, and make fun of their identity, personality, intelligence, power, and achievements. It tells you to put them down, throw their difficulties in their face, inflate their weaknesses, and highlight *your* strengths. It helps you justify yourself, prove yourself right, and prove them wrong.

"It tells you to manipulate and make them feel guilty about what they said or did, and convinces you to play the role of 'the victim.' It tells you to regret every nice word you once told them, and every nice gesture or action you once made to please them.

"It tells you to blame and accuse them. It assists while you insult them, curse them, and call them names. It tells you to punish and discipline them and get revenge. It convinces you to dare and sometimes even threaten them.

"If it feels that your words are not able to protect you sufficiently, Old Teller encourages you to turn to your whole body for help. This may be a gesture or an action of your own, in response to what you just heard them say, what you just saw them do, or what Old Teller assumed or concluded that they thought, said, or did."

At that point, Shooter cleared his throat and joined in, giving numerous examples of Human ego words-reactions:

"It's your fault. You'll never change. I knew you were going to say and do this. How could you say this to me? I can't believe what you just did to me. You're stupid. You're an idiot. What's your problem? What's wrong with you? How many times do I have to tell you? I've told you a million times. I told you, didn't I? You're irresponsible. You're just like your mother (or father). What you think, say, or do is not important. This is ridiculous. Whatever! Don't waste my time. I don't care. I wish I never helped you or did you this favor. I'm going to prove you wrong. I already know that. I said it first. I saw it first. You're a jerk. You're a loser. Go to hell. Back off. You're not going to tell me what to say or do. You won't get away with this. Don't piss me off. You'll see. I'll show you. I'm warning you. I'm going to teach you a lesson. I promise I'll make you regret this. You're going to pay for this. This is gonna cost you. You owe me an apology. You'd better... You should ... You must ... You have to ... You won't be happy if I decide to ... You have no right to ... How dare you? Who do you think you are? That's enough. Stop right there. Let's step outside. Nobody talks to me this way. There's no way I'm going to let you ... Over my dead body ..."

Shooter described several Human ego gestures-reactions and actions-reactions, such as ignoring the other person or acting indifferently towards them, rolling the eyes and turning the face, retreating into silence, or talking to someone else and making the person-trigger feel less important.

The gestures-reactions and actions-reactions could be challenging the person-trigger, confronting and threatening them by giving an odd look or pointing the warning index finger—or any other finger—in their face; sighing, using a different tone of voice while addressing them, snapping, yelling, screaming, or crying; or becoming aggressive and violent, throwing or breaking things, pushing, attacking, hitting, kicking, or fighting.

I sat there, stunned. It was scary to realize how much I could relate to so many of these ego reactions—these words, gestures, and actions—and how many of them sounded familiar.

"I just *hate* it when I react!"

"A trigger from the other person, and you react," continued Starry. "Then your reaction becomes their trigger. *You* become their trigger. It can be one word, one gesture, or one action, even in the purpose of your own defense.

"Your reaction pokes their unresolved story, awakens their pain that is their 'until now' dormant volcano, and activates their protective mechanism. Their Old Teller comes to the rescue ... and here it goes! Before you know it, this game of throwing hurtful words, gestures, or actions back and forth catches both of you, and sucks you into a vicious circle of 'who can hurt the other one more.'

"This game keeps you trapped, angry, confused, and wondering that maybe, if you took away an I-have of theirs, then you could win back what you feel they just took away from you, such as your possessions, rights, power, dignity, and the respect or love that they owe you.

"You desperately try to seek their help, empathy, approval, recognition, admiration, or pity, and desperately seek their love—especially when this person-trigger is a loved one. You feel that you may be able to prove that you are important, you are good enough, you are worthy of being loved, you deserve to be loved, and you are loved.

"Through your reaction, you think that you are attacking and hurting them, with the purpose of protecting your source of love, safety, and happiness. At the same time and through their reaction, they think that they are attacking and hurting you, with the purpose of protecting their source of love, safety, and happiness.

"Instead, you both lose even when, on the outside, one of you wins the situation, challenge, conversation, or argument, and protects their I-have (possession, right, power, dignity, respect, empathy, approval, recognition, or love).

"On the inside, it never feels like a real victory. One might win the fight, but you both lose the battle. You both stay trapped inside a painful and vicious circle. You both miss your unresolved past story's loving message that helps you grow and glow. You both pay a great price out of your physical, mental, and emotional health and well-being. You feel frustrated, exhausted, disappointed, and hurt."

"You don't feel good, Genius. You don't look good either."

"*Shooter!*" Starry interrupted, trying to limit his words.

"You actually look *crazy*," he added.

"*Shooter!*"

Ignoring Starry's attempts to keep him quiet, he continued.

"In fact, as your reaction gets more intense, and as Old Teller feeds it with more ego O'stories, your face and body look crazier and crazier ... and you also *sound* crazy!"

I laughed because, deep inside, I knew that Shooter was right.

"You know what's funny," I said, "or should I say sad? Sometimes, right in the middle of my reaction, I realize that I should stop reacting. Often, by the time I do stop, it's already too late and the damage is done. I'm feeling upset and hurt, and I know the other person is also feeling badly. Even if I apologize and say that I'm sorry, the damage cannot be undone.

"Why do we react, Starry? What's the point in reacting? What's the purpose? What good is all the damage it causes?"

"Your reaction's apparent intention is for you to protect your threatened I-have against the trigger, while your reaction's true purpose is—one more time—very loving.

"Your reaction acts like a road sign that guides you, pointing out the unresolved story of your past that needs to express itself. It highlights this story's loving message that, once understood, will help you grow and glow. The story will get resolved and released, and will then release you in return, allowing you to move forward.

"Your reacting words, gestures, and actions sometimes limit a true and complete expression of your thoughts and feelings; however, a reaction tells no lie, even when it is only expressed to yourself by you listening to Old Teller and watching the O'stories, or when it is felt as a change in your breathing and heartbeat, or a knot in your body. A reaction tells no lie, even when you try to restrain from expressing yourself with tears, words, gestures, or actions.

"Despite its apparently painful and sometimes destructive nature, a reaction is a powerful tool that is able to communicate honest emotion to you. It is an authentic translation of how you are truly feeling, and a confirmation of the presence of an unresolved story, no matter how much you try to hide this story, or run away and hide from it.

"The intensity of your reaction is proportional to how painful your unresolved story is, and a direct sign of how important the message and how significant the growth step are.

"Nevertheless, it is possible to control the intensity of your reacting words, gesture, or action, thereby reducing or eliminating the damage they cause."

"Since I can control the intensity of my reaction, then why can't I just *not* react?"

"You do not want to ignore your reaction's need to exist because it is your honest and clear lead towards the part of your past that needs to be resolved. However, you can become aware of your need to react and intercept your reacting words, gestures, or actions."

"I think it will be *impossible* for me to do that. I mean, when I react, it happens so fast! Before I even have a chance to think, or decide to stop it, the reaction has already taken over. Before I know it, I have already said or done something to trigger the other person. Before I know it, I have already reacted!"

"It is not easy to control—reduce or eliminate—your reacting words, gestures, or actions, but it is certainly not impossible!"

Starry reassured me. "It will take time, patience, and practice. It will take repetition—sometimes hundreds or even thousands of times—but you will make it possible. Meanwhile, you will be good to yourself during those times you find it more difficult not to get carried away by your reaction. You will not judge yourself and you will not give up.

"Now that you are aware of the presence of triggers and of Old Teller and its ego O'stories, and now that you understand their purpose, you will more often become aware of your reacting words, gestures, or actions.

"At first, you might become aware and catch yourself reacting *after* the reaction has already happened. Sometimes you might not even recognize yourself reacting at all.

"Later, you will catch the reaction once in a while. Slowly, you will start catching your reactions more often, one reaction at a time. You will become more aware of your reacting words, gestures, and actions. You will be able to catch your words as you actually say them, and catch your gestures and actions as you actually do them.

"One day, you will catch your words, gestures, and actions *before* you react. Gradually, your reactions will become less intense and less frequent, and will not last as long.

"There will be a day when you will remember to sit in your movie director chair, rise up, and quietly watch from above. You will no longer be sucked into the reaction's vicious circle or stay trapped in it.

"Instead, you will be able to quickly drop the situation and exit the scene. You will be able to go straight to the hidden, unresolved story and recognize it without becoming one with the trigger, Old Teller, the ego O'story, or the reaction.

"You will be able to see that the trigger is trying to steal the show, and this will no longer impress you. When you look at a person, a creature, an object, a situation, a gesture, or an action, you will be able to see that person, creature, object, situation, gesture, or action. When you hear a sound or word, you will bring it back to just a sound or word, and hear nothing else but that specific sound or word. When you smell, taste, or feel something, you will bring it back to this pure thing. The power of the trigger will melt away, and you will no longer consider it the star of the moment.

"When the trigger is someone's words, gesture, or action, you will recognize Old Teller's ego O'story of threat, fear, and loss, and you will not become one with it. You will be able to watch it, but it will no longer scare you because you now realize that the trigger cannot really hurt you or threaten your true source of love, safety, and happiness. You will understand the trigger-ego O'story-reaction game, and decide that you no longer want to play it because it is no longer fun and no longer serves you. Knowing that you have figured out this game, Old Teller will then keep quiet.

"You will recognize your need to react and, if you have already reacted, you will be able not to become one with your reaction. Your reacting words, gestures, and actions will eventually disappear, and only your reaction's true purpose—to point out the unresolved story that needs to express itself—will remain, as long as you need this story and as long as it needs you.

"One day, when the deeply hidden pain has lasted long enough, and when you get tired of hiding it and hiding from it, you will become ready to listen to your unresolved story that keeps coming back.

"You will be tired of feeling the overwhelming pain every time a trigger pokes this story. You will be tired of going with the trigger whenever it decides to take you back there, despite your agreement to go there or not. You will be tired of hurting yourself and innocent people around you every time you react.

"One day, going back to your unresolved past will simply not serve you anymore. It will no longer feel safe, comfort you, or make you feel loved. Instead, you will become aware that your unresolved past is trapping you, holding you prisoner, cutting you off from a true relationship with yourself, and preventing you from having a true relationship with the life happening around you Here and Now.

"You will be tired of feeling the pain of being stuck and closed to new opportunities. You will be bored with feeling paralyzed and will want to move on.

"One day, your need to open yourself, and accept love and happiness again, will become greater than your need to hide behind the shadow of your unresolved past.

"One day, you will finally decide to surrender and face your unresolved past. You will allow it to express itself and let it deliver its messages to you. You will be ready to look at what it wants to show you, listen to what it wants to tell you, and clearly understand its messages.

"Then, you will resolve, release, and liberate it, and it will release and liberate you in return. You will free yourself from it and move on."

"How do I do that?"

"Simply meet up with your unresolved past and kindly face it. Choose a convenient place and time to celebrate your Unresolved Past ceremony, and allow the unresolved stories of your past to express themselves.

"Sit comfortably, surround yourself with silence or soft, nostalgic music, and light a candle for the mood. It sometimes helps to use a trigger to poke the stories, such as an object, a picture, a movie scene, a sound, a word, a comment, a melody, or a song.

"Let a special scent—maybe a scent-trigger—fill the air.

"Get your happy music record ready to play 30 or 60 minutes later, once the ceremony is over. Remember that you want to visit your unresolved past, see what it wants to show you, and listen to what it has to tell you, but you do not want to stay there.

"Create your Unresolved Past chart. Using a paper and pen, write down the title of the ceremony on top of the page— Unresolved Past.

"Write your name and birth date underneath it.

"On the left side of the page, divide your life stages into periods of one, two, or three years at a time. The painful, unresolved stories you still remember today, those that highlight that specific period and still feel like a roadblock where your life does not seem to freely flow, will come to you.

"Watch and see what they want to show you, and listen to what they want to tell you. Whether these stories belong to your forever-gone good old days, to your unhappy past of absence of love, safety, or happiness, or to your apparently innocent but hurtful past, you will write them down on the right side of the page.

"Close your eyes.

"Take three deep breaths.

"Invite the noise around and inside you to leave.

"Invite the stories that are hiding to come to you. Call them out loud.

"Invite the images to parade themselves in front of you.

"Invite the sounds and the voices to speak.

"Invite the stories to show and tell you, without fighting or judging the painful emotions that arise. Welcome these emotions and encourage them to come to you. Allow them to wake up, and allow yourself to feel unhappy, no matter what face unhappiness puts on.

"The main story that needs to be seen and heard will stand out. It will quickly present itself to you. You will recognize it as the one that will change your breathing and heartbeat, and bring a knot to your throat, chest, or stomach—and maybe tears to your eyes.

"Do not be afraid to go into the emotions. Let them carry you as deeply and as far back as they want. Let this story speak as long and as loudly as it needs to speak."

"This could be very painful," I said. "I'm not sure I'll be able to do this."

"Think of it this way, Genius: A painful emotion is like an abscess. The greater the pressure, the more painful it is until it's lanced. You might not appreciate the lancing, but you always feel relieved and happy after. Right?"

"Thank you for that beautiful analogy, Shooter!"

"Any time!"

"What if I sit there and no story comes to me?"

"Oh, don't worry, Genius. I *guarantee* that, in your case, at least one story will come."

"What if too many stories come at the same time? How can I tell them apart? How will I know which one needs to speak and be resolved?"

"The stories that have a message will all want to speak," Starry answered. "They all need to be resolved. The story that affects you the most and takes the lead for the time being is most likely the one that your reaction has pointed out.

"Sometimes, the most painful, unresolved story hides deeply in your mind under a pile of other stories, which, in their turn, hide under the I-have protective shield you have built over the years.

"One after the other, those cover-up stories will unfold, deliver their message, and be resolved and released until you get to the story that is hiding the deepest. You will then be able to face this story, watch and see it, listen to it, and understand its message so it is resolved and released in its turn."

"Think of it this way, Genius: You peel off lettuce leaves, one leaf at a time, until you get to the heart."

"Thank you, Shooter. Now that's a *much* nicer picture!"

"Like I said, Genius, any time!"

"One reaction at a time, and one story at a time," concluded Starry.

Shooter reminded me that it would be a good idea to get the assistance of someone whom I trust while celebrating my Unresolved Past ceremony—maybe a loved one, a friend, a mentor, a therapist, a counselor, a religious or spiritual guide, or a member of a community or support group.

He said that, since the person assisting me would not be as touched by my past as I am, they will sometimes see, hear, and maybe even understand the loving messages of some of my past's unresolved stories, which I might not even remember.

He also reminded me of the assistance of God, Who is always present, available, and ready to help me.

"Once I have faced the unresolved story and allowed it to express itself, and once I have seen what it wants to show me and listened to what it wants to tell me, what do I do next?"

"That is it!" Starry replied.

"That is *what*?"

"That is all you have to do."

"*What's* all I have to do?"

"See and listen."

This revelation confused and exasperated me.

"I don't think I understand!"

"Becoming aware of the story and allowing it to express itself, seeing what it wants to show you, and listening to what it needs to tell you with true love and compassion, are often all that the story needs to get resolved and released.

"It wants you to accept its existence inside your life because it once *did* exist. It wants you to stop fighting and resisting its presence, and recognize it the way it happened without wanting to go back and change it. It wants you to know that it loves you. It needs you to approve of it, and acknowledge that it is important, that it is good enough, that it deserves to be loved, and that it is loved."

Starry was quiet for a moment while I silently debated if I could accept my past's unresolved stories as easily as she was claiming, and wondered how I could ever approve of them.

"Since the moment you were born," she continued, "and until the last day of your life on Earth, every part of your Human story, including the story you came with and the one you came into, has been personally and perfectly designed for you.

"Every story of your past wanted you exactly where you were supposed to be, back there and then. Every story led and brought you a step closer to where you are today. Every story was a critical and necessary station on your path of growth. Every story invested in shaping you into who you are today."

"You make it sound as if where and who I am today are so wonderful and special," I said. "Frankly, I'm not so sure about that!"

"Today," she said, "you are listening to my words, wondering about the important messages, and willing to go into your story and take a new step. For that, where you are today is a wonderful place!

"Today, you are consciously choosing to grow a little more ... and for that, who you are today is *very* special!"

"What do the messages of my unresolved past say?"

"They say that they love you and want you to be happy Here and Now. They say that they want you to grow and glow!

"Go back to your Unresolved Past chart, where you divided your life stages into periods of one, two, or three years, and look closely. For each unhappy period of your life where an unresolved story spoke, become aware of the presence of a happy period that followed sooner or later.

"Become aware of how each story of your forever-gone good old days whose loss hurts you today, how each unhappy story of absence of love, safety, or happiness that you resisted and on which you dwelled back then and there and still do today, and how each apparently innocent story that hurt you then and still hurts you today was a growth opportunity in itself!

"Become aware of the gifts that this unresolved story once offered you as well as the gifts it still offers you today."

"Ready ... get set ... *grow!*" Shooter cheered.

Shooter gave many examples of a happy period which follows an unhappy one inside a person's life, such as a hello after a goodbye, a new love relationship after a separation, a better career opportunity after a job loss, or a new home after the loss of a special place.

Other examples were a success after a failure, a victory after a defeat, a new dream and project after a lost hope, a new beginning after a bitter ending, and a new and fulfilled life after times of loneliness and emptiness.

It could also be a second chance, a new story, or a chapter, sometimes even the discovery of the person's life mission, after a painful story of poverty, addiction, violence, abuse, betrayal, disease, accident, and suffering.

"Remember that God is always in charge," Starry continued. "Have faith that He designs every period of your life, as well as the presence of every person, every thing, every place, and every event, situation, and condition, in the most profitable way for you.

"You will become aware of your unresolved past. You will accept its existence in your life, and approve of the way it happened. You will recognize its importance, acknowledge its necessity, and appreciate its positive contribution to your growth.

"When you closely watch and see, and carefully listen, you will be able to understand the messages. It will become clear to you how your unresolved past loves you.

"You will accept that it loves you.

"You will forgive it for all the pain it once caused you and still causes you today.

"Go back to your Unresolved Past chart and look deeply into each unresolved story that spoke. The messages will shine right through. These messages reside inside the opportunities that helped you glow back then and there, and still help you glow today.

"You will forgive *and* thank your unresolved past, and you will understand how the stories that come back truly love you!"

✦

"Glow? Forgive? Thank? I'm so confused!"

"Ready ... get set ... glow!" Shooter cheered again, and then shouted, "Up here! *Look up here!*"

These words were now becoming familiar. I wasn't sure if I was more excited to hear them than Shooter was to say them.

I looked up where the million stars painted another marvel for me. I gazed at the majestic sky and there it was: the full and sparkling Glow chart!

The Past

✬ ✬ ✬

The Glow Chart

The unresolved story of my past when I was:	*This unresolved story was an opportunity for me to glow through its message of:*
• Closed to love and hateful	• Love
• Unaware	• Awareness
• Empty	• Fulfillment
• Pretentious, abusive, and a liar	• Honesty, genuineness, and integrity
• Feeling guilty, overwhelmed, and resentful	• Faithfulness to my true story
• Worried and anxious	• Peace inside the empty space, the loud silence, and the deep stillness of my mind
• Lost inside the noise of the memories of my past, and my future hopes or fears	• Freedom from my past and from my future

- Disappointed, jealous, and taking the I-haves inside and around me for granted; dwelling, complaining, needing more I-haves to be happy; playing the role of "the victim," and blaming others, life, or God for being unfair

- Appreciation and thankfulness; awareness and gratitude for Here and Now

- Hopeless, confused, lost, and insecure

- Hope and clarity; guidance and direction; security that I constantly have the right people, circumstances, and opportunities; conviction that when one door closes, another one is already opening

- Mistrusting, doubtful, and desperate

- Trust that God is always in charge and I am always protected; faith that everything will turn out well

- Afraid, discouraged, procrastinating, weak in front of challenges, tired of trying again, and wanting to give up

- Courage, confidence, willpower, strength, endurance, perseverance, consistency, excitement, and enthusiasm

- Impatient, in a hurry, stressed out, insisting on finding an answer or solution when there is none, and wanting to skip stages

- Judgmental, critical, bitter, angry, vengeful, and reacting negatively

- Arrogant, pretending to know it all, always giving advice, especially when not requested; and needing to argue and always be right

- Mentally and emotionally closed, and set in my own way

- Patience, letting the answer find itself and the solution reveal itself, and taking one step at a time

- Awareness of the Human and the Being inside myself, inside others, and inside every creature; caring about the Human and the Being; awareness that every Human has a story and is trying to satisfy their own needs

- Humility; acceptance and respect of where everyone (including myself) is on their own path of growth; listening, understanding, empathy, compassion, forgiveness, tolerance, kindness, affection, and helpfulness

- Openness to learn something new, practice, adapt, and improve

- Resistant, refusing, and fighting what is; staying stubborn; wanting to control everything and everyone; always insisting on having perfection and being perfect

- Flexibility, resilience, and acceptance

- Feeling that life is a mistake, a problem, an obstacle, and a loss on the outside

- Awareness of every step I take on the inside, and that Here and Now is a growth opportunity

- Sad, dramatic, not smiling, and unhappy

- Passion, fun, humor, joy, pleasure, smiles, and happiness

I contemplated the silver sky until the last shining star faded away.

✿ ✿ ✿

"You will accept, forgive, and thank your unresolved past, one story at a time," Starry resumed. "You will accept, forgive, and thank everyone, including yourself. You will accept, forgive, and thank everything, every place, and every event.

"You will celebrate a ceremony—Unresolved Past Goodbye ceremony, one that will allow you to let go once and for all, and finally move on."

Shooter described the usual ceremony's inspiring ambiance and setup. It would be at a convenient place and time, with silence or soft background music, candlelight, a pleasant scent in the air, paper and pen, an alarm clock, and the happy music record to play once the ceremony is over.

"During this ceremony," continued Starry, "you will write a letter."

"Up here! *Look up here!*" Shooter called.

The sky lit up one more time, and the million stars wrote this letter:

☆ ☆ ☆

My Unresolved Past Goodbye Letter

A letter from me *(I write my full name)*:

_____

To you, my dear unresolved past *(I name the person, thing, place, or event)*:

_____

I acknowledge that you have been a blessed part of my life.

I accept that I was exactly when, where, and how I was supposed to be.

I truly believe that you existed because you love me.

I am aware that your true purpose was for me to grow and glow.

I forgive you for all the pain I felt then and there and may still feel today.

I thank you for my good old days and accept that they are gone and never coming back.

I thank you for what then appeared to be times of pain and absence of love, safety, and happiness.

I thank you for the apparently innocent but hurtful times.

I am grateful to you for whom and where I am today.

Now that your mission with me is accomplished, I thank you for not holding on to me or preventing me from moving on, so I continue my journey.

It is now time for me to graciously release you, just like you are graciously releasing me.

I empty my hands, and free my body, mind, and heart, making them available for someone, something, and somewhere new, and for a new experience and a new love.

I now let you go.

I send you light.

I send you love.

Today, I move on.

Today, I grow and glow a little more.

With all my love to you.

Signed, me *(I write my full name)*

✧ ✧ ✧

As the sparkles in the sky slowly started to vanish, Starry spoke.

"Once you have written the letter, it is time to let your unresolved past go, one story at a time. You can do that during the ceremony itself, if you feel ready, or at a later time, if you prefer. Just move at your own pace.

"Once you let go, you create an empty space and make room to receive who and what is new. As you are letting go, you will repeat that you trust God, for He always takes care of you in every step you take, and takes care of every situation and its outcome in your life."

"Say it, Genius! Say it out loud!"

"God, I trust You, for You always take care of me in every step I take, and take care of every situation and its outcome in my life."

"You will acknowledge and accept the fact that you are afraid because you are," Starry continued. "After you have let go of this part of your past—this person, thing, place, or event—you will repeat that you have faith that you are never alone. You will do this despite the fear of the painful loneliness and void, which letting go of this part of your past might create—this fear which has been haunting you for so long."

"Come on, Genius! Say it out loud!"

"I have faith that I am never alone."

"Talk to your unresolved past," continued Starry, "and repeat out loud, 'Today, I thank and bless you. Today, I choose to release you and let you go.'

"You can repeat these words while celebrating a ritual—an action that symbolizes letting go. One ritual would be to simply throw away the letter, or burn it and throw the ashes into running water, like a river."

"… or your kitchen or bathroom sink," Shooter added.

"You can step outside or stand by an open window and shake off your hands," suggested Starry. "While you do that, imagine that you are shaking your unresolved past out of your body, mind, and heart. Pretend that you are setting a bird free. Just open your hands and let it go. You can also get rid of an object that symbolizes the part of your past that you are now releasing.

"Sometimes, and whenever possible, it helps to physically go back to the place where the actual unresolved story happened. It would be a good idea for someone supportive to accompany you.

"Going back might be painful at first, but it helps you realize that, while the O'story still plays inside your mind, the original story of your past is no longer happening. The story no longer exists. The person inside the story has changed and moved on, or is probably no longer around. The place itself has also changed. No one and nothing stood still the way Old Teller still tells you, and the O'story still describes today.

"Going back to that same 'old' place somehow replaces the 'old' scene. It creates a new story that will mysteriously resolve and release the past one. It releases you, and you can then let go and move on."

"You can try another ritual, Genius. Roll up the goodbye letter you wrote and attach it to a doorknob with a cord. I suggest you choose the door that leads outside to your beautiful backyard. Then attach the other end of the cord to your wrist. Now open the door and start walking. Once the cord is fully extended and is preventing you from moving on, cut it with a pair of scissors."

Shooter suddenly realized something.

"Wait a minute ... I forgot the scissors! If you're already attached to the door, how are you going to get the scissors from the house? Okay, let me do this again: First, get the scissors, then get the cord, then ..."

"I get it, Shooter," I laughed. "I'll make sure that I have the scissors with me before I attach myself to the door."

"Different rituals work for different people, and at different times," Starry resumed. "You can also create your own ritual that will work for you. The idea is to perform an action that symbolizes freeing yourself from the part of your past that has done its job assisting you to grow and glow, and that no longer serves you Here and Now, but, on the contrary, is preventing you from taking a new step and moving on."

"Here's another ritual that often works for many people, Genius: Clean your house—your windows, cabinets, counters, closets, desk, drawers, and purse. Give away or throw away some of your stuff."

"Create an empty space," added Starry, "and make room to receive someone or something new. As you are letting go, tears may come. Allow and welcome them, and tell yourself that it is okay.

"As you are letting go, and as the unresolved story of your past is being released and liberated, you will feel its heavy weight actually being lifted off your shoulders, chest, and heart.

"Later, this story will come back every once in a while to talk to you. Time after time, its presence will feel lighter and lighter, and will become more and more pleasant.

"Eventually, it will come back less and less often, and will not stick around for long. It will come back only to say hello, reminding you of the growth step with which it blessed you. After it is gone, it leaves a beautiful and powerful energy inside and around you. This energy will make you feel completely fulfilled and truly happy."

✪

"What about when it does *not* do that?"

"It will, Genius. It always does ... *always!*"

"Until it does," Starry said, "until you understand its loving message, and until you are ready to accept, forgive, thank, and release this particular story of your past, remind yourself that it is okay that you are not yet ready to do so. Have self-compassion and forgive yourself, just like you have compassion and forgive Dunia.

"Have faith that, when you are ready and when it is time for you to let go, you gracefully will."

Shooter offered me these words to repeat out loud:

- I have true compassion for myself.

- I do not criticize, judge, humiliate, belittle, ridicule, insult, punish, hate, or conditionally love myself.

- I forgive myself for not always making the perfect choice or taking the ideal decision, and for not always saying or doing the right thing.

- I forgive myself for not being able to rise up and watch from above, and for not being able to go back to the stillness of my mind every time.

- I forgive myself for sometimes falling into the trap of the trigger-ego O'story-reaction game vicious circle, and for not being able to control my reacting words, gestures, or actions every time.

- I forgive myself for not being able to always clearly see, hear, or understand the language that my unresolved past speaks beyond all Human words and figure out the messages it holds inside.

- I forgive myself for sometimes forgetting compassion and forgiveness for others, for my story, and for myself.

- I forgive myself for sometimes forgetting that I am important, that I am good enough, that I am worthy and deserve to be loved, and that I am loved.

- I am proud of myself for every step I make to grow and glow.

"... and once I have let go?"

"Finally!" Shooter said, with a long sigh of relief. "I thought you'd never ask!"

"After you have let go," Starry answered, "and after you have made peace with your unresolved past, you are able to move on."

"Move on, Genius! Play your happy music record and *come back to Here and Now*. Get up, and shake and stretch your body. Move your arms and hands, and move your waist, legs, and feet. Then walk forward, and go on with your day ..."

"A new door has now opened," concluded Starry. "Move towards creating a new relationship with the life happening inside and around you.

"You are now ready to collect new I-haves. You are hopeful and look forward to having new dreams, setting new goals, facing new challenges, and living new experiences.

"There is now room for new opportunities to grow and glow.

"You are available to receive the new gifts that Here and Now offers you.

"You are able to see the empty space, hear the loud silence, and feel the deep stillness of your mind, where you are completely fulfilled and truly happy!"

CHAPTER FIVE

The Reaction

It was the last Saturday of my summer vacation. Dunia and I planned to spend the whole day together, getting her ready for kindergarten. I'd be going back to work on Monday and she'd be starting school in a week. Helen and George, Dunia's paternal grandparents, would pick her up on Sunday and take her to their cottage for a week.

First, we'd go to the hairdresser and then shop for the rest of Dunia's school supplies, a pair of black shoes, and a lunch box—a "princess" lunch box, specifically as ordered. My mother had asked to come shopping with us; she also needed to buy new shoes.

Dunia and I picked up my mother, and we all headed to the mall.

✦

As I pulled into the parking lot, a car cut me off.

"*Heeey*! *Look at this*!" I yelled, as my left hand released the steering wheel and pointed at the driver. "What is *wrong* with this guy? No courtesy *whatsoever*! This is a parking lot, not a *racetrack*!"

I turned to my mother, "Did you *see* this? Did you see what this guy just *did*?"

I turned my head back and continued shouting, "There's a *stop* sign, mister! A stop sign is not a *Christmas* decoration!"

"Why are you yelling?" my mother asked. "Do you think he can actually hear you? Stop yelling! What's *wrong* with you?"

"What's wrong with *me*?" I exploded. "This moron almost ran into us, and you're asking what's wrong with *me*?"

My mother was silent. As I drove towards a parking space that I spotted, the same driver raced me to it.

"I cannot *believe* this. Look at this! He just took my parking space! Is this guy for *real*? Is he doing this on *purpose*?"

Suddenly, I heard Shooter's voice above my tirade.

"You're looking crazy right now!"

"*Shut up*!" I snapped.

"*What*?" my mother asked, baffled and offended, as she turned and looked at me with her confused and wide-open eyes.

"I'm not talking to you," I bluntly answered.

"Grandma," whispered Dunia, "I think her head is talking to her again."

"This is great," I thought, knowing that neither my mother nor Dunia heard Shooter's comment. "All I need is for my mother to think that I'm talking to myself! All I need is for her to think that

I'm crazy! Isn't it bad enough she always says I never do *anything* right?"

"What did you just say?" Shooter asked.

"I said that all I need is for my mother to think that I'm talking to myself."

"Right after that part."

"I said that she always says that I never do anything right."

"She *said* that?"

"Yes."

"She *did*? You actually heard her *say* that?" he wondered, confused.

"Of *course* she did! Didn't you hear her ask what's wrong with *me*?"

"Yes, but I didn't hear her say that you never do anything right."

"Well, trust me, I know my mother. No matter what I do, she's *never* happy. Ever since I was little, and for as long as I can remember, she's never satisfied with anything I do. *Nothing* I do is ever good enough for her. *I* am never good enough! I mean, you just saw what happened. Even when a stranger screws up, she says that something is wrong with *me*! By the way, did you see what that *idiot* did? He almost *killed* us so he could take *my* parking space!"

"*Feel?*" Shooter asked.

"Red. *Very red!*" I answered furiously and without hesitation.

"Not only are you *feeling* red, Genius, you also *look* red. You look crazy! Your face looks crazy. Just a minute ago, your pitchy voice sounded crazy, and your hands were doing all these weird gestures and crazy things ...

"I may be far away from you, *way* up here, but I can still see and hear your rapid breathing. I can almost hear your fast heartbeat. I bet you're feeling a knot in your throat, chest, or stomach right now. Remember that when you feel red-crazy, and catch your red-rapid breathing, red-fast heartbeat, or red-knot, it means that, right now, Old Teller is speaking and you are reacting. Am I right, Genius?"

I sat still for a moment, trying to observe my breathing and heartbeat, and trying to feel the knot.

Regardless, I attempted to justify my reaction.

"Yes, but you don't *understand*! This guy just ..."

"Take a deep breath," Starry intervened.

"I mean, *really*," I insisted. "He just ..."

"Breathe, Genius! *Breathe!*"

I said nothing. I took a deep breath.

"Breathing helps your mind concentrate on the breath itself," Starry explained, "giving you a chance and just enough time to go back to the matrix of your mind, at least for the few seconds while the deep breath lasts. It gives you enough time for you to realize that Old Teller is now telling you an O'story, and that you are reacting.

"This first deep breath will make a first attempt at slowing down your breathing and heartbeat, bringing them back to their normal rhythm and undoing the knot.

"Now go back," she added.

"Well ... Genius has no choice but to go back. The parking space is already taken!"

"Go back to your *mind*," Starry clarified. "This is when a flashing red stop sign will appear and a whistle will go off to warn you to intercept your reacting words, gestures, or actions. The stop sign will read, 'Stop! That is Old Teller speaking. It is telling me an O'story, and I am reacting—this is why I feel unhappy.' Think of it as a traffic officer who puts his hand up and whistles so the cars stop.

"Then, catch Old Teller and the O'story.

"Now," she continued, "put your left hand on your stomach, right below your chest, with your palm opened and turned in against your body. Do it discreetly so your mother does not mistake your gesture for her own trigger."

I did what Starry requested. I placed my left hand on my stomach.

"Extend your right arm," she added, "and turn your palm out towards the situation that just happened."

"I can't do that *here!*"

"Just do it, Genius ... and let the distance of the extension also be discreet. Otherwise, your mother will confirm that you're *definitely* crazy."

Despite my wish to object, I decided to obey. I discreetly extended my right arm.

"Doing so," Starry explained, "keeps Old Teller, the O'story, the trigger, and your reaction at a distance. It prevents them from getting to you and taking you over. It also protects the sensitive areas of your chest and stomach against the negative energy that often accompanies a reaction.

"I want you to take another deep breath. This breath helps you go back to breathing normally again."

"It gives your face, voice, and hands enough time to stop looking and acting crazy. Just breathe, Genius ... and, while you're breathing, you can count to 10. That also helps."

"Sit in your movie director's chair and rise up," Starry reminded me. "Rise above the trigger—the action that this driver just did. Rise above the trigger—the words that your mother just said. Rise above Old Teller telling you that this man is threatening your I-have, and that your mother always says you never do anything right and you are not good enough. Rise above the O'stories, which are trying to convince you that your source of love, safety, and happiness is now in danger.

"Rise up, and watch from above. Do not become one with Old Teller, the ego O'story, the trigger, or your reaction.

"Do not become one with the situation. The situation happened outside your body and mind. Let it stay outside.

"Go back to the empty space, the loud silence, and the deep stillness of your mind, and stay there for a moment.

"Then, *come back to Here and Now.*"

My mother helped Dunia get out of the car and they both walked towards the mall. I'm not sure if she purposely decided to avoid walking next to me, but she definitely had no clue that Starry and Shooter were talking to me. She must have noticed my silence and distraction, and thought that I was mad at her. She probably decided to give me space and time to cool down, just like she does every time she pisses me off. She *always* does that!

"She *does?*"

"*Always*, Shooter! She says things to piss me off and then lets me be. First, I feel badly about what she tells me, and then I feel worse about what I say back to her. I know she's hurt right now by what just happened."

Shooter pointed out the fact that, regardless of what my mother *actually* says out loud, deep in my mind I always hear the same comments. Regardless of the present trigger coming from her, I hear that, no matter what I do, she's never satisfied. I hear that nothing I do is ever good enough for her. I hear that I am not good enough!

"Do not get involved with the situation that just happened around you," Starry said. "Do not get involved with the scene that the O'story is describing inside your mind. Do not get sucked into the details.

"For now, become aware that the true purpose of the trigger is to give an unresolved story a chance to express itself, and highlight the presence of an important growth message still waiting to be delivered.

"Trust that your reaction will lead you to that story where the message is located. Make a quick note of what just happened in your agenda. Give the situation, the trigger, the O'story, and your reaction a title and a brief description."

Shooter gave me examples of some titles and descriptions:

- The situation: Parking lot at the mall
- The trigger: (a) The crazy driver's actions
                       (b) My mother's comment, "What's wrong with you?"
- The ego O'story: (a) This man put our lives in danger, and then took *my* parking space.
                       (b) My mother *always* says that I'm not good enough.
- My reaction: (a) I yelled at the driver.
                       (b) I snapped at my mother.

"You will later choose a more convenient place and time to celebrate your Unresolved Past ceremony," Starry continued, "face the story that needs to talk to you, watch and see what it wants to show you, listen to what it wants to tell you, and try to understand the growth message it holds for you. For now, go back to the emptiness, the silence, and the stillness of your mind."

Starry was quiet for a few seconds, and then gave me the final direction.

"Now *go!*"

✫

I caught up with my mother and Dunia at the entrance of the mall.

"You know what, Mom? Go ahead and take Dunia to the hair salon. Her appointment is in 15 minutes. I'm going upstairs to the department store. I'll meet you at the hairdresser's when I'm done. Listen for your phone in case I call you, okay? I'll see you in a little while."

I gave Dunia a kiss and walked away. I thought I'd start looking for Dunia's shoes—and maybe a skirt for myself (one that hides the veins on my legs). I'd then go to the purse section. I had seen a beautiful purse last week but did not get a chance to buy it. I thought I'd take a closer look at it, since my mother was watching Dunia.

"I just hope I don't run into that man who took my parking space," I thought, still angry.

✫

On my way to the department store, I resumed my conversation with Starry and Shooter.

"What about the driver who took my parking space? What's the unresolved story there?"

"The true purpose of a trigger," Starry answered, "is to give your unresolved story an opportunity to express itself and deliver its message—especially when this trigger comes from someone you baptized as your source of love, safety, and happiness, namely your closest loved ones.

"When you react to a trigger coming from someone with whom you are not really involved, a person who is not really significant to you, or someone you do not even know, there is not always a past story that needs to be resolved, unless you find yourself often reacting to different people and situations in a similar fashion—especially when your reaction is intense.

"Since you now know and understand the game between the trigger, the ego O'story, and your reaction, you now realize that the trigger is not a true threat to your source of love, safety, and happiness. You can now easily choose not to play this game."

"Yes, but that man stole *my* parking space! He had no right to do that. I saw the empty spot first, and I'm *sure* he was aware of that. This guy is selfish and completely disrespectful!"

"In the case of true danger, such as a real threat to your safety, or the safety of your loved ones, it becomes mandatory for you to react and protect yourself and your loved ones—and even protect a complete stranger. You set your limits and request that the person-trigger stops and respects them. You can ask for the help of authorities, if required. You may also consider removing yourself from where you are—actually step back, distance yourself from the trigger and, whenever possible, simply leave. Make sure you do this with no negativity; otherwise, you will fall into the trap of the trigger-ego O'story-reaction game, and start swinging back and forth all over again.

"Now, tell me, was the fact that the man took the parking space a real danger?"

"No ... but it was *my* parking space! I saw it *first*. On top of that, this guy did not respect his stop sign. He almost caused an accident and put everyone's life in danger. He's an irresponsible, selfish *idiot!*"

"Do not become one with the trigger or your reaction," Starry reminded. "Do not become one with Old Teller or the O'story trying to convince you that this trigger is threatening your source of love, safety, and happiness.

"Let me ask you this: When this man did not stop, and then took the parking space, what exactly did you lose? What exactly did he take away from you? Which one of your I-haves did his actions *really* endanger and hurt? Is it one of your physical I-haves? Is it one of your mental I-haves? Is it one of your emotional I-haves? Go back to your Needs chart and read it over. You will quickly realize that nothing was taken away.

"No reaction—no word, gesture, or action—regardless of how hurtful it feels, can really hurt you. No matter how offensive or insulting you might think it is, it does not have a real power to challenge you. No matter how belittling, ridiculing, embarrassing, or judgmental it seems to be, it is not able to make you become any less worthy. No matter how punishing, vengeful, or threatening it looks or sounds, it can never actually make you lose anything or become a loser, make you fail or become a failure, or have the power to take anything away from you.

"In addition, your reaction has absolutely no power to take anything away from the other person either. It has no power to make you win or become more. In fact, reacting by surrendering to the act of wanting to hurt the other one and make them lose only gives you a false hope of getting something back. It might give you the *illusion* that you won, but, in reality, your reaction will only cost you.

"Even if you end up winning, and no matter what you win back—such as a parking space, an argument, money, or a lawsuit—you end up losing a lot more. You end up punishing only yourself by paying a great price out of your physical, mental, and emotional health and well-being.

"Do not allow the situation to cost you a lot more than just a parking space! Every day, you encounter an endless variety of 'parking-space' situations. Reacting to each of these situations will exhaust you, one reaction at a time. Your reactions will consume you, one small bite at a time."

Shooter described many small-bite situations from what he called "the small-bite list," such as when a driver cuts me off and takes my parking space, or when someone—including myself—races to beat a traffic light, or pass a slow driver, putting their life and other lives in danger, just to save a few seconds. He suggested that, the next time I felt tempted in these types of situations, I should ask myself, "Are my nerves not worth more than a few seconds? Is my life, as well as the other life I might be putting in danger, not worth more than a few seconds?"

Then he gave more examples of small-bite situations, such as the irritating situation with Sharon, the bank employee, who screwed up three times already. There was the annoying situation of the restaurant to which Linda and I went, and where the service was bad. He remembered the aggravating situation with that company I called the other day, where an answering machine greeted me and told me to press this button and that button. I eventually spoke with an *actual* Human, who first put me on hold *forever*, and then kept transferring me from one wrong department to the other until I was finally disconnected!

Shooter then had fun describing the many times I'd wait in line at a store, and where I'd actually take the time to count how many customers were waiting in each lane and compare the amount of goods in each shopping cart—all to make sure that I chose the shortest and fastest moving lane. Then I'd stand there and wait for my turn to pay. If, all of a sudden, *my* lane froze, I'd stretch my neck to try and see what was going on, and discover that the customer and the cashier at the front of *my* lane were standing there, either looking for something or waiting. This was usually when Old Teller would start its speech.

"Why does this always happen to *me*? Why did I have to pick *this* particular lane? There are six other lanes. Why didn't I pick one of *them*?"

I'd wait ... I'd look to my right and see that the guy who was standing *way* back in his lane was now paying his bill, picking up his goods, and leaving.

I'd wait ... I'd look ahead and see that the person holding up *my* lane was still standing there.

Meanwhile, Old Teller would start counting how many people in the lanes to my right and left were getting to the front, being serviced, and leaving, while I was still standing there, waiting, and while the small bites were consuming me, one small bite at a time.

Then I'd try to decide if I should move to another lane. I could go *all* the way to the back, behind everyone else, or choose to stay where I was and hope that *my* lane started to move soon. What if I dared to change lanes and then, all of a sudden, my *new* lane jammed while my old one moved ahead?

I heard Shooter laugh and say that this would then become a big-bite—even a *huge*-bite—situation!

"I know *exactly* what you're talking about, Shooter. These small-bite situations are everywhere. I can easily name at least one or two people who cause me to live one of these situations *every* day!"

"Of *course* you can, your Highness, and I can easily name at least one or two people whose small-bite situation cause is *you!*"

"When you are dealing with a small-bite situation," Starry said, "think of a situation where you said or did something similar to someone else that upset, irritated, annoyed, aggravated, offended, or hurt them. When you realize that *you* can also cause someone else a small-bite situation, you will be less judgmental and more tolerant. You will react less, and save yourself from some bites.

"A trigger lasts for a few seconds but, if you allow the vicious circle of the trigger, the ego O'story, and the reaction to trap you, you will only hurt yourself. You will keep on paying a great price out of your health and well-being, long after the trigger has actually left the scene. You will pay for minutes, hours, days, weeks, months, or years. The value of a parking space does not come close to that of your physical, mental, or emotional health and well-being.

"Let the parking space be nothing more than a space where you park your car. Remember that if you happen to lose one, there are plenty of replacement parking spaces out there. I am sure that you can easily find another parking space that will cost you a lot less."

"When you realize that you're in the presence of a small-bite situation—or *problem* as you sometimes call it," Shooter said, "elevate yourself way up high and look down at the rest of your life. Compared to your health and well-being and, on a lifetime scale, ask yourself, 'How important or significant is my problem? Will I remember it in a week, tomorrow, or even in an hour?'

"Then look at the life happening in the world around you Here and Now, and ask yourself this: 'On a scale from 1 to 10, how do I rate my present problem when I compare it to someone else's problem happening somewhere in the world right now, maybe somewhere not too far from here?'

"Become aware of the small-bite situation," he added, "and repeat this sentence to yourself: 'That is Old Teller speaking, and *this* is a small-bite situation!' This sentence acts like a magic wand that makes Old Teller immediately shut up and the O'stories disappear. It helps you drop the situation and exit the scene."

"Let a parking space be nothing more than just a parking space," reminded Starry. "Let a word be just a word, and nothing more. Bring the gesture or action back to its simple and pure definition. Always remember that no word, gesture, or action can actually hurt you. Become aware that no word, gesture, or action has true power over you.

"When you do not play the trigger-ego O'story-reaction game, you win a lot more than you lose."

"What do I win?" I eagerly asked.

Shooter was baffled.

"Haven't you heard a word she's *said?* You win your physical, mental, and emotional health and well-being. Weren't you listening?"

"All that and more," added Starry.

"All that and more," echoed Shooter, then realized what Starry had just said. "There's *more?*"

"You now know and understand the interaction between the trigger, the ego O'story of your mind, your reaction, and your unresolved past. In return, this allows you to understand other Humans' reactions to triggers as well as their interaction with their own unresolved past.

"Just like yours, *their* past has painful, unresolved stories that triggers reach and poke. *They* also hear their Old Teller telling them ego O'stories about how these triggers can threaten their source of love, safety, and happiness.

"You sometimes feel that they—especially your loved ones—react against you, hurt you, turn you down or reject you, and refuse to help or serve you the way in which you would like to be helped or served. You believe that they take from you and do not give you enough. You say that they do not listen to you, or acknowledge or approve of what you think, feel, say, or do. You feel that they do not understand or appreciate you, or care about you or love you.

"You can now understand that what they say or do *to you* is not necessarily meant *against* you. They are simply attempting to satisfy their own needs, protect their own source of love, safety, and happiness, and protect themselves against the pain of their own unresolved stories."

"Everyone is busy listening to their Old Teller and watching their own O'stories," said Shooter. "They hardly have enough time and energy to satisfy their own needs. They surely don't have time or energy to always satisfy yours!"

"Although you know that you are not responsible for their story or needs," Starry continued, "you are now more compassionate with them, just like you are more compassionate with yourself. Now it becomes easier for you to be more understanding of where they are on their own path of growth, just like you are with yourself."

Shooter gave different examples of questions I could ask myself to help me be more compassionate and understanding:

- What kind of a day is this person having? What are their life conditions and source of love, safety, and happiness like right now? Are they listening to *their* Old Teller and watching *their* O'stories?

- Is this man having problems with his health today? Is he in pain? Does he have problems at home with his wife or kids? Does he have trouble at work, with his finances, or with his sources of security? Is he overwhelmed with responsibilities?

- Is this woman worried about something or someone she loves? Is her family okay? Is she unhappy inside her own life story?

"You now understand other Humans' reactions," Starry resumed, "just like you understand yours. You are more accepting and patient with them, just like you are with yourself.

"When they react, you no longer reduce their whole Human Being to a word, gesture, action, or reaction. You no longer see them as a threat against which you need to defend yourself. You no longer need to protect your source of love, safety, and happiness from them.

"Without ignoring your need to react—which points out your unresolved past story that needs to express itself—it now becomes easy for you to control the intensity and frequency of your reacting words, gestures, and actions. You no longer need to judge, criticize, humiliate, ridicule, belittle, or put them down. You no longer need to manipulate, blame, accuse, insult, or punish them, and no longer need to hold grudges or feel resentful or vengeful.

"It now becomes easy for you to forgive. You choose not to react and you choose to forgive. You let the sound of their story speak louder than your reaction. You realize that this person might be hurting and, instead of your reaction, they actually need your love. Instead of your reaction, you will send them love."

"How do I do *that*?"

"You will forgive and send them a smile, not out of pity or feelings of superiority, but because you know the game now and you choose not to play it. Forgiving *them* frees both you *and* them from the grip of the trigger, the ego O'story, and the reaction, so you can both move on.

"With absolutely no negativity and with true love and compassion, you will discreetly smile, open your hand towards them, and say, 'I send you love to fill your day, your heart, and your life.'

"You are now able to see beyond their Human reaction, and the Being inside you will connect with the Being inside them.

"You are now actually making a difference by breaking the trigger-ego O'story-reaction vicious circle. You are actively limiting the useless suffering that unconscious reactions create for you, for others, and for the world. When you do, you feel completely fulfilled and truly happy!"

"*That* is how 'much more' you win by not playing the trigger-ego O'story-reaction game, Genius."

Shooter finished speaking as I arrived at the purse section of the department store. The salesman welcomed me from behind the counter.

"Good *morning*, ma'am!"

"Good morning."

"How are *you* today?"

"I'm well," I answered. "And you?"

"I'm fine, thank you. How may I help you today?"

"I was here last week and saw a purse I liked. It was right here," I said, pointing to the shelf, "but I don't see it anymore."

"What did it look like?"

"Well, it was velvety brown and about this big. The handle was dark brown, and I think it was braided."

The salesman stared at me and said nothing. I thought that maybe he was trying to imagine what I was describing, or trying to remember where the purse was.

"Actually, I'm not sure if it *was* braided. Maybe it was flat."

I waited for a comment. When he still said nothing, I assumed that he needed more details, so I continued my second attempt at describing the purse.

"No, I don't think it was flat. I think it was more ..."

"We don't have the purse anymore," he interrupted.

"Are you *sure* you know which one I'm talking about?"

"I sold the purse yesterday," he said with a dry tone.

"Well, don't you have *another* one?" I desperately continued. "Maybe someone misplaced it. Can you please verify that for me?"

The man just stood there and stared at me. He shrugged his shoulders, opened his hands, raised his left eyebrow, and pinched his lips.

"We don't *have* the purse anymore. You should've bought it when you saw it last week."

Then, he left the counter to greet another customer.

I stood there for a moment, then walked away and continued to browse, pretending that I was looking for something different. I felt my blood pressure rise and I could no longer see any purse in front of me ... I saw no purse, no shelf, no counter, and no store!

All I could hear was Old Teller starting its monologue.

"What the hell is *wrong* with this guy? What is wrong with *everyone* this morning? Is it me or something in the air? No, it's *not* me. This guy is totally arrogant and rude! What kind of a horrible *service* is that? Incompetent *loser*! You don't have the *purse*? What are you standing there for? *Look* for it! Call another store or a distributor, or try to sell me something else, but *do something*!"

Without catching its breath, Old Teller continued.

"... and that attitude! Just who do you think you *are*, mister? I'll tell you who you are. You are no more than a poor salesman who has no clue whom he's dealing with! Well, guess *what*? *I* will tell you whom you're dealing with. You'll see. I will call the manager himself and make sure he hears about what just happened. I'll let you know whom you're dealing with. I'm going to teach you a lesson that you deserve to learn—in sales *and* in manners. You'll pay for this. Nobody talks to *me* this way ... *nobody!*"

At that point, Shooter joined Old Teller.

"A salesman with a bad attitude *and* an awful service! Add *those* to your small-bite list, Genius! Maybe you should start a big-bite list, for that matter. This guy should apologize to you. In fact, the manager should *also* apologize. After all, he *is* responsible for what the employees say and do. He should find the purse and give you a discount. Better yet, he should give it to you for free, just so you don't spread the word, tell everyone about what just happened, give him bad publicity, and ruin the reputation of this place!"

"*Feel?*" interrupted Starry.

"Red, Starry," Shooter answered. "*Very* red."

"Shooter," she kindly said, "the question was not addressed to you."

I guess that was my cue.

"Red."

I said nothing more. I stayed quiet for a while. Actually, I'm not sure if "quiet" was the right word to describe how I was feeling; I think "furious" or "stunned" was more like it.

Starry and Shooter also stayed quiet.

Suddenly, it hit me.

"I'm reacting, aren't I?"

The Reaction

"The change in your breathing and your heartbeat—your blood pressure—the knot, and your crazy face are your cues, Genius. Just follow the steps of the process."

"What process?"

"The Awareness Process, which will help you stop feeling red and feel happy again."

Shooter guided me through the steps of the Awareness Process:

- *Feel?*

- Unhappy-red.

- I catch the change in my breathing and heartbeat, and I catch the knot.

- I take a deep breath.

- I go into my mind. I see the flashing red stop sign and I hear the whistle: "Stop! That is Old Teller speaking. It is telling me an ego O'story, and I am reacting—this is why I feel unhappy."

- I catch Old Teller and the ego O'story.

- I catch the trigger and my reaction.

- I discreetly place my left hand turned in against my stomach, and extend my right arm, with my hand turned out towards Old Teller, the O'story, the trigger, and my reaction.

- I take another deep breath while I count to 10: 1, 2, 3, 4, 5, 6, 7, 8, 9, 10.

- I inhale space, silence, and stillness, and exhale the ego O'story out of my mind and the reaction out of my body.

- I sit in my movie director chair, rise above Old Teller and the O'story, and watch from above.

- I do not become one with Old Teller or the O'story.

- I rise above the situation, the trigger, and my reaction.

- I do not become one with the situation, the trigger, or my reaction. The situation happened outside my body and mind. I let it stay outside.

- I see the empty space, hear the loud silence, and feel the deep stillness of my mind. I stay there for a moment.

- *I come back to Here and Now*, where I am completely fulfilled and truly happy!

"I'm not sure that I can do this. I'm not sure that I'll be able to catch my reaction before it takes me over. I'm not sure that I can rise above the situation and watch without becoming one with it."

"Be compassionate and patient with yourself," Starry comforted.

"Patience, Genius! Give yourself some time and some credit. You did catch yourself reacting. You did feel your blood pressure rise. You did feel the change in your breathing and heartbeat. You did feel the knot, *didn't* you?"

"Yeah, but Starry had to point it out for me. She had to be there."

"Starry is *always* there, and always will be. Me, too, Genius! You will *never* get rid of us! Hey! Didn't you see the flashing red stop sign? Didn't you hear the whistle? Didn't they show and tell you to stop?"

172

"I saw no stop sign and heard no whistle," I said, discouraged. "Old Teller was talking too much. I can't believe that I was actually debating how I could teach this guy a lesson. I'm so embarrassed. Boy, Shooter! I'm glad that you and Starry came to the rescue before I started sending this man to hell!"

"This man's 'bad attitude' has absolutely no power to take anything away from you," Starry reminded me. "You have nothing less, you are not less, and your source of love, safety, and happiness is not threatened, just like your reaction will not take anything away from him, make him any less, or give you anything more."

"Certainly not your purse!" added Shooter. "Your reaction will not make you more either. Teaching him a lesson will only cost you your health and well-being. This would be a painful big bite and a big price to pay—all for someone you don't even *know*!"

"Instead of losing your physical, mental, and emotional health over what this man cannot give you," Starry continued, "and instead of expecting something he is obviously not able to offer you in the present moment, enjoy what he *can* offer you."

"What exactly would *that* be?" I asked. "This man has *nothing* to offer besides his rude and arrogant attitude. How hard is it to smile and be nice? How hard is it to look for a purse or make a phone call? How hard is it for a salesman to assist a client and sell them something?"

"Do not forget that this man also has a story," Starry said. "This morning, instead of your reaction, he probably needed your love!

"Every day, you face different situations, go to different places, and interact with different people. Everyone and everything you deal with has something special to offer you. Instead of insisting on receiving what you expect from them, instead of getting mad and dwelling on what you think they will not give you, and instead of being disappointed, frustrated, and angry at what they do not offer you, enjoy what they *do* give and offer you.

"Even when you feel that they 'do not' or 'will not,' the truth is that they often do not have what you want them to give you. Just because you would like or expect them to be the source of an I-have that satisfies a need of yours, it does not mean that they are capable or know how to be that source."

"So what should I do to get service around here? The only source I expect this man to be is a source for a purse. The only need I want him to satisfy is my need to have this purse. How can I not expect him to give me that service? Isn't he the salesman?"

"I hear you, Genius. He could at least be the source of some respect and decent attitude."

"This man is who he is," Starry said, "and he gave you what he was capable or willing to give you. For the sake of *your* nerves—not only his—do not resist or fight this reality. Do not expect what he seems to be incapable of giving you at this point.

"When you are trying to collect an I-have that is not critical to your life, from a person you hardly know, or a situation with which you have to deal briefly, enjoy the acceptable I-have (service or product) that this person or situation is offering you. If you judge that it is not enough, turn to a different source that might be able to offer you more and better satisfy your present need."

"An acceptable I-have from an acceptable salesman," Shooter said. "*Less* than acceptable ... *way* below ... minimal ... flat *zero*! Let's not forget Sharon at the bank. I mean, *really*, does a person need a master's degree to figure out a bank statement? What about that waiter at the restaurant *and* the phone operator *and* the cashier? The world is full of less than acceptable people and situations, and services and products."

"... and the world keeps on turning," Starry reassured. "A parking space, a purse, a bank statement, or a service at a restaurant, over the phone, or at the cash register is not more important than your priceless health.

"For the sake of your precious physical, mental, and emotional health and well-being, do not put up a fight against the salesman's service or attitude. Accept the situation and come back another time when someone else is available to assist you, buy a different purse, or go to a different store."

"... but his *attitude*!" I insisted.

"Do not expect to receive an I-have that someone or something can obviously not offer you," Starry said. "Ask yourself, 'Does this person, thing, place, or situation have, in their possession, what I need from them? Can they be the source of the I-have that I want and that satisfies my present need?'"

Shooter gave many examples of questions that I could ask myself in different situations:

- Can this sad, angry, or bitter person offer me humor, joy, and pleasure, even a simple smile?

- Can this person, who never listens, listen to me?

- Can this busy, overwhelmed, and worried person offer me their time, attention, and support?

- Can this tired, hurt, or sick person offer me physical help?

- Can this slow person offer me fast, energetic, and enthusiastic service?

- Can I trust this person, who often lies, to always tell the truth?

- Can I expect a beginner to submit the same results as an experienced person?

- Can I expect a child or a teenager to behave like an adult?

- Can I expect a crawling baby to run?

- Can a northern country give me tropical weather?

- Can summer give me snow?

"For each person with whom you have to interact on a regular basis," Starry continued, "and for each thing, place, or situation with which you have to often deal, you will create a Happy List—a list of all the qualities that, in your eyes, make them a great person, thing, place, or situation.

"First, you will create a Happy List for the people in your life, starting with your closest loved ones. This list will remind you that every Human has their own unique story, including the story they came with and the one they came into. It will remind you that they also have their own unresolved past, which they are trying to resolve. They have unmet needs, which they are attempting to satisfy while trying to satisfy yours and fulfilling their role of being *your* source of love, safety, and happiness, to the best of their knowledge and abilities. It will remind you to be understanding and compassionate, and to accept and respect where they are on their own path of growth."

"How do I create this Happy List?"

Shooter described the usual ceremonial setup but, this time, he suggested that I choose a happy day to celebrate. I create a "good mood" ambiance, and fill the place with happy music and bright lighting. He suggested that I sit somewhere that brings out pleasant thoughts and enhances happy feelings, like in my backyard. He said to get a paper and pen ready.

On top of the page, I write down the title of this ceremony— Happy List—along with the name of the person for whom I'm creating this list.

On this Happy List, I note all the wonderful qualities that describe this person and make them, in my eyes, a great Human Being. Every Happy List description that I do not note becomes part of their personal difficulties or weaknesses, as well as the qualities they lack, which obviously make it hard for them to offer me what I sometimes expect, want, ask, and need of them.

"What does this Happy List look like?"

"Up here! *Look up here!* It's show time again!" shouted Shooter.

I looked up and it instantly struck me.

"Shooter ... I'm at the mall!"

"Oh!" he said. Then, after a brief pause, he added, "but the million stars up here are still painting!

"Hey, Genius, allow me to use Human words to describe to you what these shining stars, which have scattered and filled the sky, want to show and tell you."

Happy List

Name: _____

This person is:

Loving, nice, kind, warm, gentle, tender, thoughtful, caring, giving, generous, helpful, considerate, friendly, available, affectionate, compassionate, understanding, accepting, easygoing, tolerant, patient, forgiving, open minded, free spirited, empathic, a good listener, focused, intuitive, consistent, positive, optimistic, cheerful, happy, smiling, laughing, funny, fun, witty, pleasant, playful, courageous, brave, daring, faithful, trustworthy, simple, modest, humble, thankful, grateful, appreciative, vigilant, careful, responsible, mature, reliable, professional, determined, confident, secure, quiet, relaxed, calm, laid back, organized, productive, an achiever, efficient, dedicated, persevering, a hard worker, meticulous, expressive, communicative with opinions and emotions, rational, sensitive, practical, adaptable, mellow, compromising, flexible, resilient, cooperative, ambitious, energetic, healthy, strong, powerful, enthusiastic, curious, discreet, wise, intelligent, competent, knowledgeable, hospitable, welcoming, honest, passionate, authentic, genuine, stable, composed, sociable, respectful, talented, fair, clear, serious ...

The Reaction

This person is not:

Afraid, doubtful, insecure, easily discouraged, violent, selfish, annoying, complicated, arrogant, uselessly argumentative, overly proud, indifferent, moody, grumpy, forgetful, tense, hesitant, nervous, hyper, bad tempered, anxious, worried, irritable, stubborn, slow, lazy, nosy, greedy, ambiguous, boring, bored, dramatic, fearful, regretful, resentful, vengeful, messy, clumsy, confused, obsessed, shy, vulnerable, weak, oppressive ...

This person does not:

Betray, cheat, lie, panic, dwell, nag, play the victim, complain, blame, judge, accuse, procrastinate, manipulate others, make a big deal out of everything or nothing, hold a grudge, always feel guilty, assume, constantly listen to Old Teller and watch unhappy O'stories, react negatively ...

✫ ✫ ✫

"Wow!" I exclaimed. "This Happy List is endless!"

"You will also create your own Happy List," Starry offered.

"For myself and my *own* qualities?"

"Don't worry, Genius. This should not take you too long."

"Whenever you need it," Starry continued, "your Happy List will remind you of the great Human Being that you are. It will give you support during those times that you are too hard on yourself and expect too much—or what cannot be expected—from yourself, and when you need to be more patient and compassionate with yourself."

"Starry, you said that a Happy List can be created for anyone or anything, right?" Shooter asked.

"Of course."

"Hey, Genius, maybe this will finally help you stop complaining about almost everyone and everything."

"I don't complain about everyone and everything."

"I said *almost*," he clarified. "First, create a Happy List for your mother, one for Aunt Maryam, and then one for your friend Susan. Write one for your job, one for your colleagues, and then one for your boss at work.

"Your next Happy List will be for the weather and then for the seasons. Write one for your house, one for your neighborhood and the neighbors, and another one for whomever and whatever you say 'should give you more,' such as the public services, your city, country, and government ... the lists go on.

"Create a Happy List for everyone and everything you have to deal with and often complain about. This should not take you more than a year or two!" he joked. "Put those Happy Lists inside your Precious Box where you can refer to them whenever you feel unhappy, sad, disappointed, upset, angry, or resentful towards this particular person, thing, place, or situation."

"Reading a Happy List," added Starry, "will highlight all the happy reasons why you appreciate and are thankful for this person, thing, place, or situation.

"It reduces the negative power of the words, gestures, or actions of this particular person who just offended or hurt you, bringing each word back to just a word, each gesture back to just a gesture, and each action back to its simple definition.

"It helps you to not confuse the *whole* person with this particularly hurtful and disappointing event that just happened, and restricts your hurt and disappointment to that single situation with which you need to deal.

"Instead of listening to what Old Teller is telling you about the person, and watching the ego O'stories describing them as a heartless and dangerous monster, you will watch, see, and listen to what their Happy List is showing and telling you. Instead of diving into the pain of your reaction, it now becomes easy for you to forgive them.

"Refer to these Happy Lists, read them on regular basis, and use them as a prevention tool and constant reminder. Load your mind with an overdose of these Happy List qualities so that, whenever a trigger situation arises, your pain and disappointment will somehow feel less intense—maybe even neutralized—and the threatening power of the trigger will quickly disappear.

"These lists will help you control—reduce or eliminate—the intensity and frequency of your reacting words, gestures, or actions, and only the true purpose of your reaction, which is to point out the unresolved past story that needs to express itself and deliver its loving growth message to you, will remain."

"You will soon be able to leave Old Teller," Shooter said, "the O'story, the trigger, the reaction, the situation, and the place. You will take a step and walk away."

"I have to admit that this is not an easy step for me!" I said, in frustration, as I walked out of the department store and headed back to the hair salon.

"The step might not be easy, Genius, but it is certainly not impossible!"

"It is definitely not an easy step," Starry agreed, "but it sure is a pleasant one. Most importantly, it is a rewarding and significant step that you are taking on your path of growth.

"Go back to your mind, sit in your director's chair, rise up, and watch from above.

"Consciously choose not to mentally react. Choose to think of nothing. Stay inside the empty space and the deep stillness. Do not analyze, label, compare, dislike, despise, criticize, or judge.

"Consciously choose not to verbally react. Choose to say nothing. Stay inside the loud silence and the deep stillness, and stay above the words."

"Do not open your mouth," instructed Shooter, and then added, "*Chobolo Tobolo.*"

"What?"

"*Chobolo Tobolo,*" he repeated. "It means 'the trigger, which just happened, is no longer happening right now.' *Chobolo Tobolo!* What's done is done! What just was ruined is ruined. What just broke is broken. What just spilled has spilled. What just ripped has ripped. What just was stained is stained. What just was scratched is scratched. What just was lost is lost ...

"It is now a story of the past, and you have no control over going back there or changing anything, but you *can* control and change your reaction. You can also turn to 5W2H-O&D and ask yourself, 'What can I do *now*? How can I deal with this situation? What are my options ... or *Options?*' Right, Starry?"

"Right."

Encouraged by Starry's approval, he continued.

"What's said is said. Right, Starry?"

"Right, Shooter," she laughed.

"If words are made of silver, then silence is made of gold," he added.

Starry and I laughed some more. Inspired by our fun, he kept talking.

"Three monkeys."

"Three monkeys?" I asked. "Did you say *monkeys?*"

"No see, no hear, and no say."

Starry laughed again, and then added to Shooter's ideas.

"... *and* no do.

"Consciously choose not to physically react. Choose to do nothing— unless you are facing a dangerous situation. You are now aware that no word, gesture, or action can take from you or give to you.

"With absolutely no negativity, distance yourself from the place where the situation just happened. Leave what just happened *where* it happened. Take a few steps back and simply leave.

"Consciously choose not to react.

"Consciously choose not to think of anything.

"Consciously choose not to say anything.

"Consciously choose not to do anything.

"Consciously choose not to pay out of your precious physical, mental, and emotional health for a situation that does not deserve this costly price and is not worth that great loss.

"Whenever it is a reaction of a recurrent nature, take note of it so you can later celebrate an Unresolved Past ceremony. Choose a more appropriate place and time, watch and see the unresolved story that your reaction has pointed out, listen to it, and try to understand the growth message that it has for you.

"See the empty space, listen to the loud silence, and feel the deep stillness of your mind. Stay there for a moment. Then come back to Here and Now."

✦

"Speaking of Here and Now, there are your mom and Dunia," Shooter announced as I entered the hair salon. "Wow! Look at Dunia's hair. She looks great!"

"Baby! Look at *you*! You look like a princess! Your hair is so *beautiful*!"

Dunia moved her head sideways a couple of times, enjoying the soft curls whipping her face.

"Do you like your hair, Princess?"

"Yep," she nodded and gave me a big hug. Then she pointed at her hair. "She put sparkly stars, Mommy. *Look*! Can you see how they shine?"

"Just like home," Shooter noted.

"Just like a princess!" I said.

Then I turned to my mother.

"Who cut her hair?"

"Sandra. She's great with kids. Too bad that you missed it all. What took you so long?"

I consciously ignored her question by asking her another one.

"Did you pay already?"

I was trying to avoid another confrontation with her. I felt her question and the tone of her voice poking a painful past story. I heard Old Teller clear its throat and get ready to start telling me its one thousand and one O'stories.

"I haven't paid yet. Aren't you at least going to say hello to Sandra before we leave?"

I glanced up, desperately trying to find Starry and hoping she would rescue me.

"*Feel?*"

"Red," I whispered.

I discreetly took a deep breath, placed my left hand on my stomach, and extended my right arm.

I took another deep breath while I counted to 10.

I sat in my director's chair, rose up, and watched from above, while I quietly repeated these words to myself: "I stay above Old Teller and the O'story, the trigger, and my reaction."

I consciously chose not to react. I did not think of anything. I did not say anything. I did not do anything.

I went back to the empty space, the loud silence, and the deep stillness of my mind, and stayed there for a moment.

Then, I turned to my mother and looked into her eyes. For the first time in a very long time, I *really* saw her. I smiled and asked her to go find Sandra while I paid.

I looked up and smiled again, and saw Starry wink at me.

"Don't forget to celebrate your Unresolved Past ceremony, and write your mom's Happy List soon," Shooter yelled as he zoomed away.

"I will. I promise."

CHAPTER SIX

The Future

The plan was for Dunia to spend all of next week at the cottage with Helen and George. She had asked to sleep with me the night before she left.

I held her closely and watched her beautiful face while she fell asleep in my bed. My hand caressed her soft skin and her wild curls spread all over the pillow. I could not get enough of her scent. I listened to her breath and felt its warmth on my face. I must have kissed her a million times.

Starry and Shooter never showed up. They probably wanted to give me some privacy so I could savor the precious moments I spent with my daughter. They probably also realized that I hadn't gotten much sleep lately, spending most of my nights listening and talking to them, and I was tired.

✦

Morning came so fast! I wished that I could've stayed in bed and cuddled with Dunia for the rest of the day. I wished that I didn't have a million things to do before tomorrow.

Helen and George arrived at the house earlier than expected. We were to spend part of the morning together. After breakfast, I went upstairs to prepare Dunia's suitcase. George wanted to leave before noon to make sure they got to the cottage before sunset. The cottage was about a six-hour drive—eight when George drives!

I stood at the front gate and watched their car slowly drive away. Dunia kept turning around to see if I was still there. She was excited to be going to the cottage where she knew that she'd have a good time. She would play with the dog, go horseback riding with her grandpa, and swim in the lake. Still, her eyes could not hide her confused sadness about not being with me for a while. She waved her little hand goodbye until she could no longer see me.

I went back inside, trying to get ready to do my million things. Dunia's face and little hand waving goodbye kept flashing in my mind.

"I miss her *already!*" I thought. "I don't know if I did the right thing by letting her go away for a whole week before starting school. Maybe it's too much stress for her. Maybe it's too much stress for *me* ... but what was I to do? I have to go back to work, and someone would've had to watch her all week anyway. At least her grandparents will take better care of her. Plus, she'll be entertained when her cousins get there tomorrow. She'll have fun with the dog and the horses, and have a blast at the lake.

"Oh, God! The *lake*! I don't like lakes and I don't trust them. They seem calm and safe but, every year, I hear of so many accidents. I know her grandparents are responsible and careful. I know that her cousins will watch over her, but still ...

" ... and the horses! I don't like *that* idea either. I know that George is great with horses. I know he's been riding for years, but horses are so *unpredictable*. What if Dunia's horse decides to go *crazy*? What can George do? What if she falls? What if she gets hurt?

"Oh, God! What did I *do*? Maybe I should join them and make sure that everything is under control. That's it! I'll join them!"

I hesitated for a moment.

"What am I *thinking*? I can't join them! I'm *working* tomorrow. I'll just call and ask them to bring her back."

I rushed to the phone and started to dial the number.

"Good morning!"

"Oh, Starry! What a morning!"

"What happened?" Shooter wondered, concerned.

"I'm going *crazy*!"

"Why?" he asked. "What *happened*? What did I miss?"

I sighed deeply as I put the phone down.

"I'm afraid that Dunia went to spend a whole week with her grandparents."

"And?"

"They went to the cottage."

No one said anything for a few seconds.

"There's a *lake* there," I added.

Expecting the rest of the story and wondering what bad thing had happened to Dunia, Shooter insisted, "... *and?*"

"There are horses, too!"

At that point, realizing that nothing bad had happened, he sarcastically added, "*Really!*"

"Really," I confirmed.

I was so absorbed in my mind that I didn't notice that Shooter was not exactly being sympathetic.

"How could you send Dunia to a place where there is a lake *and* horses?"

"Shooter!" Starry warned, trying to limit his insensitive words.

"*What?*" he rebelled. "How can she be afraid of something that has not happened yet or that may not even happen at *all?*"

"I'm really afraid that my baby might get hurt there."

All of a sudden, Shooter's question got my attention.

"Shooter's *right!* What kind of a crazy thought is that? To be afraid of something that has not happened yet or may not happen at all?"

I tried to make some sense out of this. I tried to stop that thought, but it was useless.

Anticipating another long explanation from Starry, I stepped out to the backyard and sat on the swing.

"Starry, say something ... *please!*" I was hoping that her wisdom would explain my fear and help me understand.

Starry remained quiet.

"Maybe she's trying to make some sense of it herself," I thought. "Maybe she's trying to figure this out."

"You think so, Genius? I think she's trying to figure *you* out!"

Then, saving me from Shooter's mockery, Starry finally spoke.

"Do you remember what a trigger is?"

"A trigger," Shooter rushed to answer, "is something you see, hear, smell, taste, or touch and feel. It exists in the life happening inside or around you. It could be something you remember or think of, or something that someone says or does. It could be anything—a situation, an event, an object, a movie scene, an article, a sentence, a word, a sound, a song, a scent, a flavor ..."

He paused to catch his breath, and then continued.

"It could be an action, a gesture, a handshake, a smile, a laugh, a glance, a blink, a wink ..."

"Okay, Shooter," I interrupted. "I get the picture."

"A lake ... a horse," he added, amused.

"Do you remember what a trigger does?" Starry asked.

Shooter again rushed to answer.

"It all depends on the trigger. Some triggers are good and some are bad. When the trigger is good, Old Teller tells you O'stories that make you feel happy; when the trigger is bad, Old Teller tells you O'stories that make you feel unhappy."

"A trigger is not good or bad," I corrected. "A trigger is neutral."

"No, it's *not*! Maybe when it's a lake or a horse, but it's not neutral when it threatens your source of love, safety, and happiness. Like the time you lost your job a few years ago. Do you remember *that* trigger, Genius? Do you remember how afraid you were that you wouldn't be able to pay your bills at the end of the month? How neutral of a trigger is that? What about when Susan's husband left her? Was *that* trigger neutral?"

Without waiting for my answer, he kept charging.

"No, it's *not!* Those triggers are not neutral. They are bad ... *very* bad!"

"Every chance it gets," Starry explained calmly, "Old Teller puts on a different face and tells you different O'stories. Some O'stories are about your past, some about your present, and others about your future.

"Old Teller sometimes puts on its Future Promise and Salvation face to tell you O'stories about a future that would save you from a present you judge as unhappy.

"Sometimes, when it wants to warn you about the pain that a future absence—lack or loss—of a certain I-have out of your source of love, safety, and happiness might cause you, Old Teller puts on its Fear face.

"Let us go back to the lake for a moment. A lake is a body of water surrounded by land, where different plants, fish, and other creatures live. That is a lake's simple and objective definition. A lake is not good or bad.

"Sometimes, the lake triggers Old Teller to put on a Happy face, and tell you O'stories about the lake being a source of joyful and pleasant times spent with your family and friends, having fun, eating together, swimming, cooling off, and playing games and exciting water sports. It tells you O'stories about being outdoors, surrounded by nature, and about the lake being a beautiful, quiet, calm, soothing, mysterious, romantic, and inspiring place to dream and relax.

"Old Teller puts on its Future Promise and Salvation face, and tells you O'stories about how times spent at the lake will save you from a present you say is unhappy.

"Other times, Old Teller puts on its Fear face and tells you fear O'stories about the lake being a dangerous source of accidents and terrible outcomes for you or your loved ones, and about getting hurt—maybe even dying.

"Can you see how the lake, in itself, is just a lake? It is not good or bad. An O'story of your mind can make you feel happy when it is joyful and pleasant, while another O'story can make you feel unhappy when it is one of fear, loss, and pain."

Starry paused for a moment, allowing me to absorb what she just demonstrated.

"Now let us talk about the horse," she continued. "By definition, a horse is a wild or domestic animal. Sometimes, Old Teller tells you O'stories about the pleasures of interacting with this beautiful animal, and about touching, petting, and taking care of it. It describes the physical, mental, and emotional pleasures of being outdoors in nature, and feeling the soft breeze while slowly riding the horse in the fields or mountains, or along the ocean shore. It describes the pleasures of running fast and feeling the thrill of speed, and the power and freedom of the wind.

"Other times, Old Teller tells you fear O'stories about the horse being a possible—and maybe a sure—source of accidents and terrible outcomes, such as getting injured, hurting, suffering, or becoming paralyzed—maybe even dying.

"Can you see how the horse in itself is just a horse? It is not good or bad."

Not quite convinced by what Starry claimed, Shooter asked another question.

"What about *real* problems? What about a real job loss or a painful divorce? How are *these* not bad triggers?"

"A job loss," Starry replied, "means that the Human no longer has an assigned job and is no longer working for the time being, while a fear O'story of the mind goes something like this: 'I was laid off because I am not good enough. I do not have what it takes to find another job. I am too old to find a new job and no one will hire me. The economy is bad and no one is hiring right now. I will never find a job. I will not have enough money to pay the bills. I will lose my house and become homeless. I will not be able to buy food and I will starve. I will suffer—maybe even die.'

"By definition," she continued, "a divorce is when two married people legally separate and end their marriage, while a fear O'story of the mind goes something like this: 'My marriage failed because I am a failure. No one cares about me and no one loves me. I am so unlucky in love. I am not good enough. I do not deserve to be loved. No one will ever love me. I do not trust anybody and I do not want to love again. I will never love again. My love life is over. My life is over—and I will die.'"

Trying to find a *real* problem and bad trigger situation in which to challenge Starry, Shooter came up with a scenario.

"Okay. What about a *real* accident that happens to someone or their loved ones, and not like the one Genius is afraid of? What about when someone is *really* sick? How can an accident or being sick be neutral? How can *those* triggers not be bad? A real accident is bad and being sick is bad ... and that's a *fact!*"

"When a Human or their loved one gets into an accident or becomes sick," Starry said, "it means that a certain part of their body is not healthy and may be suffering, or has a limited function for the time being. Meanwhile, a fear O'story of the mind goes something like this: 'I am—or my loved one is—so sick. I am in so much pain. My body does not function properly. I do not function normally and I am limited. I will never get better. I will suffer forever. I will never heal. I will never be able to perform my normal activities anymore. I will never have a normal life like I once did and like other people do. I will never enjoy life again. My life is over—and I will die.'"

I pondered what Starry explained, and then came to a conclusion.

"Then Old Teller can tell me fear O'stories all the time!"

"The life happening inside and around you is a succession of arising needs and a collection of satisfying I-haves," she said. "When a need arises, whether it is a need that you create for yourself or one that life creates for you, you feel that you are being bumped outside of your comfort zone. This need may concern any aspect of your life, such as your personal life, your love life, your family life, your social life, or your health, career, hobbies, or lifestyle. The need requires your attention and care, so you collect an I-have that satisfies it— one that takes you back to your comfort zone.

"Collecting an I-have starts by taking a step to change something, transform an idea of your mind into a new project, make a new move, meet a new challenge, move in a new direction, live a new experience, or make a dream come true.

"Remember that the nature of something new is unknown, and what is unknown is often judged as something bad and confused with something unsafe, scary, and painful.

"The need arises and Old Teller is alert. It starts warning you about the risk of you being kicked out of your comfort zone, in case you actually took that step to collect the satisfying I-have.

"The need arises and a fear O'story is born. A fear O'story is temporary. It is never constant or permanent. It will only last until you have collected the I-have and gone back to your comfort zone, until the need gracefully resolves itself and disappears, or until the feared situation that the O'story is describing actually happens."

Starry gave many examples of what a fear O'story might describe:

- The costly price I will pay out of my physical, mental, and emotional health and well-being, in order to collect an I-have and satisfy my need

- A chance I cannot afford to take because, if I do, I will jeopardize and lose at least one of my I-haves

- How someone or something will rob me of my source of love, safety, and happiness, and cause me to suffer

- The scary results with which I will end up, in case my present situation has changed

- How, if I step outside of what I am accustomed to and follow my dream, something bad will happen

- How, if I (or my loved ones) take a new step, I (or they) will catch some kind of virus, have an incurable disease, face dangerous situations, get into a terrible accident and be injured, disfigured, dismembered, and paralyzed— maybe even die

- How, if I say this or do that, I will disappoint someone and hurt their feelings, or I will be disappointed and hurt

- How, if I make a specific move, I will not be worthy of the respect, esteem, and recognition of the people in my life—especially my loved ones, who I feel are my reason for living—and I will lose their approval and love

- How I cannot move from where I am Here and Now, and leave everyone and everything behind

- How I need to have more guarantees, and secure every aspect and angle before I take a risk

- The not-so-perfect results with which I will end up, reminding me that I am not perfect or even good enough

- The big mistake I am making by saying this or doing that, confusing me that I am a mistake

- How I will lose this game, competition, case, or deal, leading me to think that I am a loser

- How I will surely fail this attempted move, making me believe that I am a failure

- How my application, request, project, idea, or proposition will be rejected, and I will believe that I am a reject

- How I will waste my time and energy trying to go for it— especially if it does not work out in the end

- How, if I do not take that step, chance, or risk, or make that move, I will surely regret it one day, and feel even unhappier than I already am

- A misfortune that will happen one day anyway, so I might as well stay where I am.

✦

"Why does Old Teller do that?" I asked.

"Old Teller loves you," Starry answered. "It speaks and warns you so you are careful."

"If it notices that you're not listening," Shooter interrupted, "Old Teller will speak louder, and its fear O'stories will become scarier.

"You listen to Old Teller," he added, "you believe the O'stories, and you keep yourself safe ... and scared, anxious, stressed, angry, frustrated, bored, empty, unfulfilled, living with lost passions and forgotten dreams, and missing out on life. You keep yourself safe ... and just existing instead of living, stuck, trapped inside the fear O'stories, and not moving forward.

"Old Teller keeps talking, the fear O'stories keep playing, and you keep playing it safe, Genius, while Dunia plays and has fun with the dog and the horses, and while she swims in the lake having a splash and a blast!"

"Old Teller loves you," Starry repeated. "It wants to prevent any painful, unhappy outcome, and protect you against feeling the pain and unhappiness.

"When a need arises, Old Teller instantly goes through its repertoire and pulls out a fear O'story that describes the painful, unhappy outcome of a similar step once taken to satisfy a similar need, just to warn you and keep you safe.

"The fear O'story could describe an unresolved story of absence—lack or loss—of love, safety, and happiness. This story could have belonged to your own past, or to the past of a loved one or someone whom you may or may not even know. It could have been a story you witnessed, read, or heard, and which affected you.

"The fear O'story could describe an unresolved past story still repeating that you are not important, you are not good enough, you are not worthy of being loved, you do not deserve love, and you are not loved.

"Old Teller tells you to stop. You obey, and stay exactly where you are—stopped and frozen with fear. You no longer dare to take a chance or a risk, even the smallest one. You no longer dare to take a step, move forward, and live the passionate life you want to live."

✦

"How can I keep Old Teller quiet and the fear O'stories away?" I asked.

"Either alone or with the assistance of someone you trust," Starry answered, "you will celebrate an Unresolved Past ceremony where you will become aware, accept, forgive, thank, and release the unresolved past story.

"You can also celebrate a Fear Goodbye ceremony, where you write a goodbye letter to your fear, and then celebrate a ritual to release it."

"Burn the letter and throw the ashes into running water," added Shooter, "or roll it up and attach it to your wrist and a door knob ... and don't forget the scissors!"

"Doing so," continued Starry, "will help remove the roadblock that this fear O'story had become on your path, so you can finally take a step and move forward."

"This will help for sure," I said, "but I'll bet that Old Teller will *not* keep quiet and the fear O'stories will *not* go away!"

"Throughout your life," Starry elaborated, "every I-have you once collected satisfied a need of yours. Every collected I-have around you today is proof that the danger or terrible outcomes that Old Teller's O'stories described, and which you once feared, did not really happen ... Let us go back to your life story."

"Up here! *Look up here!*" shouted Shooter.

"It's broad daylight, Shooter!" I noticed. "The stars are not here yet."

"The stars are always here, Genius! Close your eyes, you'll see ..."

I closed my eyes, and watched the million star avalanche once again cover the sky.

✫ ✫ ✫

"Watch every scene where you wanted to take a step," Starry said, "and Old Teller started telling you fear O'stories. Watch how every need ended up being satisfied or resolved, one way or another, and how the terrible outcomes, which these O'stories described, did not end up happening.

"If, every once in a while, one unhappy outcome did happen and *became* the new need that life just threw at you, watch how this new need—the unhappy outcome itself—became resolved or satisfied eventually.

"Let us go back a little to that day when you were trying to ride your bike for the first time."

"That's not going back a little, Starry!" Shooter teased.

"Let us go back," Starry continued, "and remember what Old Teller told you when you decided to satisfy your need to ride your bike."

"Look, Genius! It was your red bike with the funny horn."

"Oh, I remember *that* bike! I also remember Old Teller telling me how I was going to fall and hurt myself. It said that I would never be able to ride alone and that my dad would be disappointed in me. It told me that he would not be proud of me or love me anymore."

"Do you really remember Old Teller telling you all *that*, Genius? You were no older than *three!*"

"Back then, I could not express my thoughts or feelings with words. Now, after spending these few nights and days with you and Starry, it's a new game for me.

"I clearly remember the O'stories. I also remember being embarrassed that I could not ride. I was afraid that my dad would make fun of me and that I would not be worthy of his love or deserve it anymore."

"You ended up riding your bike," Starry said, "even though you fell off a couple of times."

"A *couple* of times?" Shooter interrupted. "Keep watching, Starry, because I'm not sure that you saw the whole thing!"

"You hurt yourself," Starry laughed. "You got up and tried again. You did it, and your dad was proud of you and still loved you."

"Hey, Genius. Look here when those kids took your doll and ran away. It was heartbreaking to see you scream and cry the way you did."

"I remember *that* doll! It was pink and squeaked when I squeezed it. It was during our summer vacation. We were staying in an upper-floor apartment and I was on the balcony playing with the doll when it accidentally fell over. I looked down through the bars of the balcony and watched those kids pick it up and leave. I remember screaming my lungs out and crying my eyes out. I was the most miserable kid in the whole world. I can still feel the pain I felt after I lost that doll. I thought I was going to die!"

"... but you did *not*, Genius! You later got a new doll and a bunch of new toys, even nicer ones."

"Look here when you tried to drive a car for the first time," Starry noted, "and Old Teller started telling you fear O'stories about how you will have an accident, destroy the car, and hurt yourself—maybe even die … but look at how you ended up driving and did *not* have an accident, did *not* destroy the car, and did *not* hurt yourself or die."

Starry, Shooter, and I kept watching my life story, as told by the million stars.

"Look at this time when you wanted to tell this popular guy that you liked him," Starry continued, "and Old Teller told you that you were not worthy of this guy's time or consideration, how you would make a fool of yourself, and how a guy like him would not be interested in someone like you. You ended up talking to him. You even dated him and had a great time!"

"Now *wait* a minute, Starry!" Shooter again interrupted. "Are we looking at the same scene? Which guy are you talking about? If it's Kevin, that's not how *I* remember it. Need I remind you that he actually took Genius out and dumped her the next day?"

"Kevin from college?" I asked. "Oh, God! I was *so embarrassed!* I thought I was going to die."

"You obviously did not, Genius. You went on with your life, dated other guys, and moved on to new experiences and new love stories."

Shooter then spotted another scene.

"Do you remember when you lost your job a few years ago? Look here, right after Dunia was born."

"Please don't remind me, Shooter! Those were *horrible* times. I was so afraid that I wasn't going to be able to pay my bills. I was afraid that I wasn't going to find a job or be able to take care of my daughter. I was afraid that I was going to lose my house, my car, and everything I had. I thought that we were going to starve. I was afraid to lose all control over my life. I really thought it was the end of my world."

"... but it was not, Genius! You actually ended up finding another job, and everything worked out."

I said nothing.

I watched the rest of my life story and soon began to realize that almost all of what Old Teller's fear O'stories described never came true, and my needs ended up being satisfied or resolved, one way or another. I also realized that every need I created for myself, and every one that life created for me, was indeed not the end of my world!

"No, it was *not* the end of my world," I admitted out loud, "and yes, I *did* end up finding another job and everything *did* work out."

"Remember that things always have a way of working out in the end," Starry said. "What looks and feels like a *problem* always has a solution. Every need has a satisfying I-have—one way or another.

I quietly watched my life story until the last star slowly disappeared.

✫ ✫ ✫

"You will choose a convenient place and time to celebrate your Encouraging List ceremony," Starry added. "It is a list of your successes, attained goals, and personal achievements that made you feel like a hero. It includes every obstacle that you overcame, every challenge that you met, every problem that you solved, every I-have that you collected, and every need that you satisfied.

"Create a pleasant atmosphere for the ceremony. Surround yourself with silence, or let nice music play in the background. Light a candle and let a pleasant scent fill the air. Prepare your paper and pen, your alarm clock, and your happy music record, which will play once this 30- or 60-minute ceremony is over. Be sure to sit comfortably.

"On top of the page, write down the title of the ceremony— Encouraging List—and your full name and date of birth underneath it.

"On the left side of the paper, divide your life stages into one-, two-, or three-year periods.

"In the middle section, and for each period, list the needs you created for yourself or that life created for you, and remember the fear O'stories born along with them. Give each need and O'story a title and a brief description.

"On the right side of the page, and for each need, become aware and note that the terrible outcomes and painful results Old Teller's fear O'stories described never came true.

"Close your eyes.

"Take a deep breath.

"Invite the noise around and inside you to leave.

"Invite the stories of your past to come to you."

Shooter suggested that I start as far back as I could remember, such as the first day I got on the school bus alone, or the many times I stood in front of the whole class and read out loud. I would remember the times when I wrote and passed my school exams and graduated every school year. I would note the time when I brought back the medal from my dance competition, got my driver's license, experienced my first kiss, landed my first job, bought my first house, and started my family.

He said to remember the many times I expected to hear that something bad had happened (or is happening, or will happen) or assumed that someone thought, felt, said, or did something bad (or is, was, or will be thinking, feeling, saying, or doing something bad) and I was afraid to suffer and be unhappy.

He told me to become aware of how all these expectations and assumptions almost never came true. He said that the next time Old Teller is tempted to tell me to expect or assume something bad, all I have to do is ask Old Teller to shut up by saying, "*Shhh!*"

Shooter then invited me to keep my Encouraging List in my Precious Box, where I could refer to it every time I wanted to take a step and Old Teller starts telling me its one thousand and one fear O'stories.

He said that my Encouraging List will remind me that most—if not all—of what Old Teller's fear O'stories described never really happened, just like what the fear O'stories describe today will also not happen. Through the language it speaks beyond all Human words, my Encouraging List will help me keep Old Teller quiet and the fear O'stories away.

"I agree that my Encouraging List will also help me, but I still doubt that *my* fear will go away. I don't think that this list will be enough to make Old Teller leave me alone so I can take a step,

HOW TO BE HAPPY

move forward, and start living the passionate life that I want to live."

"Guess what, Genius? I have news for you. Old Teller loves you and will never leave you alone!"

"Then how am I going to move forward?"

"Remember that what is new is unknown," Shooter answered, "and what is unknown is often judged as scary and unsafe.

"Sometimes, all you have to do is make what is new and unknown more known."

"How do I do *that*?"

"Wave your magic wand," he said, "*or* ... get your paper and blue and red pens."

"Either alone or with someone who can help you," Starry offered, "use *5W2H-O&D* to gather the facts and figure out the unknown factor—or guilty factor—that triggered Old Teller to speak and tell you fear O'stories.

"*5W2H-O&D* will help you make this factor more known, and then do something about it, instead of letting Old Teller dwell, and instead of letting this factor stay in your way, preventing you from moving forward. It will help you calculate and evaluate the risk before you take a step. Your step will then be enlightened and therefore more known and less scary.

"Every once in a while, Old Teller will insist on telling you a fear O'story that describes the possible loss of an I-have in case you took that step.

"Remember that a fear O'story is temporary and will only last until the new need is either satisfied or resolved, or until the feared loss of the I-have actually happens.

"Welcome the fear O'story, accept the possibility of the loss, and build on that. Ask Old Teller, 'So *what* if this bad—or even the worst—outcome really happens? So *what* if I lose this I-have?'

"Then, kindly thank Old Teller for warning you, take that step, and move forward."

"If kindly doesn't work," Shooter added, "ask Old Teller to shut up. Just say, '*Shhh!*'

"Let me explain something to you, Genius. From 1 to 10 on the fear scale, your fear of taking a step will often score 10 the first time around. It will score 9 the second time, and the third time it will be 8, and so on.

"If you want to wait for your fear to score 0, or have it disappear before you take a step, you'll wait forever! You'll wait until it's too late. You'll stay exactly where you are: safe and frustrated, worried, and just existing instead of living.

"If you think that taking a step is scary, I assure you that staying where you are is much scarier!"

"Let the resolved stories of your past," Starry resumed, "your Fear Goodbye letter, your Encouraging List, and your 5W2H-O&D answers encourage you. Go to your Precious Box, refer to the Glow chart, and find courage and faith. Ask them to take your hand and walk next to you. Take a step, move forward, grow, and glow!"

Shooter had words for me to repeat out loud:

- Today, I say *enough*!
- Today, I stop putting the passionate life I want to live on hold.
- Today, I move forward with my courage and faith next to me.

- Today, I take a chance *and* a step. *So what* if I lose a certain I-have? I know that my true source of love, safety, and happiness is untouchable.

"Remember that you are never alone," Starry continued. "Have faith that God always takes care of you in every step you take. Trust that He takes care of every situation and its outcome in your life.

"God is in charge, every step of the way. He designed this step and allowed it to be in your life, and He will, without a doubt, take care of you.

"Take that step, and keep the step small. Do the best you can, and trust the rest in God's hands.

"Take that step, and stay with it.

"Stay Here, and stay Now."

Starry walked me through the Awareness Process, one safe step at a time:

- *Feel?*

- Unhappy-red.

- I catch the change in my breathing and heartbeat, and I catch the knot.

- I take a deep breath.

- I go into my mind. I see the flashing red stop sign and hear the whistle: "Stop! That is Old Teller speaking. It is telling me a fear O'story, and I am afraid—this is why I feel unhappy."

- I catch Old Teller and the fear O'story.

- I discreetly place my left hand turned in against my stomach, and extend my right arm, with my hand turned out towards Old Teller and the O'story.

- I take another deep breath while I count to 10: 1, 2, 3, 4, 5, 6, 7, 8, 9, 10.

- I inhale space, silence, and stillness, and exhale the fear O'story out of my mind.

- I sit in my movie director chair, rise above Old Teller and the O'story, and watch from above.

- I do not become one with Old Teller or the O'story.

- I see the empty space, hear the loud silence, and feel the deep stillness of my mind. I stay there for a moment.

- *I come back to Here and Now*, where I am completely fulfilled and truly happy!

CHAPTER SEVEN

Fatigue

I wondered about how happy I felt "Here and Now." It was past noon and I had not heard from Helen or George. Less than half a day remained of my summer vacation, and the million things I had to do were still a million.

I was tired from running around and not sleeping well lately. I wished that I didn't have to go back to work. I wished that I could've stayed home another week to do my million things—or to do absolutely nothing. I was tired from trying to keep Old Teller quiet, but Old Teller would not shut up!

"Why does Old Teller talk so much?"

"You mean besides the fact that it loves you, Genius? Who knows?"

211

"Many factors," Starry explained, "affect the presence of Old Teller's O'stories inside your mind, as well as their actual content and the frequency of their recurrence. These factors belong to your own story, including the story you came with and the one you came into.

"Among these factors are your own past experiences that affected you, as well as those of your loved ones or someone you may or may not know. It may be stories you witnessed, read, or heard, and that left an impression on you.

"Heredity and genetics could also be factors. Others include your personality, lifestyle, responsibilities, habits, culture, or religion or belief system. It could be the environment that surrounds you at home or out in society, the geographical place where you live, and the weather and the seasons."

"It could even be the alignment of the stars," added Shooter.

"That's exactly what I said, Genius ... *who knows?*"

"Factors are endless," continued Starry. "Sometimes only one factor is involved, but more often it is a combination of many. Try to identify these factors and, whenever possible, deal with and resolve them.

"It is important for you to help your body, mind, and emotions stay healthy and strong, so you can handle Old Teller and its unhappy O'stories in an efficient way.

"One way is to eliminate and prevent fatigue. When your body is tired, your mind becomes tired and an easy target for Old Teller and its O'stories, and you feel unhappy. The more tired your mind is and the unhappier you feel, the more tired your body becomes. It is a vicious circle.

"Fatigue reduces your ability to quiet down Old Teller and control the unhappy O'stories, and you feel 'stressed out'—as

Human words say. It can discreetly sneak up and settle in your body, reducing the level of your energy and performance. When left unnoticed, and if you do not deal with the cause behind it, fatigue can become chronic and rob you of healthy and happy living."

✦

"What causes fatigue?"

"Besides the noise of Old Teller and its O'stories, many factors could be the cause. There could be an underlying medical condition, such as a metabolic, endocrine, immune, infectious, cardiac, pulmonary, or drug-related problem. You may feel tired when a part of your body is injured or trying to compensate for a certain limitation in movement or function.

"Regardless of the medical cause, always listen to your body and become aware of its signs of discomfort, pain, or limitation. These signs can be your friend. Through the language they speak beyond all Human words, they try to inform you of something important. They direct and point your attention to the area of your body that needs your care.

"Instead of ignoring them, carefully see what they are trying show you, listen to what they are trying to tell you, understand their message, and thank them for it."

" ... before you shut them up with painkillers and different pills like you sometimes do, Genius."

"Whenever necessary," continued Starry, "consult with health professionals—a medical doctor or an alternative medicine practitioner, such as an osteopath, a homeopath, a naturopath, a chiropractor, or an acupuncturist. Get the proper checkup and the right diagnostics, and then receive the appropriate treatment to try to eliminate the medical problem causing this fatigue."

"Make sure you also eat right," Shooter advised, and then suggested questions to ask myself:

- Have I been kind to my body lately?
- Am I eating or drinking too much or not enough?
- Am I getting enough protein, vitamins, carbohydrates, fiber, and minerals?
- Am I eating and drinking what my body needs to stay healthy and give back to me?
- Am I eating and drinking—and inhaling—what hurts my body and prevents it from staying healthy and giving back to me?

"Get the right information about a healthy diet," Starry invited, "by consulting with a nutritionist, and referring to reliable sources on nutrition, such as articles, books, or the Internet. You can use the help of 5W2H-O&D to get to know what your body needs for it to stay healthy and full of energy. The answers to the questions will help you figure out which part of your diet is healthy, which part you need to change and improve, and which part you need to eliminate."

Shooter had words for me to repeat out loud:

- Today, I say *enough*!

Fatigue

- Today, I stop doing what no longer serves my body.

- Today, I stop doing what has cost my body enough of its good health.

- Today, I eat less _____ ; I eat more _____ .

- Today, I drink less _____ ; I drink more _____ .

"Start by changing one nutritional habit at a time," Starry suggested. "Every day, either add one healthy element to your diet or remove an unhealthy one. Practice your new diet for one week before you modify it again. One habit at time, one small change at a time, and one step at a time.

"Eating right keeps fatigue down, keeps Old Teller quiet, and keeps the unhappy O'stories away."

"Eat right and sleep well," Shooter added.

"During sleep," Starry explained, "your body is able to recuperate the energy it has spent while helping you collect your daily I-haves and satisfy your needs. While you sleep, your body—for example, your brain, heart, lungs, stomach, muscles, and immune system—recharges itself. It rejuvenates, re-energizes, strengthens, repairs, and restores the cells of every organ and system.

"A lack of amount and quality of sleep, especially when it is chronic, reduces your ability to fight and resist physical, mental, and emotional fatigue. Make sure you get a healthy and sufficient number of sleep hours every night (or day).

"Ask yourself if it has been a while since you had a good night's sleep, and how many times a week you get the adequate amount and quality of sleep."

"Don't stay up too late," Shooter said. "Don't stay up thinking, working, reading, watching television, or using the computer ... but it's okay if you're up talking to a *star!*"

Shooter offered me more encouraging words to repeat out loud:

- Today, I say *enough!*
- Today, I say enough of not sleeping well.
- Today, I say enough of staying up late—past this certain hour.
- Tonight, I go to sleep early.

"Easier said than done."

"It might not be easy, Genius, but it is certainly not impossible! Remember that you are blessed with plenty of time and patience for you to practice sleeping well."

"Start by going to sleep 10 or 15 minutes earlier than usual," Starry said. "Repeat your new sleep schedule for one week before you modify it again. Remember, one step at a time ... *always!*

"You can also use the help of your alarm clock. Let it remind you when to go to sleep, just like it reminds you when to wake up."

"... and do not *snooze*, Genius!"

"Stop all distractions at least 10 or 15 minutes before your bedtime," Starry continued. "This includes any argument, intense discussion, work document, television show, or computer session. Take a warm bath or soak your feet in warm water. Drink something warm, or place a hot water bottle against your stomach. This can be very soothing and relaxing."

Shooter listed more questions to ask myself:

- Do I suffer from insomnia?
- Is my sleep environment friendly and does it help me get a good night's sleep?
- Is my bedroom comfortable?
- Is it quiet enough or would I rather hear relaxing music in the background? Is an irritating noise preventing me from sleeping deeply?
- Is the lighting of my room adequate?
- Is the temperature comfortable?
- Is the quality of the air good?
- Is my room clean and orderly?
- Is my bed spacious enough?
- Is my bed—the mattress and pillows—comfortable for my head, neck, shoulders, arms, back, and legs? Does a part of my body feel sore while I sleep or right after I wake up?
- Does the person next to me snore? Do I snore? Do I suffer from sleep apnea? Do I grind my teeth while I sleep?
- Do I have a headache when I wake up? Do I feel tired in the morning, even when I think that I just had a long and full night's sleep?

"Do not postpone improving your sleep environment," Starry advised, "and allow yourself a better amount and quality of sleep.

"You can research and read about sleep disorders and their solutions in designated books or on the Internet. Remember to use the help of *5W2H-O&D*. If necessary, you can go to a sleep clinic and consult with a sleep expert or therapist, a doctor, or an alternative medicine practitioner. These professionals can inform you about other possible sleep problems—such as insomnia—as well as their causes and possible treatments.

"Sometimes, despite a quiet mind and a comfortable sleep environment, insomnia might still visit you every once in while. When this happens, Old Teller will be awake and will want to talk. It is important that you do not get upset or angry with yourself, Old Teller, or your insomnia.

"Do not fight your insomnia because doing so will tire you out. It will exhaust you more than the insomnia itself. Just stay in bed with your eyelids closed, and look far into them.

"Look at the empty space and the deep stillness of your mind, and repeat these words to yourself: 'I am aware and accept that I am not deeply asleep and it is okay because I know that my body and mind are resting.'

"Remind yourself that God takes care of you. Pretend that your bed is His hand where you are safely sleeping, and let the sheets be His other hand that covers and holds you.

"Then calmly breathe and relax. Kindly wish Old Teller a good night, and tell it to go to sleep."

"If kindly doesn't work," Shooter added, "ask Old Teller to shut up. Just say, '*Shhh!*'"

Starry described a body and mind relaxation breathing technique, which would help me relax and fall asleep:

- Calmly breathe, and relax the body from the top of the head all the way down to the toes.

Fatigue

- Take a deep breath. Inhale slowly while counting to five: 1, 2, 3, 4, 5.

- Hold the breath while counting to five: 1, 2, 3, 4, 5.

- Exhale slowly while counting to five: 1, 2, 3, 4, 5.

- Inhale again and, this time, carefully observe the air going into the nose.

- Observe how it fills the lungs. Notice how the chest and stomach expand.

- While exhaling, feel the warm breath through the nose or mouth.

- Inhale ... exhale.

- Repeat the breathing, and continue to observe every breath.

- Concentrate on the count and the rhythm of each breath.

- Continue to breathe slowly.

- Repeat breathing five times while concentrating on each breath.

- Feel the mind starting to clear up and relax.

- Inhale and send the breath to the head. Let this breath fill every muscle and help the head relax.

- Exhale.

- Inhale and send this breath to the muscles of the forehead. Let them relax.

- Exhale.

- Repeat this relaxing breathing technique for every muscle of the face: eyelids, eyes, cheeks, nose, jaw, and tongue.

- One after the other, continue sending a relaxing breath to every muscle group of the body: neck, shoulders, arms, hands, chest, stomach, back, legs, and feet—all the way down to the toes.

- Inhale ... exhale.

- Watch the breath. Observe the rhythm.

- Relax the body and mind.

"... and have a good night's sleep, Genius! If this still doesn't work, you can always count sheep!"

We all laughed at Shooter's comment.

"By the way, Starry," I said, "I've always wondered about how this ritual of counting sheep works."

"The mind cannot do two things at the same time," Starry explained. "While you are counting sheep, your mind cannot think of anything else. In the same way, the body and mind relaxation breathing technique prevents Old teller from speaking and the O'stories from playing, and helps you relax.

"Here is another suggestion: Always keep a note pad and pen by your bed. Whenever Old Teller starts to speak, and the O'stories start to play and prevent you from sleeping, turn on a dim light and make a quick note of the O'stories. Writing the O'stories down empties them from your mind onto paper, bringing you back to the empty space, the loud silence, and the deep stillness, and allowing you to fall asleep."

"What about fatigue and exercise?" I asked.

"Yeah, Starry. What about fatigue and exercise?" Shooter echoed. "Somebody here—I will not say *who*—needs to go back to the gym, and not only for fatigue elimination and prevention purposes!"

After waiting for a comment and not getting one, he continued. "Guess who that somebody is, Genius?"

"It must be Starry," I answered, laughing.

"Genius!"

I tried to justify myself.

"Do you know how many times a day I tell myself that I should exercise? I mean, really ... I know all about the benefits of exercise. I know that it helps prevent, reduce, and even eliminate my fatigue. I know that it gives me energy and a better appetite. I know that it allows me to have a better quality of sleep.

"I'm aware that it clears my mind and helps my body be in healthier shape so I can be more productive and perform better. I know that it enhances my mood so I feel happy. I know all that, and I try to exercise ... I *swear*! You have no idea how much money I've wasted over the years on gym memberships that I never used, and on exercise machines that ended up sitting in the corner of the room collecting dust."

"... and clothes."

"This is not *funny*, Shooter! I know that I have to exercise. Every time I make a resolution, I get motivated at first, just enough to start. My motivation lasts for a little while. Then, after a few workouts, I quit."

"That's because you're lazy."

"I'm *not* lazy!"

"Yes, you are. You even said it yourself the other morning."

"I just *hate* to exercise. I hate going to the gym. It's just not my thing, no matter how hard I try."

"Hey, Genius, exercise doesn't only mean going to the gym, lifting weights, and using machines."

"For people who like it," Starry explained, "working out in a gym can be a wonderful way to exercise. For those who do not—like you, for example—that is also fine. It simply means that this type of exercise is not a need of yours."

Encouraged by Starry's understanding, I continued.

"I *hate* to exercise, regardless of the activity. I've tried *every-thing*, every activity out there. Exercise is not my thing!"

"That's what I said, Genius. You're lazy!"

"No, I'm *not*, Shooter! I'm just not motivated. I don't have the will for it."

"Then take a *will* pill. Take this pill whenever you don't feel like doing something—like exercise, for example. The pill will give you the necessary dose of *will* that you need. Take it once a day with breakfast, and keep taking it until the day you feel enough out of shape or, in your case, until grace comes along."

"*Grace?*"

"Grace *will* happen to you one day! By the way, Genius, quit saying that you've tried all the activities because it's not true. You've only tried a few, and there are many more. Besides, for the ones you've already tried, maybe going to a different gym, or being around different people, could make a difference. Try that!"

"Well, if I find an activity I like, I know I won't find the time for it."

"One of the reasons for exercise is to have fun," Starry explained. "Another one is to keep your body healthy and energized—move your body, and stretch and keep it flexible, tone your muscles, strengthen your bones and joints, burn your extra caloric intake, and maintain an adequate blood circulation.

Fatigue

"Another reason is for you to relax and energize your mind and emotions. When you already feel overwhelmed by your busy schedule, adding an extra activity, like exercise, could be an extra task you 'should' or 'have to' do. It would be another responsibility you 'must' fulfill, and another thing to do on your task list. This will stress you out, which goes against the benefits, goal, and purpose of exercise.

"Until you lighten up your schedule and reserve more time to exercise, you can start enjoying the benefits of baby-step exercises."

✦

"I hope that you're not going to hit me with 'walking instead of driving' and 'taking the stairs instead of using the elevator' because I won't do that. I've already tried it many times. It just doesn't work."

"When you wake up in the morning," Starry suggested, "and while you are still in bed, start by simply stretching your arms above your head and stretching your legs."

"Like Max does," Shooter said.

"Max *who*?"

"Max ... the dog at the cottage, Genius! Haven't you ever seen him stretch his legs in the morning? The front paws first, and then the back ones?"

"Stretch your arms and legs," continued Starry, "and hold them there, stretched, while you count to five: 1, 2, 3, 4, 5.

"Relax them and again count to five: 1, 2, 3, 4, 5.

"Stretch them for another five seconds. Make sure you feel that your whole body is stretching.

223

"Relax for five seconds.

"Repeat this movement five times.

"Then, after you get out of bed, stand up and stretch again. Raise your arms above your head, try to reach the sky with your fingers, and imagine that your feet are growing roots deeply into the earth.

"While you are getting ready to start your day, play your favorite rhythmical music for five minutes and move to the beat. Prepare your dance music the previous night. That way, all you have to do in the morning is press 'play.' Whether you are in your bedroom, bathroom, or kitchen, just move to the beat."

"Play the music!" added Shooter. "Let the sound and the beat of the music flow from the source of the music straight into your ears.

"Let the music move your head and turn your neck front, back, left, right, and around.

"Let it flow into your shoulders and shake them.

"Let it grab your arms, lift, and fly them.

"Let it hold your hands and wave them.

"Let it run through your body, reach your waist and hips, and shake and sway them.

"Let it go down your legs, and walk, hop, and turn front, back, and sideways.

"Let it get to your feet and dance ... one musical baby step at a time.

"Play the music, even for only five minutes. Music works like magic! You'll see that your feet will not only dance, Genius, but they will walk *and* climb the stairs ... they'll even climb mountains!

"Trust in the mysterious power of music. Let it be your *will* pill until grace happens!

"Every day, take five musical breaks," Shooter continued, eagerly. "You can set your alarm to remind yourself to stop, play the music, and dance. I suggest that you take your first musical break right after you wake up. The second one will be two hours later. For example, if your first musical break was at 8 a.m., then your second one will be at 10."

"You want me to dance at work? What would people say?"

"Maybe they'll be jealous and decide to join you. Maybe you can be *their* will pill, Genius! If you prefer, you can dance in a private space, like a closed office; if this space is not available, take your music player and go to the restroom. No excuses!

"Your third musical break will be two hours later, which would bring you to noon. The fourth break will be another two hours later at 2 p.m., and the fifth one will be at 4."

"I have to pick up Dunia at 4. I don't have time for a break."

"Great! Pick her up and let her dance to the music, too. Your fifth musical break may even be after dinner. Put on a pair of comfortable shoes, play the music, stretch, dance, or take your dog for a walk around the block. Discover your neighborhood and meet your neighbors."

"I don't *have* a dog, Shooter!"

"Then adopt one!" he promptly proposed. "Trust in the power of music, and trust in the power of dogs! Walk your dog or, I'll tell you what, Genius ... let your dog walk you!

"Five-minute musical breaks, five times a day," he concluded.

"I'll play the music," I finally agreed. "I'll try it."

"You see? I told you that you haven't tried everything. Here's another suggestion: Get on your bike and play the music."

"I don't have a bike!"

"Well, ask for one for your birthday. The list of activities is endless: walk, jog, bike, rollerblade, golf, swim, ski, play ball or racket sports, practice yoga, do tai chi, dance the tango ..."

Shooter suddenly stopped and said, "Hey! I got one for you, Genius. Why don't you join a boot camp near you?"

"You must be kidding! A boot camp? *Me?*"

"You have no idea how much fun those can be."

"No, thanks! Not for me ... no *way!*"

"Why not? It's great exercise and great fun! It's like playing games. It can also be great for your social life."

"What's wrong with my social life?"

"It's boring! You said so yourself. Besides, you've been talking to a star for the past few days and nights, for God's sake, and you're asking me what's wrong with your *social* life?

"All right, forget the boot camp, Genius! Go online. You'll find a million activities out there. You're bound to find at least one you have the will to do. Contact your city or local sports or activity centers. Try everything and choose something ... *one* thing!"

"Throughout the day," resumed Starry, "you can take as many musical breaks as you want. Stretching and dancing *are* a form of exercise.

"Exercising frequently and repetitively, even if only for a few minutes, is extremely beneficial. It is, in fact, an efficient way to prevent, reduce, and eliminate fatigue, and relax and energize your body, mind, and emotions.

"Like Shooter said, it could be the pill with just the right dose of *will* that you need for now."

✦

"I can take as many musical breaks as I want ... still, a break is just a break. I don't think that these breaks will get rid of *my* fatigue."

"Wherever you are and whatever you are doing," Starry explained, "different muscles need to work in order for your body to keep certain postures, achieve certain movements, and make certain actions.

"A muscle works by contracting and tensing up, and then releasing. Sometimes a muscle is required to work and offer more than what it can offer comfortably. Other times, it is required to work overtime—or work for too long, like when you spend long hours sitting down or standing up in the same posture, or when you repeat the same movement or action.

"Sometimes a muscle discreetly works when it is not required to do so. Instead of relaxing and recharging, this muscle uselessly contracts and tenses up, without you noticing it. These contractions and tensions can become a great source of fatigue, irritability—and sometimes pain—especially when they have been occurring over a long period.

"In order to compensate for this fatigue or pain, other muscles, which have nothing to do with the initial posture, or the original movement or action, try to support this now tired or painful muscle, and start to contract and tense up in their turn. This newly affected part of your body can now become tired, stiff, weak, painful, or sometimes even numb. Its function becomes limited, and your body, mind, and emotions become tired."

"When you use your computer, for example," Shooter said, "the only muscles that really need to work—to read or type—are those of your eyes, fingers, hands, and arms.

"Ask yourself, 'Do I need my shoulders, neck, chest, back, and leg muscles to assist me while I read or type? Do I need my whole face to read or type? Do I need to frown? Do my eyes need to squint? Do my cheeks and jaw need to be tense? Do I need to clench or grind my teeth?'

"You know, Genius, when you're in front of your computer, your face looks crazy."

"That's because I'm thinking and concentrating on what I'm reading or typing."

"All you need is for your brain to think, your eyes to see, and your arms, hands, and fingers to type. You don't need the muscles of your *whole* face—or your neck, shoulders, chest, back, legs, feet, and toes—to uselessly work hard, tense up, and assist you to do something that does not involve or even concern them. You don't need your crazy face to read or type!"

I thought for a moment about Shooter's observation.

"I never noticed that I had this problem."

"I assure you that you *will* have a problem," he said, "when you start feeling pain in your neck, shoulders, chest, and back, or when you start having headaches."

"You do not have a problem per se," reassured Starry. "It is simply a habit you picked up along the way, and a habit can be replaced with one that is more beneficial to you."

"How can I replace a habit of which I'm not aware in the first place?"

"You are now aware and able to catch the red feeling whenever Old Teller is speaking and an unhappy O'story is playing," she explained. "In the same way, you will become aware and be able to catch the useless tension in your muscle, especially when this muscle is not involved with your present posture, movement, or action.

"In the same fashion as you are now able to go back to the empty space, the loud silence, and the deep stillness of your mind, you will be able to bring back your tense muscle to its initial, natural, and relaxed state.

"At first, you will catch the tension every once in a while—maybe after this tension has greatly built up, or after you have started feeling pain or numbness. Slowly, you will more frequently become aware of its presence, and then release it and relax the muscle.

"Just like you set your alarm clock to help you practice becoming aware and catching Old Teller and the O'stories of your mind, you can also set it to remind yourself, every hour, to become aware and catch the tension of your muscles. When the alarm goes off, do not move. Keep the same posture in which you are sitting, standing, lying down, or moving, and observe your muscles.

"First, observe the muscles of your face. Then go through the muscles or muscle groups of the rest of your body, all the way down to your toes. For each muscle, ask yourself, 'Is this muscle tense right now? Do I really need this muscle to work in order for me to keep my posture, achieve my movement, or make my action?'

"You then conclude if this muscle is uselessly tense and needlessly working, causing you to feel tired. You will give this tense muscle or muscle group your complete attention. You will catch the tension, and release it and relax the muscle or muscle group.

"Observe the muscles of your forehead and eyebrows. Catch the tension and release it, and relax these muscles. Hold the newly relaxed position for five seconds while counting to five: 1, 2, 3, 4, 5.

"Observe the muscles of your eyes—the eyelids as well as the eyeballs themselves. Catch the tension and release it, and relax these muscles. Hold the newly relaxed position while counting to five: 1, 2, 3, 4, 5.

"Observe the rest of your face—your cheeks and jaw. If they are tight, open your mouth, massage your jaw, and move it sideways a few times to relax it. If your tongue is tense, relax it while counting to five: 1, 2, 3, 4, 5.

"Observe, catch, release the tension, and relax the muscles of your neck, shoulders, arms, hands, fingers, chest, stomach, back, legs, knees, feet, and toes.

"Once every hour, repeat this exercise of observing, catching, releasing, relaxing the uselessly tense muscles or muscle groups, and holding the newly relaxed position for five seconds.

"With time, patience, and practice, you will become more and more aware of the presence of the tension. You will release this tension, and your muscles will stay relaxed."

✪

"What more can I do to stop being tired?"

"You want to do *more* to stop being tired, Genius? Do *nothing!* Stop! Take a break!"

"Whether you are at work or at home doing housework," Starry explained, "every hour, and with the help of your alarm clock, take a five-minute break and step away from your workstation."

"... even if only to go to the restroom," added Shooter.

"Taking regular breaks helps prevent, reduce, and eliminate physical, mental, and emotional fatigue. During this five-minute break, if you were working standing up, sit down and, whenever possible, lie down. If you were working sitting down, stand up or walk around, and stretch your body, one muscle at a time.

Fatigue

"Divide the muscles of your body into five groups: (1) head and neck; (2) shoulders, arms, hands, and fingers; (3) chest and stomach; (4) back, waist, and hips; and (5) legs, feet, and toes.

"Stretch the muscles of every group. Hold the stretched position for five seconds, relax for five, and repeat five times."

Shooter suggested that I refer to books and the Internet to find stretching exercises that suit my body. He also reminded me of the option of consulting with a physical trainer.

"Give your eyes a break," continued Starry. "During this break, look away from their point of focus and concentration, whether it is someone or something, such as an object, a product, a computer screen, or a document.

"Whenever possible, look far outside a window, or simply close your eyes and stretch them by looking up, down, and sideways, and rotating them to the left and then to the right. Keep them closed for a while and look far into your eyelids. Look at the empty space of your mind."

"How about a 10- or 15-minute power nap whenever you can, Genius? A power nap is *powerful*. Dance, stretch, and nap!"

"Give your ears a break," Starry added. "If you were working in a noisy place, retreat to somewhere quieter."

"… even if it is the restroom, Genius."

"Try to find a quiet place away from the noise around you," Starry continued, "where you are able to hear the silence. Find a place where you can go above the noise inside you—the noise of Old Teller and the O'stories—and listen to the loud silence of your mind.

231

"Give your mind a break. Just like your body, your mind also needs frequent breaks to prevent fatigue from building up, and to help keep Old Teller quiet and the O'stories away. Take the time to go back to the empty space, loud silence, and deep stillness of your mind."

"It's a time for a time out!" Shooter announced. "A time out ... where you stop and think of nothing ... where you stop and say nothing ... where you stop and do nothing. The only thing you *can* do, Genius, is breathe and give your mind a break. Breathe ... five breaths ... one breath at a time.

"Inhale and, while you do, count to five: 1, 2, 3, 4, 5.

"Exhale and, while you do, also count to five: 1, 2, 3, 4, 5.

"Repeat this five times. Concentrate on your breathing and prevent Old Teller from speaking and the O'stories from playing." Starry concluded.

"It is time for a physical time out, to reduce—maybe even eliminate—some of the tension that built up in your muscles, and dissipate some of the accumulated fatigue, so your body feels more relaxed and energized.

"It is time for a mental time out, to go back to the stillness, so your mind feels more relaxed and energized.

"When you go back to what you were doing, you will feel recharged with a new energy. Your body and mind will feel fresh, and you can do and accomplish more."

"God knows how much more I need to do and accomplish ... a *million* things more!"

"While you do that, Genius, pay attention to the posture of your body—the way you sit or lie down, stand up and walk and move, reach and pick something up, and carry and lift things. Pay attention to each muscle of your body, starting from the top of your head, all the way down to your toes. Feel if your clothes and shoes are comfortable. Notice if your purse or briefcase is too heavy."

"Wherever you are," Starry said, "whether at home or at work, and whatever you are doing, examine the ergonomics of your work environment and workstation: your chair, desk, counter, computer screen and keyboard, and tools and machines—especially the ones you use on a regular basis. Analyze the setup itself—the design, shape, size, height, and weight—as well as the way you use and handle everything. Study the lighting and the background sounds or noise, and the room temperature and air quality.

"Do not forget to use *5W2H-O&D*, which will assist you to ask yourself the right questions. With this technique, along with the Internet and related articles, you will find the answers that will help you eliminate any ergonomic factor causing your fatigue. Remember to turn to someone who can help you, such as an environmental and posture specialist or ergonomist.

"Chronic discomfort can quietly sneak up on you and, before you know it, fatigue has built up in your body. You then find yourself irritable and sometimes even in pain. Your mind becomes an easy prey for Old Teller and its unhappy O'stories, which invade and take it over.

"Make sure you take regular and frequent small breaks *every day*. Make sure you stop enough times *every day*. Set your alarm once every hour, and stop for five minutes."

"Play the music," reminded Shooter. "Exercise has never been so easy with only one number for you to remember: *five*!

"Take a five-minute break, five times a day. Dance for five. Stretch for five. Breathe for five. Release and relax for five. Repeat for five ... and a high five to you, Genius!"

"Every weekend," Starry proposed, "take a long break and spend some precious time *with* yourself. Block two hours from your schedule, and enter your name. This time off is reserved especially for you to spend with yourself.

"Go to the park, sit, watch the empty space, and listen to the loud silence that surrounds you. Watch, listen, smell, and touch and feel ...

"Let your eyes wander. Contemplate the majesty of every rock, the pride of every tree, the freedom of every bird, the glitter of every drop of water in a fountain, and the glow of every Human Being walking by or sitting there.

"Let your ears discover the deep secrets of these rocks and the rustle of the leaves of these trees. Let them enjoy the happy melodies of those birds, the soothing song of that water, and the glow of every Human Being.

"Take a deep breath and smell the scent of the fresh air, the grass, and the earth.

"Feel the warm sun, the soft breeze, or the strong wind.

"Sit there, and become one with nature and the park."

"Take off your shoes," said Shooter, "get up, and walk around. Let the grass tickle and massage your feet. Then stop, and lie down."

"Lie down? On the *grass*? In the *park*?"

"In the park ... in your backyard ... anywhere!"

Fatigue

"I can lie down on the swing in my backyard. Why would I lie down on the grass in the park?"

"Go wild, Genius! Get Dunia to teach you how to do that. Choose a day when clouds are scattered in the sky, and play the cloud game together. Lie down on the grass, look up, and watch the clouds float up there ... or should I say *up here!*" he joked. "You and Dunia can find an endless variety of shapes in these clouds. You can find a car, a bike, a deer, a cat, a rabbit, a seahorse ... maybe you can even find *me!* This game can never be boring. It's always great fun!"

"Since you are lying down," Starry added, "this game relaxes your body. While you are focusing on the clouds, your mind is busy trying to remember and match the shapes. Since the mind cannot think of two things at the same time, the cloud game also relaxes your mind, and keeps Old Teller quiet and the unhappy O'stories away."

"If the clouds get thicker and it starts to rain," said Shooter, "and unless there's lightning or you're sick, just stay there for a few minutes. Don't hurry back into the house. Stay there and feel every raindrop on your face and body."

"... and if it keeps raining, what do I do with myself for two hours?"

"Satisfy your 'need to relax,' Genius! Go to a spa and get a massage. How about that?"

"Now you're talking. I second *that!*"

"... or stay home, light some candles, and take a bubble bath," he added.

"These are great ideas, Shooter. I haven't had a massage or taken a bubble bath in months ... maybe years!"

Shooter's "weekend break with myself" suggestion list continued: Draw, paint, carve, garden, or cook. Learn something new, like a new language, for example. Read a magazine, an article, a poem, or a book. Write, or listen to music. Watch a movie or some funny videos. Go to the theater, a concert, a comedy club, or a karaoke bar. Play the tourist and visit my city. Go to museums, attractions, and events. Go to the mall and indulge myself. Treat myself to a delicious meal at my favorite restaurant.

"You want me to spend two hours at a restaurant *by myself*?"

"*With* yourself! Hey, Genius, your company is quite pleasant, you know ... even for longer than two hours!

"Once a month," he added, "block half a day from your schedule and enter your name. One half-day reserved just for you. Leave your phone and watch at home, go for a long drive, and repeat out loud, 'Today, I say enough of putting off time I spend with myself!' Then play the music, and sing as loudly as you can.

"At least once a year, take a one- or two-week break. Stop and take a vacation. Go away on a trip. Take a cruise. Browse the getaway and travel destinations of your dreams, and call your travel agent.

"Every seven years," he continued, excitedly, "take one year off."

"You mean take one *month* off," I corrected.

"I mean take one *year* off," he repeated.

"A *whole* year? What are you talking about, Shooter? I can't take a whole year off. I can't even take one afternoon off, not even when I'm *sick*!"

"Taking a whole year off once every seven years is called a 'sabbatical.' I hear that even God took the seventh day off after He spent six days creating the world. Do you think your life is more complicated and hectic than creating the whole world?"

"Well, God obviously did not have any bills to pay! I'll tell you what, Shooter. I'll take a sabbatical when grace happens."

"Grace?" he asked, amused.

We all laughed.

"Do yourself and everyone around you a favor, Genius. Don't wait to be sick to take some time off!"

"Taking frequent breaks," Starry resumed, "prevents, reduces, and even eliminates fatigue. It recharges your body, mind, and emotions. Take frequent breaks and play. Take frequent breaks, have fun, and laugh. Having fun and laughing are powerful ways to get rid of fatigue. They enhance your ability to deal with Old Teller and its unhappy O'stories."

"Ask the fun experts," suggested Shooter.

"There are experts who can tell me how to have fun?"

"They don't even charge for it. Their service is completely free, and they are available whenever you need them, 24/7. Do you want me to tell you how to contact them?"

"Of course, Shooter!"

"I know a girl who's very talented. She's a natural! She can show you how to have fun again. Her techniques are simple and inexpensive. They don't involve any high-tech tools or costly products. I'm sure it will be her pleasure to spend time with you and show you the details, the rules, and the way 'fun' works."

"Who is she?"

"Her name is Dunia," he announced. "You see, the repertoire of Dunia's Old Teller is not developed, so no O'story distracts her from having fun.

"You might need to buy a skipping rope, maybe some coloring chalk or drawing pencils, and a ball to roll, throw, catch, and kick around.

"Actually, you don't need to buy anything at all. You can play the music and dance together. You can make silly and funny faces—maybe imitate Old Teller's happy *and* unhappy faces. You can play the cloud game. You can make shadows on the wall with your hands, or just blow bubbles with soap and water and watch them float around and shine. You can go to the park, and build castles with nothing but sand and dirt—like *you* used to do, Genius.

"I'll bet that you can have fun simply by watching Dunia. Observe the details and expressions on her face when she speaks, smiles, and laughs, and when she concentrates or gets upset. Watch her while she sits, moves, skips, runs, or rolls around. Listen to her when she speaks, screams, giggles, and laughs.

"The energy of this little girl is contagious. Her enthusiasm and aliveness will definitely keep Old Teller quiet and the unhappy O'stories away, and will prevent, reduce, and even eliminate your fatigue."

✬

I thought for a moment and remembered the many times Dunia had actually tried to save me from Old Teller and its unhappy O'stories.

"I remember one time, not too long ago, when I was sitting alone at my kitchen table, staring at the floor, and looking at absolutely nothing.

"Dunia walked into the kitchen, looked at me with her curious eyes, and, out of nowhere, asked, 'Mom, what do you do for fun?' I'm sure that she saw my tension and fatigue, and read the despair and boredom on my face."

"There you go, Genius! Dunia knows about fun, and she can tell when it's not there. She sure could teach you a thing or two about it."

"This happens especially when I'm not busy," I continued, "or when I'm in between tasks, like while I'm driving or trying to relax. The worst is when I put my head on the pillow after I've gone to bed. The O'stories of my mind go crazy! They're like a group of wild horses that are set free and run all over the place. This must be what Dunia saw on my face."

"She saw the *horses*? Do you think she saw George's horse?" he joked.

"The *O'stories*, Shooter! She saw the O'stories when I was sitting alone."

"Then don't sit alone, Genius! Get busy. Do something and keep busy. Keep your mind busy, too, and don't give Old Teller a chance to speak! Since the mind cannot think of two things at the same time, when you keep your mind busy and focused on one specific project, activity, or task, Old Teller will keep quiet and the O'stories will disappear.

"Read, write, paint, or take pictures. The list of what you can do to keep busy is endless. Keep your mind happily busy, Genius, and don't sit alone!"

Starry made an important distinction.

"Do not sit *lonely*!

"Remember that, just like your body, your mind also needs frequent breaks to rest, relax, and recharge with energy and stillness. Sitting alone *with* yourself, staying inside the empty space of your mind, and enjoying the loud silence and feeling safe, fulfilled, and happy inside its deep stillness is a happy kind of solitude and a healthy time out.

"Unhealthy solitude or loneliness, on the other hand, while Old Teller's unhappy O'stories swing you back and forth between your sad past, your unhappy present, and your promising or scary future, can make you feel unhappy-red."

"From up here, I see a lot of lonely people ... *everywhere!*" said Shooter, with a sad tone of voice. "From up here, I see loneliness spreading fast ... men, women, children, young adults, and older adults ... rich and poor ... people of all shapes and colors."

"Why is that?" I asked. "Why are so many people lonely in the world today?"

"Let me tell you about a few reasons I see from up here," he answered, and then sighed deeply. "Once upon a time, parents had many children, and the family—babies, young children, teenagers, adults, and older adults—lived together.

"Everyone shared their mornings, days, and evenings. They sat, ate, talked, played, laughed, and had fun together. Many family members shared the same space, maybe one small bedroom and sometimes even the same bed. They shared each other's possessions. They stayed together and took care of each other. They helped, supported, entertained, and kept each other company. There was no time or room for unhappy loneliness.

"Nowadays, in what Human words describe as a more 'modern' world, many parents have fewer children because, according to them, life is expensive. They need to buy a big house where each child has their own bedroom, television, and computer.

"Instead of sharing time and space, and instead of sitting, eating, talking, playing, laughing, and having fun together, everyone goes to their own room inside their big house.

"You know, Genius, from up here, I sometimes see big houses where loneliness is the master. The bigger the house, the more room loneliness occupies. I see big parties, every day and night, where sad past, unhappy—worried and bored—present, and scary future O'stories meet, dance, and go wild!

"Those kids grow up. They are in a hurry to leave their homes, become independent, and start their own life, only to sometimes fall into the trap of loneliness shortly thereafter. In this more modern world, just like their parents, they soon become busy running after different I-haves, and are ready to do whatever it takes to collect them.

"Sometimes, they invest all their time, including the time they could spend with their loved ones—their family and friends—in order to pursue a career, achieve a business success, and reach a goal.

"Sometimes, they leave and move away for an opportunity they believe will lead them to higher financial security and a better lifestyle, which they hope will make them happy. After a long, hard day at work, they come back to an empty house, which they share with their roommate—loneliness—while their loved ones are missing them and feeling lonely as well."

Shooter stayed quiet for a few moments, and then took a deep breath before he continued.

"In this more modern world, you sometimes try to call and speak with someone on the phone, and then find out that you have to interact with a machine. You sit in front of a screen, watch what it wants to show you, and listen to what it wants to tell and sell you "so you can be happier" as it tries to convince you.

"You sometimes talk back to it, type, play, and spend hours communicating through it. Doing all this decreases human interactions, such as personal conversations while people look into each other's eyes and smile. It limits the social activities and get-togethers."

"... but Shooter," I interrupted, "that's technology, and we need it."

"Of course you do," Starry intervened. "The purpose of technology—the main reason for which it was created—is to make your life easier and more efficient, and bring people together ... and it does! Technology is there for you. It is happy to offer its services to you and help you.

"However, when you become distracted from this purpose, technology is not proud to see you abuse it, or allow it to invade the time and space that was designed and must remain designated for other aspects of your life. Technology is not pleased to replace the sacred time and space reserved for you to spend with the people in your life, namely your loved ones. Technology is not happy to see you lonely!"

"From up here," Shooter added, "I've never seen a television hold someone's hand, or a computer screen give them a big, comforting hug. I've never seen one take the time to listen to them, touch them, and make them feel better.

"Listen to me, Genius. Do not spend hours in front of your screen. Get physically and emotionally involved with people, animals, and nature.

"Block regular times from your schedule to spend with your loved ones. Let these times be sacred and do not erase them. Do not knock them down your priority list, and do not take care of them only when you have some spare time. Do not wait until your million things to do are done.

"Join a class or enroll yourself in a group activity. If you can't find anything to do out there, or if nothing fits your schedule or lifestyle today, organize an activity yourself. Create occasions and events, and invite your family and friends. Get together in the evenings and on weekends. Share lunches, dinners, and coffee or tea breaks. Celebrate birthdays, throw parties, play games, go to picnics, plan outings, and organize trips. The list of what you can do is endless!

"Don't blame the weather. Don't say that it's bad, or that it's grey, cold, messy, humid, or hot. It doesn't matter! Get together indoors. Just make a phone call, and you *and* they will be happy you did.

"Don't use the excuse that you have no one to spend time with. Reconnect with your old friends. Pick up the phone or send everyone an e-mail and invite them to an event, even if you end up spending this precious time with only one person. Use the help of 5W2H-O&D, choose one option, and set a date to get together.

"Everyone suffers from unhappy loneliness every once in a while and, like you, everyone wants to be with loved ones. Nobody wants to be lonely, Genius, and everyone wants to be happy.

"If your family and friends are not available, get busy helping someone who needs your help. God knows how many people out there need it! Help a friend, do community work, and volunteer with people. Volunteer at a hospital or school, or with a cultural or religious organization. Volunteer to take care of animals or the environment. Call your city, or search the Internet or phone directory for different associations.

"Make a list of their names, phone numbers, and addresses. Get busy calling or personally visit them and ask how you can help and what you can do for them."

"Do not become one with unhealthy solitude or loneliness," concluded Starry. "Do not let your mind become an easy prey for Old Teller and its unhappy O'stories.

"Get interested in other Humans instead. Look at them and see them, instead of watching the unhappy O'stories of your mind. Hear them and listen to them, instead of listening to Old Teller. When you do, you will feel completely fulfilled and truly happy!"

"Pick up the phone and call someone, Genius, or pick it up and answer to someone who's calling you."

As soon as Shooter finished saying these words, the phone rang.

CHAPTER EIGHT

The Million Things to Do

I got up from the swing and ran into the house to answer the phone.

"Hello?"

"Hi, Mommy!"

"Baby! How *are* you? Is everything okay?"

"Yep. I'm here with Grandma. She bought me chocolate!"

"She *did*? Are you having fun?"

"Yep. Grandma wants to talk to you."

Before I got a chance to say anything else, Dunia handed the phone to Helen.

"Hello, Helen. Is everything okay?"

"Everything's fine. We just stopped at a rest area to stretch a little. There was a bit of traffic right before the bridge. We'll be back on the road in a few minutes."

"Did Dunia go to the bathroom?"

245

"Yes, she did."

"Be careful, please. Take your time getting to the cottage."

"Don't worry! No one is more careful and drives more slowly than George," she reassured me, laughing.

"Don't forget to call me when you get there. Be safe. Goodbye!"

"Be careful ... be safe. Did Helen say 'bridge'? Now there's a lake, a horse, *and* a bridge?"

"This is not *funny*, Shooter!"

"Your Old Teller never shuts up, Genius! Does it?"

Somewhat relieved to know that everything was under control with Dunia, I ignored Shooter's question, got my agenda, and sat at my kitchen table. I was hoping to find out that some of my million things I had to do before tomorrow had miraculously disappeared!

"Your Old Teller is so creative," Shooter continued. "Remember that, if you allow it, it will speak forever and tell you one thousand and one O'stories that keep you well entertained."

"Sometimes," Starry said, "Old Teller puts on one of its many Unhappy faces, and talks to you about your past, dwells, blames this past for your unhappy present, and tries to explain how and why you ended up here.

"Other times, it puts on a different Unhappy face, and talks to you about your future, dwells, accuses this future for your unhappy present, and tries to justify how and why you are still here.

"To dwell on your unhappy present even more, Old Teller puts on its Worry face, and tells you worry O'stories that make you feel unhappy. Human words describe this unhappiness by saying that you worry or you are worried.

"Worry O'stories describe the million things you have to do. They describe your heavy load of appointments, overwhelming responsibilities, and unfinished tasks.

"You worry because you have no time to deal with this heavy load and are unable to meet deadlines.

"You worry when you have too many options and cannot make up your mind, or when you have few options or no choice at all, which prevents you from starting something.

"You worry when you have no clue what to do or where to start.

"You worry when you do not have enough money and cannot afford something.

"You worry when you do not have what it takes to make it—enough resources, such as looks, health, age, courage, intelligence, education, knowledge, experience, or connections.

"You worry because you have at least one unmet need or *problem*—as Human words call it."

"Hey, Genius, do you know that I can tell which worry O'story is playing on your mind, just by looking at your face?"

"You *can*?" I wondered, surprised.

"Oh, yeah!" he bragged.

"*Really*, Shooter?" Starry doubted.

"Well, not exactly *which* O'story, but I can sure tell when Genius is watching one. I'll bet *she* knows how I do that. Don't you, Genius?"

I thought for a moment, and then dared to ask, "Is it my crazy face?"

"You got it! It *is* your crazy face ... the one with the lines."

"*What* lines?"

"The lines on your forehead, especially the ones between your eyebrows."

I made no comment, which Shooter interpreted as a green light to elaborate.

"... and the ones around your lips."

"*Shooter!*" Starry warned.

"It's *true!*" he rebelled, and then addressed me. "I'm serious, Genius. When you're listening to Old Teller and watching an O'story, the lines on your face suddenly multiply and become deeper. Sometimes, I can see them all the way from up here!"

"*Shooter!*"

Ignoring Starry's second warning, and still taking pleasure at describing my crazy face, he continued.

"Your twinkles really tell me that you're having a worry O'story moment."

"My *what?*"

"It's your twinkles," he repeated. "I can see them from up here."

"*Wrinkles*, Shooter," corrected Starry. "They are called wrinkles."

"Oh, yeah. That's what I meant to say: *wrinkles*."

"I'm not sure if it was a good idea for Starry to correct him," I thought to myself. "I think I prefer twinkles!"

I heard Shooter humming, "*Twinkle, wrinkle, little star ...*"

"Listening to Old Teller and watching the worry O'stories," Starry explained, "can be harmful for the body, mind, and emotions. "The Human feels and looks unhealthy. More wrinkles show on the face. The eyes lose their shine. They look at the life happening around them but do not really see it. The Human looks absorbed in their mind. They lose their smile. Their face looks harsh and tense, and the happy vibration that used to emanate from them disappears. Their body could become less resistant to disease and more prone to problems, and some parts could become painful or have a limited function."

Shooter named some problems that could occur, such as muscle tension in different parts of the body—neck, shoulders, back, chest, or stomach.

He said that listening to Old Teller and watching the worry O'stories could affect the appetite—the person starts eating more or not enough. The amount and quality of sleep could be affected. Insomnia kicks in. Fatigue settles in the body, and the person feels tired and lacks energy.

Headaches or migraines could develop. Allergies, diabetes, blood pressure or heart problems, and digestive, respiratory, immune, or nervous problems could arise—maybe anxiety attacks, or even a breakdown or a burnout.

"The mind is distracted," Starry continued. "The Human cannot concentrate or focus properly on what they are saying or doing. They cannot control or organize their thoughts. They cannot think straight or fast enough. They are confused and cannot make a decision. They hesitate, make more errors, and forget more. Their mind is tired and loses its stillness.

"The Human is emotionally tired. They feel overwhelmed, anxious, stressed, worried, and unhappy."

"Wow!" I said. "Old Teller and the worry O'stories can cause some serious damage!"

"A lot more damage than the unmet need or problem on which Old Teller is dwelling can cause you. Listening to Old Teller and watching the worry O'stories could be more harmful to your health than the missing satisfying I-have is to the unmet need, or the unfound solution to the problem.

"Old Teller can dwell as long as the need remains unsatisfied or the problem unsolved. So, for those needs or problems that may not have a prompt I-have or solution, Old Teller may dwell for minutes, hours, days, months, or years, and you can worry for a long time."

"... and Genius, for those that may not have any, you can worry forever!"

"While Old Teller dwells, and the worry O'stories play inside your mind," Starry continued, "you no longer see the empty space, hear the loud silence, or feel the deep stillness. You are no longer connected with yourself or with the life happening around you Here and Now."

"So how can I stop Old Teller from dwelling? How do I get rid of the worry O'stories?"

"Old Teller sometimes tells you to get involved in situations that you cannot really change and ones over which you have no control. It insists on dragging you to fight battles that are not yours. They are battles that you will never win and which fighting will only exhaust you. When the worry O'stories play and describe these battles, you feel unhappy."

"What battles are those?"

"Up here! *Look up here!*" shouted Shooter.

"Night or day," I thought to myself, "whether I'm in my back-yard, at the mall, or in my kitchen, I now know that the million stars are always shining!"

I looked up, closed my eyes, and read a long list of battles that glistened in the sky.

✫ ✫ ✫

Battles That Are Not Mine

- Go back to my past, including the story I came with or the one I came into.
- Go back to a place that is no longer Here.
- Go back to a time that is no longer Now.
- Be with someone who is no longer Here and Now.
- Bring back someone or something.
- Rewind time and change what has already happened.
- Take back what was already said or undo what was already done.
- Become upset and blame myself or someone else for what has already happened.
- Regret what happened, and why or how it did, and feel that it could have, would have, and should have happened differently.

- Regret my good old days, hold on to them, and resist letting them go.

- Fight the presence of my unresolved past inside my life.

✬

- Fast forward time (seconds, minutes, hours, days, or years).

- Skip stages and be today where I am supposed to be tomorrow.

- Make a dream come true, reach a goal, and get to the finish line while I am still at the beginning.

- Collect an I-have when it is not yet time to do so, forgetting to have faith that no one can take away what is meant to be mine.

- Eliminate fear or expect it to disappear before I take a step.

- Know the unknown, predict future results, and guarantee happy outcomes.

✬

- Resist what is Here and Now.

- Be at two places, and think of, say, or do two different things at the same time.

- Collect an I-have and satisfy a need simply by dwelling instead of doing something about it.

- Fight and resist the one and only possible I-have option.

- Find an answer to every question, and find a solution for every problem when there is none or when it is not yet time for the answer or solution to reveal itself.

- Always know and understand what, why, or how someone is thinking, feeling, saying, or doing something—or what, why, or how they did or will think, feel, say, or do something.

- Discover life's secrets, and always understand how or why something is happening, or did or will happen.

- Always discover the blessing under the disguise.

- Always understand the language spoken beyond all Human words, and figure out every message.

- Stop time, and prevent life from moving forward and change from happening—whether this change is sudden or gradual.

- Resist change, and stay stubborn and want everyone and everything to stand still.

- Stop myself and my loved ones from aging.

- Escape the inescapable day that will separate me from my loved ones or separate them from me.

- Stop life's natural flow and cycles.

- Stop the seasons from changing and control the weather.

- Stop and prevent every natural disaster from happening, such as floods, earthquakes, tornadoes, or hurricanes.

- Stop and prevent every problem, misfortune, and tragedy from existing.

- Stop poverty, disease, accidents, violent acts, crime, and war.

- Protect and save myself and my loved ones everywhere, every time, and from everything.

- Protect and save the world.

✿ ✿ ✿

"It's everyone's duty to save the world," I disagreed as I opened my eyes. "We're *all* responsible to make it a better place."

"Save yourself first, Genius ... and you will help save the world!"

"Every Human's story and every need," Starry said, "including those of your loved ones, belong only to them. The only story and needs for which you are responsible are your own. Stay true to your story and to your needs. Stay true to yourself.

"Old Teller and the worry O'stories sometimes try to convince you that you should solve and remove someone's problems, and take up their challenges and responsibilities. By doing so, by wanting to take a step on *their* path instead of them, you forget that you might be intruding and interfering with *their* opportunity to grow and glow.

"Feeling badly or guilty about what appears to be their sad fate, absorbing it into your own story, and insisting on saving them—even when you cannot—is exhausting. You can listen to them, support, encourage, and help them while *they* fight their battles, collect their I-haves, and satisfy their needs.

"You can help change and improve the world with one cause at a time. While helping others is indeed a battle of yours, saving the whole world is not. Your share of the battle is limited to what you can *really* change, and to the task you can actually accomplish in order to give back to the world ... one idea, one word, one gesture, and one action at a time."

The words that Shooter told me to repeat out loud were some of his ideas about how I could help save the world:

- Today, I put a smile on someone's face.
- Today, I say one more nice word than I usually say.
- Today, I do one more nice gesture or action than I already do.
- Today, I am nicer to the life happening inside and around me.
- Today, I treat myself kindly.
- Today, I treat everyone kindly, as well as nature and all living creatures.
- Today, I take care of every thing.
- Today, I choose one cause, which is close to my heart and serves my story and me, and help improve it, one step at a time.

"... and you will, Genius. You *will* save the world!"

"Sometimes," Starry continued, "Old Teller and the worry O'stories try to convince you to always say 'yes' and please everyone—or at least someone."

"I have *that* problem," I interrupted. "I can never say 'no' to anybody."

"Of course you can," Shooter disagreed. "You did say 'no' to your mom the other day when she asked you to visit or call your aunt.

"Someone might ask you to do something you don't want or can't do, even if it's a favor, Genius, or go somewhere you don't want to go, even when it's an invitation to go to a nice place or attend a pleasant event. All you have to do is say 'no.'

"This person you just turned down may be surprised, disappointed, and even hurt, upset, or mad when they receive your 'no' to their request. On a scale from 1 to 10, their surprise and disappointment will score 10 the first time around. Then, it will only score 9 the second time they ask for something and you say 'no.' Slowly, their surprise and disappointment will decrease and eventually disappear.

"All you have to do is say 'no,' and all the other person has to do is turn to a different source to help them find the I-have that will satisfy their need. One day, hopefully soon, they will create a Happy List about *you* and keep it in their Precious Box."

"Still," I insisted, "it's not easy for me to say 'no.'"

"It may not be easy, Genius, but it is certainly not impossible! All it takes is time, patience, and practice.

"You can actually learn and practice saying 'no.' Find someone who already knows how to do that and let them help you.

"You can even practice saying 'no' by yourself. Stand in front of your bedroom mirror and pretend that your reflection is someone asking you for a favor that you don't wish or feel like doing. Ask for the favor, and then look yourself straight in the eyes and answer out loud, 'No!' Ask for another favor, and again answer, 'No!' Ask for as many favors as you please, until you become familiar with saying 'no.'

"On a scale from 1 to 10, the next time you are tempted to say 'no' to someone, your unease will score 10. It will only reach 9 the second time around. Time after time, it decreases. With time, patience, and practice, saying 'no' will become much easier."

"When you say 'no,'" Starry continued, "Old Teller will want to speak and warn you that saying 'no' will cost you the love of the person you just turned down. If this happens, reassure Old Teller and reassure yourself that you will never lose the love of a person who truly loves you. Remind Old Teller and remind yourself that your source of true love is always safe!"

Starry and Shooter stayed quiet for a few moments while I listened to Old Teller insisting that saying 'no' is not easy.

"Ask Old Teller to shut up, Genius. Just say, '*Shhh!*'

"Now, close your eyes again and keep reading. The stars are still shining up here, and the list goes on ..."

I closed my eyes, and resumed reading the list of battles that are not mine.

✫ ✫ ✫

- Always expect a "yes" from others.
- Blame others for my unhappiness.
- Expect others, especially my loved ones, to constantly have time for me and be available to listen to me, guess what I am thinking, guess how I am feeling, guess what my needs are, and then save me from my unhappiness.
- Expect others to always care about my feelings, take care of me, and satisfy my needs—forgetting that every Human is busy satisfying their own needs.

- Expect others to love me how I want them to love me.

- Expect others to make me happy.

- Expect to receive an I-have from a person, place, or situation that cannot or will not offer me one.

- Expect what cannot be expected.

- Control every small-bite situation.

- Control or change someone's personal story, looks, character, personality, talents, strengths, weaknesses, habits, attitude, behavior, thoughts, ideas, points of view, emotions, feelings, needs, words, actions, reactions, taste, decisions, and choices.

- Change someone so *they* are happier.

- Change someone so they fit my expectations and *I* am happier.

- Assume what someone is thinking, how they are feeling, and what they will say or do.

- Expect gratitude and thank yous from everyone at every time.

- Resist the fact that my story is the *only* story I have and will ever have during my life on Earth.

- Resist what my story is, and how it is happening Here and Now.

- Resist the presence of what I feel are my weaknesses.

- Expect to always be right, never make a mistake, and never lose.

- Expect to hold a perfect record everywhere, with everyone, and in everything I think, say, do, give, or receive, instead of being flexible, patient, compassionate, and forgiving, and forgetting that this need for perfection is an exhausting battle to fight.

- Expect all my needs to always be completely met and satisfied.

- Prevent needs from arising or changing.

- Ignore and resist needs that come back.

- Resist times of emptiness.

- Resist what feels like a painful need or problem inside my story, forgetting that this need or problem is my perfect growth opportunity.

- Always keep Old Teller quiet and the unhappy O'stories away.

- Resist my true thoughts, emotions, and feelings, which tell me to stay true to my story and to myself.

- Clearly know and always remember where I came from and where I am going, what I am doing here, and what I want.

- Always remember who I am.

"Back to Earth, Genius!"

I slowly opened my eyes. I was fascinated to realize how many of these battles, which are not mine, I try to fight ... *every day!*

"What do I do with these battles?" I asked. "Do I file them away for now and deal with them later, like I do with an unresolved past or a fear O'story? Is there a ceremony to celebrate at a more convenient place and time?"

"The only ceremony to celebrate, at a more convenient place and time in the honor of such battles, is a *Goodbye* ceremony, Genius!

"When a battle is not yours, don't file it away. Hurry to your movie director's chair. Sit, rise up, and watch from above. Then, turn the spotlight off Old Teller and the worry O'story.

"Stop this O'story from playing and describing the battle, just like you stop a television show you don't want to watch by turning off your television. Stop Old Teller from telling you to fight this battle, just like you stop a song or a radio program you don't want to hear by turning off the radio.

"If this doesn't work, ask Old Teller to shut up. Just say, '*Shhh!*' Then, replace the worry O'story with empty space and loud silence, or wave your magic wand and replace it with an image. What pretty image would you like it to be?"

"Let's see," I answered. "A butterfly or a bird ... maybe a puppy ..."

"A horse," Shooter interjected.

"... a flower, a tree, a mountain," I added.

"A lake," he playfully offered.

"... the sun ... the moon," I continued.

I heard Shooter clear his throat and proudly announce, "A star ... a *shooting* star!"

"... or just delete it," suggested Starry.

"Delete the shooting star? You want Genius to delete *me*?"

"The worry O'story," Starry laughed. "Keep the list of battles that are not yours in your Precious Box. Review this list often until you become familiar with these battles and can quickly and easily recognize them.

"At first, you might not be able to recognize a battle before you have felt unhappy-red for a while and before you have probably exhausted yourself trying to fight it. Slowly, with time, patience, and practice, you will be able to catch the battle every once in a while—maybe while Old Teller is still in the midst of telling you to fight it. Eventually, you will catch it as soon as Old Teller starts to speak.

"You will also notice that, among the battles on this long list, it is the *same* battles that often come back to your mind, which makes it easier for you to recognize them.

"As you replace or delete the worry O'story describing the battle, ask for God's assistance and repeat the serenity prayer written by Reinhold Niebuhr:

'God, grant me the serenity to accept the things I cannot change, courage to change the things I can, and wisdom to know the difference.'

"Then, *come back to Here and Now*."

"What about when the battle *is* mine to fight? Like my million things to do at home, at work, and for myself and Dunia? What about when I *do* have control over it, and *can* change something about it?"

"Stop saying that you have a million things to do, Genius. You *don't!*"

"Yes, I *do!*"

"It's just like when you said that you had tried *every* exercise and activity. That is Old Teller speaking! Stop repeating Old Teller's 'drama' words and expressions because you're starting to believe them. These words and expressions, which you repeat to yourself, to others, and to God, sustain you in the role of 'the victim' and hurt only *you!* When you catch it telling you a dramatic O'story, ask Old Teller to shut up. Just say, '*Shhh!*'

"You do *not* have a million things to do!"

"Yes, I *do*, Shooter!"

"... and you have no clue where to start," Starry interrupted.

"Exactly," I confirmed.

"... and you do not have enough time to do everything," she continued.

"Right!" I agreed, relieved to know that at least Starry sympathized with me.

"It's Old Teller telling you that you have a million things to do, Genius—which, by the way, *you do not.* Old Teller sure knows how to exaggerate and dramatize an O'story, and how to set it up, produce it, and present and sell it to you."

"I wish Old Teller was exaggerating and dramatizing, Shooter. I wish that I did not have to do all these things. I wish that I did not have to go back to work tomorrow, or at least had a few extra hours a day ... *that* would help for sure!"

"Let's wave that magic wand and give you some extra time to do your million things even if, knowing you, Genius, you'll probably make them a million and *one!* How many more hours would you like?"

"Two," I answered, amused. "No wait ... make that *three*."

"Think of the purse you bought," Starry intervened.

"You mean the purse I *tried* to buy yesterday?"

"The one you bought last month," she said. "Do you remember why you bought it?"

"Because the old one she had was getting too small to fit all of her junk."

"What I have in my purse is not *junk*, Shooter! Everything I keep in it is important. I need everything I have in my purse, and my old one could not fit everything anymore."

"Of *course* it couldn't. Isn't this exactly what you had said about the purse you bought before this one ... *and* the one before that? You keep buying bigger purses, and finding more important *things* to stuff into them, until these things start falling out because you can no longer close this purse, or you force it to close until it tears."

"That's exactly why I bought *this* one. This one should be just perfect. This one can fit everything."

"That's why you wanted to buy another purse yesterday, right, Genius? These purses you keep buying might be perfect for your junk, but they sure are not perfect for your back.

"Haven't you noticed how heavy this perfect purse, which you stuff with important things, has become lately? Haven't you noticed how you've been complaining that your neck, shoulder, and back hurt every time you carry it?"

I thought for a brief moment and admitted to myself, "Shooter is right! I *have* been feeling pain in my neck, shoulder, and back lately. I *did* notice that my purse was getting heavier and heavier."

Quickly erasing that thought from my mind, I held my ground.

"Well, I need all these things." Then, addressing Starry, I asked, "What about the purse, Starry?"

"Think of this purse as the space where you put things that you judge important to you, and compare it to your schedule where you try to fit the things that you have to do."

"... *all* million of them!" Shooter quipped.

"The more things you put in your purse, the heavier it becomes," Starry continued. "The more things you have to do are put on your schedule, the heavier your schedule becomes. You feel as if you are going to break down under the physical, mental, and emotional charge, and under the heavy load of these things and your busy schedule that leave you no time for yourself.

"You say that you have a crazy life, and you do not know where to start or put yourself. You cannot figure out how or when to do all these things, or if you *can* do them and deliver on time. You feel worried, overwhelmed, anxious, nervous, stressed, tired, and unhappy.

"The more you load your purse, the heavier it becomes, and carrying it becomes painful. The more you load your schedule, the heavier it becomes, and living becomes painful."

"Meanwhile," Shooter added, "your million things to do inspire Old Teller to dwell and tell you its *million and one* worry O'stories."

"So what can I do? What's the solution?"

"Unload your purse, Genius! Clean it up. Get rid of a few things.

"Unload your schedule. Clean it up. Get rid of some of your million things to do."

I firmly rejected this suggestion.

"I *can't!*"

"Why not?"

"Because I have a lot of responsibilities."

"As long as you are alive," Starry explained, "you will always have needs to satisfy, whether they are needs you choose and create for yourself or ones that life creates for you.

"New situations arise and new needs are born, pushing you outside your routine and comfort zone. They require that you answer to them, deal with them, and, whenever possible, satisfy them, bringing yourself back on track. This is how your task list is born. You call them 'things to do'—tasks, responsibilities, or obligations.

"The moment a new task comes up and is put on your list, a new worry O'story is born along with it. The task in itself is not necessarily the source of the worry O'story. The real source is the fact that this task is not accomplished yet, which means that the satisfying I-have is not collected and the need is not satisfied.

"Old Teller will dwell and the worry O'story will play inside your mind as long as the task remains on your list. The more tasks accumulate and load your schedule, the more worry O'stories are born, which leads you to feel worried, overwhelmed, anxious, nervous, stressed, and unhappy.

"Old Teller will dwell and the worry O'story will play until the moment you stop avoiding this task and accept its presence on your list, and until you seriously face it, take action, and actually do something about it. The worry O'story will harass you until the satisfying I-have is collected and the need is met and satisfied.

It will haunt your mind, irritate and stress you, and drain your energy until you actually *do* the new thing.

"Once it is done, this thing to do is released, leaving a light yet powerful energy behind it. You will then feel liberated, free, and energized. Old Teller will keep quiet and the worry O'story will disappear. You can then go back to the empty space, the loud silence, and the deep stillness of your mind, where you are completely fulfilled and truly happy!"

Shooter had encouraging words for me to repeat out loud:

- Today, I say *enough!*
- Today, I stop dwelling on this thing I have to do.
- Today, I do something about it.

"No matter how many things I do and accomplish, others always pop up and load my list again. It never ends! I'm tired of living and carrying this heavy weight!"

"Living and traveling heavy is physically, mentally, and emotionally tiring," Starry confirmed.

"So what can I do?"

"Don't travel heavy, Genius. Travel light! Put down some of your million things to do. Unload! Make them a thousand instead. How does one thousand sound to you?"

"I *can't* unload, Shooter. I *have* to do these things. These things have to be done!"

"Fine, then. Keep the things you have to do ... *done!*"

"That's what I said! I have to do these things. I have to get them done!"

Shooter kept quiet for a moment, and then spoke.

"Keep your task list as empty as possible. Keep your things to do done and forgotten. Goodbye ... *ciao* ... *adios!*"

Now I was confused *and* annoyed.

"Starry, what is Shooter talking about? How do I keep my million things to do done? How do I travel light?"

Starry explained.

"There are tasks you choose to delete as soon as they come up—such as battles that are not yours, or tasks that do not serve you or your story. You remove such tasks from your list. Then, you delete the worry O'story from your mind.

"There are tasks you choose to delegate and remove from your list. Then, you delete the worry O'story from your mind.

"There are tasks you choose to break down. Then, you delete the worry O'story from your mind.

"There are tasks you choose to accomplish immediately, as soon as they come up, and remove from your list. Then, you delete the worry O'story from your mind.

"There are tasks you choose to file away for the time being. You set a date to accomplish such tasks. Then, you delete the worry O'story from your mind."

"*That* is how you keep your million things to do done, Genius. *That* is how you travel light!"

"Every day," Starry elaborated, "a certain amount of energy is available for you to invest in accomplishing each one of your tasks.

Your physical, mental, and emotional health as well as your time, money (or material possessions), and Human assistance represent the resources of this energy. These resources work together, and support and complement each other.

"This energy is measured by a unit—the 'energy-unit.' The energy-units to invest in each task are: physical health-units, mental health-units, emotional health-units, time-units, financial-units, and Human assistance-units.

"These energy-units each belong to a budget: physical health-budget, mental health-budget, emotional health-budget, time-budget, financial-budget, and Human assistance-budget.

"Every budget has an available number of units that you can spend to accomplish your task. As long as you do not exceed this number, you feel happy. When you go beyond this number, instead of listening to Old Teller's happy O'stories of fun and excitement and feeling happy, you start listening to its worry O'stories and you feel unhappy.

"Your physical health-budget's comfortable limit is determined by how much your body can help you to accomplish your task, while it still feels healthy and pain free, and while it still moves freely and functions with no limitations. When you exceed this limit, your body might become injured, sick, or painful, its functions might be limited, and you feel tired, tense, and unhappy.

"Your mental health-budget's comfortable limit is determined by how much your mind can help you to accomplish your task, while it stays healthy, sharp, focused, and still. When you exceed this limit, your mind feels tired and loses its stillness, and you feel worried, stressed, and unhappy.

"Your emotional health-budget's comfortable limit is determined by how much your emotions can help you to accomplish your task, while you still feel relaxed and calm. When you exceed this limit, you feel tired, worried, stressed, and unhappy.

"Your time-budget's comfortable limit is determined by how much time—minutes, hours, days, months, or years—you can spend to accomplish your task. When you exceed this limit, you feel worried, stressed, and unhappy.

"Your financial-budget's comfortable limit is determined by how much money you can afford to spend to accomplish your task. When you exceed this limit, or the amount of money that you had initially decided to spend on this task, you feel worried, stressed, and unhappy.

"Your Human assistance-budget's comfortable limit is determined by the Humans who are available and willing to spend their own energy-units to help you accomplish your task. When no one is available to assist you properly, you feel worried, stressed, and unhappy."

✦

"When a task which could be a battle of yours comes up and is put on your list," Starry continued, "start by deciding if you *want* to fight this battle.

"Ask yourself these questions: 'Do I really want to fight this battle? Do I want to accomplish this task? Will the I-have that I will collect serve me? Will the collected I-have satisfy a need that belongs to me? Will I feel happy once this I-have is collected and this need is satisfied?'

"Then, carefully watch and see your true story, and listen to the answers it honestly gives you. If you decide that you *want* to accomplish this task, then evaluate if you *can* accomplish it.

"To recognize such a task, start by evaluating the number of required energy-units. Then, evaluate if you have enough energy-units to spend. If you do, then you can choose to accomplish this task while feeling happy. If you do not, evaluate how many energy-units are still missing, and try to collect them."

"How do I evaluate? How do I know?"

"Get out your paper and pen, and do the math, Genius! Use the help of 5W2H-O&D as well as an existing source of information—like an article in a book or on the Internet—to collect the necessary information about this task.

"Always remember that, if necessary, you can ask someone whom you trust and who is knowledgeable on the subject to help you, such as a physical, mental, or emotional health specialist, a therapist, a time manager, a financial advisor, a Human resources agent, a coach, a mentor, a colleague, a friend, or a loved one."

"For each energy-unit category," Starry continued, "ask yourself these questions: 'How many energy-units does this task require to be done?' and 'How many energy-units can I afford, within the limits of my energy-budget, to give to this task?'

"Once you have answered the questions, the next step is, as Shooter said, to do the math. For each category, ask yourself, 'Is the number of energy-units that this task requires within the limits of my energy-budget?'

"If the answer is 'yes,' then go ahead, accomplish the task, and keep feeling happy.

"If the answer is 'no,' ask yourself, 'How many energy-units are still missing? How can I increase and reach this missing number? Where can I find these units? What are my options? *Options?*"

"This one-word question—*Options?*—acts like a magic wand," Shooter added. "Whenever you catch Old Teller dwelling, just ask

Options? This question will instantly make Old Teller shut up and the worry O'stories immediately disappear."

Shooter had many suggestions for me:

To increase the number of my physical health-units, I could improve my eating and sleeping habits, exercise, take more breaks, stretch, and dance.

To increase the number of my mental health-units, I could increase my knowledge and experience, research and read on the subject, take a course, get a degree, and learn by watching or assisting someone who has successfully accomplished a similar task.

To increase the number of my emotional health-units—and since my thoughts affect my emotions—I could practice more often to become aware of the presence of Old Teller and its O'stories in my mind, and learn how not to become one with them. I could practice to relax, and go back to the empty space, the loud silence, and the deep stillness of my mind.

To increase the number of my time-units, I could unload my schedule and create more time for the new task.

To increase the number of my financial-units, I could find a way to save money, earn more money, work more hours, get a second job, change my current job and find one that pays more, get a loan from an institution, or borrow money from a friend.

To increase the number of my Human assistance-units, I could hire someone, or ask a relative, friend, or colleague to help me.

"Turning one of your already satisfied needs of your comfort zone into a source for the required energy-units that are still missing," Starry explained, "might trigger Old Teller to start speaking and warning you that you just got kicked outside your comfort zone. This leads you to feel angry, frustrated, resentful, worried, stressed, and unhappy."

As an example, Shooter said that, when I try to use the time I spend with my family as a source for the required time-units that are still missing to accomplish the new task, then my family time will feel invaded and threatened, which triggers Old Teller to speak.

"Make sure," Starry continued, "that the already satisfied need to which you turn for help can afford to give you what you are planning on taking, without it suffering and without you feeling pushed outside your comfort limits, so Old Teller keeps quiet."

"What about a task that is important to me and would help a dream of mine come true? I can't live within my comfortable limits. I have to push beyond them, right?"

"When a task is important to you," Starry answered, "the already satisfied need to which you turn will not feel invaded or threatened. It will not put up a fight against your request and will not resist giving to you. Instead, it will happily support you, and gladly give up some of its own energy-units in order to help you make your dream come true.

"This already satisfied need is proud to assist and accompany you while you reach a goal that is dear to you. It is pleased to watch you collect the I-have that satisfies your new need. It is understanding and patient. It believes in you and encourages you.

"All satisfied needs to which you turn for the required energy-units work together and support each other. They stay satisfied because you are satisfied. They are happy because you are happy.

"Old Teller will not tell you any fear or worry O'stories or make you feel angry, frustrated, resentful, stressed, or unhappy. Pushing beyond the limits will only trigger Old Teller to tell you wonderful and encouraging O'stories of excitement, perseverance, fun, enthusiasm, passion, satisfaction, fulfillment, and happiness."

Shooter suggested that I go back to my Precious Box, find my balance equation that the million stars and my Needs chart helped me write down, and update and complete it with the assistance of 5W2H-O&D and my energy-budget limits.

"What about a task whose outcome is important to me and which I could but do not want or have the time to accomplish?"

"You can get this task done without actually doing it yourself, Genius! Someone else is bound to want or have the time to accomplish it for you. Just hand the task over to them. *Delegate* it! Assign it to someone who is available and knowledgeable on the subject. Whenever possible, you can even teach and train someone. At home, for example, you can get someone to help with your house cleaning."

"Oh, *no*! Not that. I can't delegate *that*!"

"Why not?"

"Because I'll have to clean the house after this person does, or maybe even before."

"*Before?*"

"I can't let people see the mess—or worse, the *dirt*! Besides, I don't trust anyone to clean my house."

"Why not?"

"They never clean it the way I like it to be cleaned."

"They never clean it *enough*, you mean?"

"I'd rather do it myself. It's just better and easier this way."

"*Better?* Maybe, Genius, if you say so and if it makes you happy, but don't try to convince me that it's easier ... and stop trying to fool yourself, too!

"Don't you hear yourself complaining that you're sick and tired of always having to clean up? Do you realize how many times a day you say that your work is never done? If you insist on not letting anyone help you clean your house, you can at least get someone to help you with Dunia, even for only a few hours a day or a few times a week.

"How about your neighbor who offered to help you the other day? She said that she would come after you arrived home from work. She would cook for you and stay until after dinner to help you do the dishes and clean the kitchen, and help Dunia get ready for bed. She told you that she could use the job *and* the money. Since her kids have grown up and gone, she could also use the company. She even told you that she feels the 'need to be useful.' Helping you would help her at the same time and, by letting her help you, you'd be doing yourself *and* her a favor. Actually, you'd be doing everyone around you a favor by being less tired and worried, and more pleasant and happy.

"But no! You insist on taking care of Dunia *and* the house by yourself. You go shopping for grocery *and* school stuff. You cook, pick up, clean the kitchen, do the dishes, do the laundry, clean the bathroom, dust, and vacuum. You pay the bills. You cut the grass. You even plant your own *trees*, for God's sake!

"Then, you complain that your back hurts, you're exhausted, and you don't have a minute for yourself. You worry because you have a million things to do. You nag and say that the work is never done, the work never ends, and it's an ongoing battle with housework and other responsibilities."

I heard Shooter take a deep breath and say nothing more. Perhaps he was waiting for me to make a comment, but what could I say? He was right. Everything he said was true!

"Of course, I'm right!" he continued. "Then you go to work and, instead of asking someone to assist you, instead of delegating and assigning certain tasks, you insist on doing everything *yourself*.

"You answer phone calls. You reply to e-mails, prepare documents, write reports, meet with salespeople, and place and check orders. You organize projects, meetings, and events. You make decisions, and follow up on every detail ...

"Then, you complain that you have a million things to do, your work is never done, and the work never ends. You're tired and overwhelmed. You're mad, frustrated, and resentful towards your boss, colleagues, and employees. You judge them and talk behind their backs. You call them losers and say that they're useless and don't help."

"I just can't delegate work that easily, Shooter, because someone always manages to mess something up, and the work never ends up being perfectly done like I expect it to be."

"I guess you can't expect perfection all the time, Genius. You should know that by now. Remember that your need for perfection is an exhausting battle to fight!"

I said nothing, although I knew that Shooter was right—again. I still felt that where I can give perfect results, I just *cannot* and *should not* settle for less. It has to be perfect—at least for me.

"Working hard and delivering 'perfect' results," Starry elaborated, "gives you a great sense of achievement. You give 'perfect' results and, in return, you receive—or hope to receive—financial rewards, and personal physical, mental, and emotional satisfaction, along with the approval and recognition of others.

"When the results of the task you are trying to accomplish, the action you are performing, or the product or service you are offering are critical—such as when it is a matter of life, safety, or security—you give your undivided attention, full energy, and complete effort and investment. Perfect results are your only and nonnegotiable option.

"For every other task, which is the case most of the time, no results are perfect. As long as the results are satisfactory and acceptable, and meet the main purpose of what is needed and expected out of this task, they are in this way perfect—perfect for your physical, mental, and emotional health and well-being."

"All I know is that the results of what *I* do need to be perfect," I insisted. "Satisfactory is not acceptable to me."

"Your need for perfection," Starry reminded, "could be the loud echo of an unresolved story of your past, confusing your not-so-perfect results with the idea that *you* are not perfect or good enough, and scaring you that these results will cost you one or more I-haves.

"In this case, whether alone or with the help of someone, celebrate an Unresolved Past ceremony to release the story, so the story releases you in return.

"Perfection is relative," she continued. If you look closely, no result is equally perfect for everyone."

"... not even when you clean your house yourself, Genius! Look closely—actually, you don't even have to look that closely," he grumbled.

"No result is equally perfect for everyone," Starry repeated, "but it can be good enough to meet the main requirements and expectations. In order to do so, you need to spend a certain amount of energy-units. If you exceed this amount, trying to reach a perfect result starts feeding off the energy-units of your already satisfied needs, and maybe even those of survival, such as rest and sleep.

"Old Teller starts telling you worry O'stories. Your body feels tired and nervous, your mind loses its stillness, and your emotional well-being disappears. Stress, resentment, and unhappiness settle in. You pay the price out of your body, mind, and emotions for that perfect result, which now becomes more harmful to your health than the not-so-perfect outcome is to the task itself."

Shooter suggested some interesting questions to ask myself:

- What do I lose if this business project is not flawless?

- What do I lose if I don't make the perfect phone call or have the perfect conversation?

- What do I lose if I don't write the perfect letter or e-mail, submit the perfect document, or offer the perfect I-have (service or product)?

- What do I lose if my house is not spotless and shining all the time?

- So *what* if I don't prepare the perfect dinner, throw the perfect party, organize the perfect trip, or get the perfect tickets or seats to an event?

- How perfect will this perfection feel after it has cost me my body's physical, mental, and emotional health and well-being?

- How would this perfect result serve me at that point?

- How happy would I be?

"Asking for someone's assistance and delegating a task," Starry resumed, "whether partially or totally, and receiving acceptable results will always perfectly serve you by keeping your body, mind, and emotions healthy.

"Remind yourself of the possibility that the results of this task may only be acceptable, and not the perfection you expect. You are flexible and you accept this possibility. You are open to it and welcome it. You are thankful for this person's help and the services they offer you to the best of their knowledge and abilities. You appreciate the results they give you. You are grateful for their presence and assistance, which lightens the heavy weight of your tasks, and allows you to travel light and feel happy.

"Have faith that everything will go on like it always has in the past, when not every result or outcome, not every service or product, and not every situation were necessarily perfect.

"Gracefully delegate this task that you do not want or have the time to accomplish anymore. Remove it from you schedule and delete the worry O'story from your mind.

"Go back to the empty space, the loud silence, and the deep stillness of your mind, and stay there for a moment. Then come back to Here and Now."

✦

"What about when I *personally* have to accomplish a task that requires many energy-units when I cannot, do not want, or am not ready to delegate it?"

"When you are in the presence of such a task," Starry answered, "Old Teller will tell you worry O'stories about the scary size of the task itself, as well as the great number of energy-units it will cost you to accomplish it. Old Teller will tell you how difficult it is to collect the satisfying I-have, and how unreachable the goal seems to be. This task now looks like a long road and feels like a strenuous walk. Whenever possible, break down this task."

"... before the task breaks you, Genius!"

"You can break it down into smaller tasks that consume less energy-units," Starry continued. "Taking smaller steps, accomplishing smaller tasks, and reaching smaller goals require less energy-units at a time. These smaller tasks seem easier, trigger less or no dramatic worry O'stories, and feel less overwhelming and less stressful.

"Each small step you take, each small task you accomplish, and each small goal you reach releases an encouraging energy that pushes you forward and helps you take the next small step, accomplish the next small task, and reach the next small goal.

"One task at a time ... one step at a time."

"Hey, Genius! Think of it this way: Your million things to do are, in reality, one million times only *one* thing. Instead of one huge task, like cleaning your whole house on the same day—which, in your case, is usually your day off—this overwhelming task becomes many small tasks that you can accomplish on different days of the week. For example, you can dust on Monday, vacuum on Tuesday, do the laundry on Wednesday, and so on.

"Here's another proposition for you: Split your house into smaller areas to clean on different days. For example, you can clean the living room on Monday, the kitchen on Tuesday, the bathroom on Wednesday, and so on. Just do one small house task at a time, or clean one room at a time ... one step at a time.

"There are many tasks that you can break down, such as cleaning your house, working on a project, renovating, decorating, gardening, shopping, exercising, or losing weight."

Shooter paused for a moment and then came up with another smart comment.

"*Somebody*—I will not say who—has been talking about losing weight for a *long* time."

"No hear, no say, and no do," I thought, while I made sure that I did not react to these words.

"Whatever amount of weight you decide to lose often seems overwhelming," Starry elaborated. "The number of pounds often looks big, scary, intimidating, and seems unreachable. Breaking down this task—losing weight—into losing a small number of pounds weekly makes losing the weight a more attainable goal."

"Remember to do the math, Genius. Just like one million things to do are one million times only *one* thing ... 20 pounds to lose are, in reality, 20 times only *one* pound to lose.

"One pound at a time ... one step at a time."

✦

"Then I will feel overwhelmed by my list's endless number of small tasks!"

"Some small tasks are the result of the breakdown of one bigger task," Starry explained, "but many other tasks are born small. The number of your list's small tasks can, in fact, overwhelm you and trigger Old Teller to start telling you all kinds of worry O'stories.

"A task that is born small usually requires few energy-units. Accomplishing such tasks immediately and as they come up daily—when you personally have to accomplish them because you cannot, do not want, or are not ready to delegate them—eliminates them from your schedule, and prevents them from adding up and remaining on your list. This keeps Old Teller quiet and the worry O'stories away, and allows you feel free and happy."

Shooter gave some examples of small tasks that I could accomplish immediately—instead of "later"—and remove from my list and my mind, such as making a quick and final decision about something, deleting or delegating a task, contacting the person to whom I want to delegate, asking this person, and setting the date to start delegating.

I could answer or make a phone call, or send an e-mail. I could ask a question, look up information, find an answer, schedule an appointment, make a payment, pick something up, or put something away.

"I usually use sticky notes for these small tasks," I proudly shared. "I have these notes all over the place."

"These notes surely are helpful reminders," Starry kindly approved. "Having them 'all over the place,' though, continually reminds you that the tasks are unfinished, therefore remaining on your list and on your mind, and you feel worried, stressed, and unhappy.

"Instead, immediately accomplish a task that requires very few energy-units as soon as it comes up, and prevent Old Teller from repeating its worry O'stories wherever you are and whatever you are doing."

"Sometimes when I'm at home in the middle of doing something, my million things to do for work haunt me. Then, when I'm at work, my million things to do for home and Dunia drive me crazy!

"I mean, *really*, what can I do about work when I'm at home doing housework, running errands, and taking care of Dunia? What can I do about a business meeting? How can I resolve a problem I have with a colleague? How can I meet with a salesperson?

"... and what can I do for home or Dunia when I'm at work taking care of business? How can I vacuum the house or clean the bathroom? How can I finish the laundry that's piled up? How can I go grocery shopping or cook dinner? How can I take Dunia to the hair salon or take her shopping for her school supplies?

"The worst is when I go to bed. As soon as I put my head on the pillow, my million things to do invade my mind, and Old Teller starts telling me its one thousand and one worry O'stories. They are all kinds of crazy O'stories about my things to do for work, for home, for Dunia, for myself, for my finances, for my mother, for my aunt, for Susan, for what I have to do or not do, and for what I have to say or not say ... battles that are mine and others that are not!

"I toss and turn for hours—sometimes even all night. Old Teller will not keep quiet. It is so loud and makes so much noise. It keeps me up and I can't sleep."

"You know that you cannot physically be at two different places," reminded Starry, "or think of or do two different things at the same time. When you are somewhere, trying to accomplish a task, and another one from your list sneaks into your mind and starts to harass you, you are aware that you cannot attend to this other task right Here and Now.

"For the time being, all you *can* do is stop this task from distracting you, quiet down Old Teller, keep the worry O'stories away, and bring back your concentration to the task of Here and Now—even when this task is 'sleeping.' All you *can* do is file away the intruder task, and then delete the worry O'story.

"Create a file, in your mind, where you send this task that does not belong to Here and Now and on which Old Teller is dwelling."

Shooter suggested that I create different files, give each one a title, and send each intruder task to the appropriate one. He compared creating these files in my mind to creating computer files or folders in a filing cabinet.

For example, I create one file for my home tasks called "Home," and another one for my work tasks called "Work." Whenever a task that does not belong to Here and Now and to which I cannot attend right away pops up in my mind, I can visualize that I am "dragging and dropping" it into its designated file for the time being. I could deal with this intruder task at a more appropriate place and time.

"Take note of this task that just invaded your mind," added Starry. "Taking note actually transfers the task from your mind into your agenda, and prevents Old Teller from dwelling and warning you about the risk of forgetting to accomplish this particular task, and about the pain of losing a certain I-have in case you did forget. Taking note allows you to go back to the empty space, the loud silence, and the deep stillness of your mind."

Shooter reminded me to keep a paper and pen by my bed. Whenever an intruder task visits my mind while I'm trying to fall asleep, I write it down. Doing so actually helps fight insomnia, and allows me to get a healthy and good night's sleep.

He proposed that, somewhere between my house and my work place, I choose a specific landmark, such as an intersection, a traffic light, a store, a bridge, or a building. This landmark will be the designated spot where I catch and file away all intruder tasks and delete the worry O'stories.

On my way to work, for example, this landmark is where I file away—in their appropriate "Home" file—all tasks and responsibilities for home. This landmark is where I delete the worry O'stories, while I repeat out loud, "This is where all tasks and worry O'stories about home stop."

On my way back home, this same landmark is also the point where all tasks for work are sent to their designated "Work" file, and where worry O'stories are deleted while I repeat out loud, "This is where all tasks and worry O'stories about work stop."

He suggested that my bedroom door, walls, and windows can also be the barrier that blocks all intruder tasks and unhappy O'stories while I rest and sleep, keeping them outside my bedroom—this sacred place where only happy O'stories are allowed and welcome.

If this doesn't work, Shooter reminded me—one more time—to ask Old Teller to shut up, by saying "*Shhh!*"

"What about a task I cannot delete, delegate, break down, or immediately accomplish, and which I keep filing away and avoiding?"

"You keep filing away and avoiding a task often because its nature and outcome are not very clear to you, and sometimes even unknown. Remember that what is unclear, unknown, and not guaranteed, and what feels unfamiliar, is often judged as scary and confused with something that is bad, dangerous, or painful. Demystifying the unknown nature of the task will take the drama out of it, and reduce—even eliminate—the fear of dealing with it as well as the fear of its cost or outcome. Reducing or eliminating the unknown factor helps you stop wanting to file away and avoid this task. It encourages you to face it and deal with it.

"There are many tools that can help you do so, such as the *5W2H-O&D* technique with which you are now familiar. This technique translates your task from your mind onto paper, and elaborates its true nature, clearing up your confusion about it and reducing your fear of it.

"This technique is a valuable tool that helps you in an efficient, constructive, and productive fashion. It breaks down the complexity of the task. It reveals and clearly shows you the details of *What?*, *Why?*, *Where?*, *When?*, *Who?*, *How?*, and *How much?* It lays the different aspects on the table and helps you analyze them. It also helps you single out the one or few areas—or guilty factor—responsible for the worry O'stories. It sets the spotlight on the one or many components you need to address.

"5W2H-O&D helps you find different options and choose the most convenient and appropriate one for you, for the time being. It helps you come up with an action plan, and set a date to start accomplishing the task, instead of letting Old Teller dwell on it. This technique is powerful and helps you feel less intimidated by the task.

"Whenever you feel unhappy-red because Old Teller is dwelling on a task you keep filing away and avoiding, set a date to face this task and actually deal with it, with the help of 5W2H-O&D, and ask someone to assist you, if required. Note this date—as well as a convenient place—in your agenda, and then delete the worry O'story from your mind."

At this date and convenient place, as I'm getting my paper and blue and red pens ready, and before I start asking the 5W2H-O&D questions and answering them, Shooter suggested that I repeat these words out loud:

- Today, I say *enough!*
- Today, I stop dwelling on this task. I stop going back and forth about it in my mind.
- Today, I stop filing away and avoiding this task, and calmly face it, despite a feeling of fear or resentment I might have, and for the sake of my physical, mental, and emotional health and well-being.
- Today, I deal with this task to the best of my knowledge and abilities.

- Today, I ask myself, "What can I do about this? What are my options? *Options?*"
- Today, I have faith that I have the necessary tools, guidance, protection, courage, and energy to find the most convenient option that serves my story and me, for the time being.

"Skip a question whenever it does not apply," reminded Starry, "or whenever you cannot seem to find the answer, even after you have researched it or consulted about it. Move on to the next question, and let the answer find itself.

"After you have answered all the 5W2H-O questions, choose only one option. Do not hesitate, reconsider, or go back on your decision; otherwise, Old Teller will start speaking again. Stick to the one option you chose and move forward, for the sake of your physical, mental, and emotional health and well-being."

Shooter had more inspiring words for me to repeat out loud:

- I do not stay stubborn with the idea of finding the perfect solution.
- I accept that it is not always possible to have a perfect solution.
- I am flexible. I am aware that there are no guarantees, regardless of which option I choose.
- I choose one option and welcome it as the most convenient one for me, for the time being.
- I am thankful for the outcome this option will bring me.
- I am aware that, regardless of an I-have I may lose on the outside, I always win on the inside because I am always taking a step forward on the path of my growth.

"Once you have chosen the option," resumed Starry, "set the date to take action, go back to your Precious Box, refer to your Encouraging List, and take the first step. Start somewhere ... start *anywhere!*

"Remember to keep the step small. Do the best you can and trust the rest in God's hands. God planned this step for you, and He takes care of you. Keep your faith that He always makes sure you have the necessary courage, patience, and energy, every step of the way. Keep your faith that He puts the right people, opportunities, and circumstances on your path.

"Let each step guide and direct you. Look at what it is trying to show you, listen to what it is trying to tell you, learn the language it speaks beyond all Human words, and try to understand its message. Let it help you grow and glow ... one step at a time.

"Before you know it, you will find yourself at the finish line. Meanwhile, enjoy each step you take. Stay Here, and stay Now."

"Step after step after step ... you know, Starry, taking all these steps is *exhausting!*"

"When you feel exhausted, it means that you have exceeded the comfortable limits of your energy-budget. Insisting on accomplishing a task—a battle that *is* yours—is now harming your physical, mental, and emotional health and well-being.

"There comes a time when you decide to bail. Choose an energy-unit value—a number or point—beyond which you stop fighting the battle and drop the task."

"... before the task drops you, Genius!"

Shooter told me to ask myself these questions:

- Has trying to accomplish this task cost me too much?

- Have I spent too many energy-units in order to do this thing?

- Have I lost enough of my precious physical, mental, and emotional health and well-being?

- Have I spent enough time or money?

- Have I lost enough I-haves in order to reach this goal?

- Have I already paid too high a price for this success?

- Is trying to accomplish this task feeding off the already satisfied needs of my comfort zone—such as my family life, social life, career, leisure, or rest and sleep—and creating suffering for them?

- Is trying to complete this particular project taking over my life?

- Have I dwelled enough on this situation?

- Have I allowed Old Teller and the worry O'stories enough space, silence, and stillness?

- Have I felt unhappy-red long enough?

"At one point," resumed Starry, "it is more important to reduce and limit your energy-unit loss, and eliminate the worry O'stories, than to collect the I-have and reach the original goal you had set. Choose a number to limit your loss and drop this task. Set a point where you just say 'enough.'"

"How do I recognize this number? How do I set this point?"

"You'll recognize the number, Genius. You'll *feel* the point. You'll know ...

"It's like when you go shopping. You will soon be going back to the mall to buy yourself a new and smaller purse, right? When you go shopping, you have a budget—a certain amount of dollars you want to spend and don't want to exceed. Well, that's how you set that point."

There were more inspiring words from Shooter for me to repeat out loud:

- Today, I say *enough*!
- Enough damage to my precious physical, mental, and emotional health.
- Enough loss of my time and money.
- Enough of "more money" I have to earn and more possessions I have to own.
- Enough of this success I have to achieve.
- Enough of this case, prize, or award I have to win.
- Enough of this relationship I have to work out and save.
- Enough of this lesson I have to teach.
- Enough of this feeling of resentment and revenge.
- Enough time wasted while waiting for someone to change or something to happen.
- Enough of my energy-units wasted listening to Old Teller and watching its unhappy O'stories.
- Enough of remembering, regretting, crying, and being stuck in the past.

- Enough of hesitating and fearing to move forward.

- Enough of complaining, resisting, and fighting Here and Now.

- Enough of dwelling on something instead of doing something about it.

- Enough of feeling unhappy-red and doing what no longer serves me.

- Enough of not being true to my story and myself.

- Enough of existing instead of living.

- Enough of waiting to live completely fulfilled and truly happy.

Starry guided me through the Awareness Process with which I was now becoming more and more familiar ... one step at time:

- *Feel?*

- Unhappy-red.

- I catch the change in my breathing and heartbeat, and I catch the knot.

- I take a deep breath.

- I go into my mind. I see the flashing red stop sign and hear the whistle: "Stop! That is Old Teller speaking. It is telling me a worry O'story, and I am worried—this is why I feel unhappy."

- I catch Old Teller and the worry O'story—the battle or task.

- I discreetly place my left hand turned in against my stomach, and extend my right arm, with my hand turned out towards Old Teller and the O'story.

- I take another deep breath while I count to 10: 1, 2, 3, 4, 5, 6, 7, 8, 9, 10.

- I inhale space, silence, and stillness, and exhale the worry O'story out of my mind.

- I sit in my movie director chair, rise above Old Teller and the O'story, and watch from above.

- I do not become one with Old Teller or the O'story.

- I stop dwelling and I do something about the O'story—the battle or task.

- *Options?*

    - I do not fight this battle because it is not mine. I delete the battle and replace it with a beautiful image—like a shooting star.

    - I delete this task that does not serve my story or me.

    - I delegate this task.

    - I break down this task.

    - I immediately accomplish this task.

    - I file away this task, and set a date to face it and deal with it.

    - I drop this task.

- I see the empty space, hear the loud silence, and feel the deep stillness of my mind. I stay there for a moment.

- *I come back to Here and Now*, where I am completely fulfilled and truly happy!

"Somewhere along the way," Starry continued, "after you have deleted, delegated, broken down, immediately accomplished, filed away and set a date to face and deal with, or dropped a task, you might feel unhappy-red again because Old Teller has more to say.

"It wants to warn you about the big mistake you just made, the not-so-perfect and maybe even terrible results with which you will end up, and the I-haves you will lose. It wants to tell you that you will regret your decision about doing the task the way you chose to do it.

"If this happens, thank Old Teller for warning you. Send it love and a smile, remind it and remind yourself that those not-so-perfect results are perfect for your precious physical, mental, and emotional health and well-being. Kindly reassure it and reassure yourself that, even if you lost a certain I-have, your true source of love, safety, and happiness remains untouchable."

"If 'kindly' doesn't work, Genius, ask Old Teller to shut up. Just say, '*Shhh!*'"

Starry concluded.

"Choose your battles, keep your things to do done, and keep travelling light!

"See the empty space, hear the loud silence, and feel the deep stillness around each battle, each thing to do, and each worry O'story, and between all battles, all things to do, and all worry O'stories.

"*Come back to Here and Now*, where you are completely fulfilled and truly happy!"

CHAPTER NINE

Here and Now

"Come back to Here and Now, where you are completely fulfilled and truly happy!"

✦

"Starry often repeats these words," I quietly thought. "What exactly do they *mean*?"

At the risk of sounding stupid, I decided to ask.

"What do you mean when you say, 'Come back to Here and Now, where you are completely fulfilled and truly happy?'"

Starry explained.

"While the O'story plays inside your mind, it describes a scene—the players as well as the stage. It describes you and everyone in there. It describes your—as well as their—looks, words, gestures, and actions. It describes the place itself, every thing, and every creature.

"When the O'story describes a scene that happened in the past, Human words say, 'I remember.' When it describes a scene that might happen in the future, Human words say, 'I imagine.' Regardless of where or when the scene is happening, Old Teller speaks, the O'story plays and describes, and you remember or imagine Here and Now.

"*Here* is the only place where you can truly be and *Now* is the only time that truly exists. The only people with whom you can truly be are the ones who are present Here and Now."

"This is obvious," Shooter said.

"Except to Old Teller," Starry pointed out. "Old Teller can tell a lot except the difference between the place where you are now and the place where you were before or where you might be later. It confuses the place where the O'story of your mind is happening with Here, and convinces you of that.

"Old Teller cannot differentiate between yesterday, today, or tomorrow—or before, now, or later—and considers every time to be Now.

"It believes that the people from the O'story of your mind are present Here and Now. It also believes that your—as well as their—looks, words, gestures, and actions from the O'story of your mind exist Here and Now.

"You get busy watching the O'story. You believe it and react to it as if it were truly happening Here and Now.

"All of a sudden, one O'story brings back a happy past story to your life of Here and Now—a pleasant memory, as Human words call it—and you actually feel happy. Another one brings back an unhappy past story to your life of Here and Now—a sad, painful memory—and you actually feel unhappy.

"One O'story brings a happy and promising future story to your life of Here and Now, and you feel happy. Another one brings a future story that is full of pain and fear to your life of Here and Now, and you feel unhappy.

"Regardless of the details of the O'story, you are convinced that what you are watching is actually happening Here and Now. The O'story sucks you in deeply and keeps you trapped in it. It distracts you and cuts you off from the real life happening inside and around you Here and Now.

"The O'story disconnects you from Here. The place around you disappears. You look, but you do not see anything anymore. You do not hear anything either. Sounds and voices disappear. You no longer smell, taste, or feel anything. All of a sudden, you find yourself where the O'story of your mind is happening, either where a past story once happened or where a future one might happen.

"The O'story disconnects you from Now. The date and time—the moment, minute, hour, day, month, and year—disappear. All of a sudden, they become the date and time when the O'story of your mind is happening, either when a past story once happened or when a future one might happen.

"The people around you disappear. They might be right in front of you, talking to you, but you do not see them anymore. You do not hear their words. You do not even hear their voices. All of a sudden, the people from inside the O'story of your mind are present, the people from a past story come back to your life of Here and Now, or those from a future one appear and surround you.

"Your own body disappears. You no longer see any part of your body, or realize what you are doing anymore.

"When you are transported to a place and time of back there and then, or later where and when, you are no longer connected with the life happening Here and Now, and you start feeling unfulfilled and unhappy."

"I'm tired of feeling unfulfilled," I said. "I don't want to be unhappy anymore."

"Then *get* connected, Genius ... and *stay* connected!"
Starry elaborated.

"Come back to the place of Here, and stay inside this place.

"Come back to the time of Now, and stay inside this time.

"Come back to the people who are present Here and Now, and stay with these people.

"Come back to what you are saying or doing Here and Now, and stay with your words, gesture, or action."

"Are you talking about 'living in the present moment'? Is that what you mean by 'come back to Here and Now'? Is that what Shooter meant by 'get and stay connected'? If it is, I often try to do that but never succeed for more than one moment!

"How do I *do* that? How do I get and stay connected?"

Starry presented a powerful way to practice *getting* connected with Here and Now:

- I ask myself these questions and answer them, using very few words: "Where am I Now?" and "Where is the O'story of my mind happening?"

- I become aware, conclude, and repeat, 'The O'story of my mind is definitely not happening Here."

- I come back to Here.
- *This is how I get connected with Here.*

✪

- I ask myself these questions and answer them, using very few words: "What is today's date, and what time is it Now?" and "When—what date and time—is the O'story of my mind happening?"
- I become aware, conclude, and repeat, "The O'story of my mind is definitely not happening Now."
- I come back to Now.
- *This is how I get connected with Now.*

✪

- I ask myself these questions and answer them, using very few words: "Who is present Here and Now?" and "Who is present inside the O'story of my mind?"
- I become aware, conclude, and repeat, "The person or people from the O'story of my mind are not present Here and Now."
- I come back to Here and Now.
- *This is how I get connected with the person or people who are present Here and Now.*

✪

- I ask myself these questions and answer them, using very few words: "What am I saying or doing Here and Now?"

and "What am I saying or doing inside the O'story of my mind?"

- I become aware, conclude, and repeat, "I am not inside the O'story of my mind."

- I come back to Here and Now.

- *This is how I get connected with myself Here and Now.*

"Once you get connected with Here and Now," Starry added, "your body's senses will help you *stay* connected, through what your eyes see, your ears hear, your nose smells, your mouth tastes, and your hands and skin touch and feel.

"Look at the empty space around you where all people, creatures, and things exist.

"Then, look at the things that occupy this space, and count as many of these things as you like. Staying with the count and with these things helps you stay connected with Here and Now. If there are any, look at the living creatures—animals and plants—and count as many of these creatures as you like.

"To enhance this connection, choose one thing or creature. Contemplate it as if it were the only thing or creature that exists around you, and describe it to yourself. Describe its color, shape, size, and pattern. If it is a creature, describe how it sits still or moves, and feel the energy of life flowing through its body.

"Always remember to see the empty space around each creature and thing, and between all creatures and all things.

"Whenever present," Starry continued, "look at the people who occupy this space around you, and count as many of these people as you like. Then, choose one person—maybe the one with whom you are interacting. If you know their name, say it. Contemplate this person as if you were getting ready to draw or paint them. Observe them as if you were seeing them for the first time, and describe to yourself what your eyes see. Describe this person in an objective way, without giving your personal opinion. Do not label, judge, prefer, like, or dislike them.

"Describe what they look like. Describe their face—eyebrows, eyes, ears, cheeks, nose, lips, and mouth. Describe their facial expression. Describe the way they breathe. Describe how they keep quiet, and how they speak, smile, laugh, or cry. Then, look at their body and describe it. Describe their hair, skin, neck, shoulders, arms, hands, chest, stomach, back, legs, and feet. Describe what they are wearing. Describe how they sit or stand, how they walk and move, and what they are doing and how they are doing it.

"Observe how the Being inside them glows. Feel the aliveness of their body, namely their eyes, mouth, and hands. Feel the energy of life flowing through their every glance, breath, word, and expression, and through their every gesture and action.

"Always remember to see the empty space around each person and between all people."

"Hear the loud silence where all sounds and voices exist," Starry added. "Then, listen to those sounds and voices, and count as many of them as you like.

"To strengthen your connection with Here and Now, close your eyes. Choose only one sound, focus your attention on it, and describe it to yourself. If you are interacting with someone, concentrate on their voice. Listen well and describe it in detail. Describe its tone, melody, and level of energy. Listen to the person's words, and stay with them."

"Stay with their *words*?" I wondered.

"Listen to that person telling you their story," she explained. "Stay focused, one story at a time ... one word at a time. Watch their face and body talk to you through their expressions and gestures—this language spoken beyond all Human words. If Old Teller of your mind starts to speak and the O'story starts to play, catch Old Teller and the O'story, and bring back your attention to the words that this person in front of you is telling you Here and Now."

"Easier said than done!"

"It might not be easy, Genius, but it is certainly not impossible! You just have to be patient. All it takes is time and patience."

"Time, patience ... and practice," added Starry. "You can learn, practice, and even master listening by staying focused on the words that the person in front of you is telling you, without drifting off to listen to Old Teller and watch an O'story of your mind.

"Different techniques can help you. Here is one you can easily practice anywhere, any time, and with anyone: You will sit down, facing your practice partner, and look into their eyes. Your partner will speak continuously for one minute while you carefully listen and stay focused on their words and story.

"While listening, if an idea of your own, or one word or gesture from your partner, triggers Old Teller of your mind to speak and an O'story to play, catch Old Teller and the O'story. Place your left hand turned in against your stomach, and extend your right arm with your palm turned out towards Old Teller and the O'story. Then, *come back to Here and Now.*

"When the minute is up, repeat out loud what you just heard, using your partner's exact words, or as close to them as possible. Do not hesitate, analyze, give an opinion, or judge them. Do not input any words of your own. Avoid using expressions, such as 'I think,' 'I am sure you said,' or 'you meant that.'

"Always remember to hear the silence around each sound, voice, and word, and between all sounds, all voices, and all words."

"Smell the place," Starry added. "Count as many scents as you like. Then, close your eyes, choose one scent, and concentrate on it. Stay with this scent, and describe it to yourself.

"Always remember the emptiness around each scent and between all scents."

Shooter had another idea.

"If a scent can keep you connected with Here and Now, I'll bet that a flavor can also do that. Bring the food or drink to your mouth and close your eyes, and you'll quickly get connected. Make sure you don't close your eyes *first*, Genius. Otherwise, you're in for a messy and quick disconnection, and you'll forget all about the emptiness around each flavor and between all flavors!"

Starry laughed, and then continued.

"If you touch the person, creature, or thing, or if the person or creature touches you, close your eyes and describe to yourself what your hand and skin feel.

"Watch and see, hear and listen, smell, taste, touch and feel, and stay connected with the life happening around you Here and Now."

✫

"Stay connected with the life inside you, too," Starry continued. "You can strengthen this connection by watching and describing yourself. Focus your attention on your own body. Look at every part that your eyes can see, and describe to yourself what this part looks like. Touch every part that your hands can reach, and describe what you feel.

"Become aware of how your body automatically sees, hears, breathes, smells, tastes, thinks, feels, talks, and moves.

"Become aware and describe your aliveness inside your every breath, word, expression, gesture, movement, and action. Feel the energy of life flowing through you. Feel the warmth of your body—a physical sign of this energy.

"Become aware of the presence of the Being inside you, and let this awareness connect you and keep you connected with the life happening inside you Here and Now."

✫

"If I were to describe myself and everyone and everything to get and stay connected with Here and Now, I'll be describing all day. It's impossible to do that!"

"Since the mind cannot do two different things at the same time," Starry explained, "it could describe who and what is no longer or not yet Here and Now, or who and what is Here and Now. In other words, you can either watch an O'story and listen to Old Teller, or watch and listen to the life happening inside and around you Here and Now.

"At first, it might take you a few minutes to count and name different things, creatures, or people, and then describe only one thing, one creature, one person, or yourself for you to be able to get and stay connected with Here and Now.

"Slowly, with time, patience, and practice, you will be able to see, hear, smell, taste, touch and feel, and describe many things, creatures, and people, including yourself, in just a few seconds. You will soon master the art of observation, and quick and detailed description, which helps you build a bridge that you can use to instantly get and stay connected with Here and Now."

"Whenever Old Teller shifts you back to a past time and place," added Shooter, "or projects you into a future one, you'll hop on that bridge and use it to quickly cross over from the place and time of the O'story of your mind to Here and Now. Building this bridge sometimes means describing a full room or a whole town, or maybe one simple, tiny detail ... like a phone ringing."

The phone rang.

"How does Shooter *do* that?" I thought, as I got up to answer the phone.

It was Helen. She informed me that everybody got to the cottage safe and sound. She said that Lisa and John surprised them and were already there waiting. She also said that Dunia was outside, playing with Max.

Reassured by that phone call, I came back to Here and Now. Starry resumed.

"When you become aware that the O'story of your mind is not happening Here, then you come back to Here. You get connected with Here—the only place where you can truly be.

"When you become aware that the O'story of your mind is not happening Now, then you come back to Now. You get connected with Now—the only time that truly exists.

"When you become aware that the person or people from the O'story of your mind are not present Here or Now, then you come back to Here and Now. You get connected with the person or people who are present Here and Now.

"When you become aware that your words, gestures, and actions from the O'story of your mind are not happening Here and Now, then you come back to Here and Now. You get connected with yourself Here and Now.

"Count, name, observe, and describe the people who are present, as well as the creatures and things that exist in the life happening around you Here and Now. Observe and describe yourself and stay with the details. Keep busy describing the life happening inside and around you—look and see, hear and listen, smell, taste, and touch and feel.

"Doing so keeps your mind busy and focused on Here and Now, instead of leaving it free for Old Teller and its O'stories. Old Teller will then keep quiet. The O'stories will disappear, and will no longer distract you, or absorb and trap you. They will fade away, allowing you to bring back your attention and concentration on yourself and on the place, time, people, creatures, and things that are present Here and Now.

"The O'stories will vanish, leaving only empty space, loud silence, and deep stillness where life freely flows, and where the Being glows Here and Now."

Here and Now

The Awareness Process that would help me get and stay connected with Here and Now was almost complete. Starry walked me through the steps ... one step at time.

- *Feel?*
- Unhappy-red.
- I catch the change in my breathing and heartbeat, and I catch the knot.
- I take a deep breath.
- I go into my mind. I see the flashing red stop sign and I hear the whistle: "Stop! That is Old Teller speaking, and the O'story is describing what is happening in the past or future, away from Here and Now, and I am disconnected from Here and Now—this is why I feel unhappy."
- I catch Old Teller and the O'story.
- I discreetly place my left hand turned in against my stomach, and extend my right arm, with my hand turned out towards Old Teller and the O'story.
- I take another deep breath while I count to 10: 1, 2, 3, 4, 5, 6, 7, 8, 9, 10.
- I inhale space, silence, and stillness, and exhale the O'story out of my mind.
- I sit in my movie director chair, rise above Old Teller and the O'story, and watch from above.
- I do not become one with Old Teller or the O'story.
- I see the empty space, hear the loud silence, and feel the deep stillness of my mind. I stay there for a moment.
- *I come back to Here and Now.*

- I get connected with Here and Now:

    - Where am I Now?

    - What is today's date and what time is it?

    - Who is present Here and Now?

    - What am I saying or doing Here and Now?

- I stay connected with Here and Now:

    - Who or what am I seeing Here and Now?

    - Who or what am I hearing Here and Now?

    - What am I smelling Here and Now?

    - What am I tasting Here and Now?

    - What am I—my hand or skin—touching and feeling Here and Now?

- I am completely fulfilled and truly happy!

"It will certainly not be easy to keep Old Teller quiet and stop the O'stories from playing and happening in the past or the future. It will not be easy for me to get and stay connected with Here and Now."

"It might not be easy, Genius, but it is certainly not impossible! Remember, time, patience, and practice. Besides, Old Teller can speak all it wants. Don't mind it. Keep counting, naming, observing, and describing. It will eventually shut up. The O'stories can play all they please. Don't watch them. Ignore them. They too will leave you alone."

"What about when Here and Now is unhappy? I'd *rather* listen to Old Teller and watch a happy O'story. I *want* to escape and retreat to my happy good old days, or dream of a happy and promising future. I don't want to stay *or* get connected. I don't want to be Here *or* Now."

"You are exactly where you are supposed to be, doing exactly what you are doing," Starry said.

"Remember that God is in charge, and always takes care of you. Have faith that He designs Here and Now—the presence of every person, every thing, every place, and every event, situation, and condition—in the most profitable way for you."

"Here and Now is what it is, Genius. When you feel that it's unhappy, remember to ask Old Teller to shut up. Just say, *Shhh!*

"Then, sit in your movie director chair and rise up. Elevate yourself to where I am, and look at the life happening inside and around you.

"From up here, it's easy to look and clearly see that this 'unhappy' Here and Now occupies a limited space and time inside your life, and you'll no longer reduce your whole life to it.

"From up here, you can look and clearly see that this 'unhappy' Here and Now is a minuscule and temporary station on the long track of your life, and you'll no longer become one with it, or confuse it with your whole life."

Shooter offered me these words to repeat out loud:

- I am aware that I may have a problem, but I am not this problem nor is my whole life—I name 10 blessings in my life.

- I am aware that a part of my body may be unhealthy (painful or limited), but I am not this pain or limitation. My whole body is not painful or limited nor is my whole life—I name 10 healthy parts of my body.

- I am aware that I may have an unmet need, but I am not this unmet need nor is my whole life.

- I am aware that one or more satisfying I-haves may be missing, but I am not this missing satisfaction nor is my whole life.

- I am aware that I may have an unhappy feeling about someone or something in particular, but I am not this unhappiness nor is my whole life.

"Just like your unmet needs, emptiness, and unresolved past," Starry continued, "Here and Now also loves you and is a blessing in disguise.

"You are now aware that, thanks to your unmet needs, your life is in constant evolution. You are aware that emptiness brings you back to yourself. You are aware that every period of your unresolved past was a necessary growth station for you.

"In the same way, Here and Now is also a necessary station. Accept it in your life, and become aware of the abundant gifts it offers you."

"Remember that resisting Here and Now is an exhausting battle to fight," said Shooter, "and a great source of pain and unhappiness."

"Here and Now is born to serve you and be your opportunity to grow and glow," Starry added. "Acknowledge its positive contribution to your life.

"Here and Now has a mission to accomplish: to help you be the great Human Being that you are. Welcome it into your life because it is important, it is good enough, and it deserves to be loved.

"Here and Now has one ultimate purpose: to make you happy. Allow it to express itself. Watch closely, listen carefully, and try to understand what it is trying to let you know. Let it deliver its message—this priceless gift—to you.

"Ask *Feel?*, answer unhappy-red. Come back to Here and Now, and ask yourself, 'What is Here and Now trying to show and tell me? What is it trying to make me understand? What blessing does it want me to discover? What growth message does it have for me?'"

"These questions act like a magic wand, Genius. They instantly turn every 'unhappy' Here and Now into a happy one!"

Starry presented a summarized yet complete, powerful, and practical version of the Awareness Process:

- *Feel?*
- Unhappy-red.
- I take a deep breath.
- Stop! That is Old Teller speaking, and the O'story is describing what is happening away from Here and Now—this is why I feel unhappy.
- I catch Old Teller and the O'story.
- *I come back to Here and Now.*
- I get connected with Here and Now: "Where am I? What is today's date and what time is it? Who is present Here and Now? What am I saying or doing Here and Now?"

- I stay connected with Here and Now: "Who or what am I seeing and hearing Here and Now? What am I smelling, tasting, and touching and feeling Here and Now?"
- I ask myself, "What is Here and Now trying to show and tell me, and make me understand? What loving growth message does it have for me?"
- I am completely fulfilled and truly happy!

"Slowly," Starry continued, "with time, patience, and practice, you *will* understand the loving growth message, and be grateful for this priceless gift—the message—that Here and Now offers you."

"When you do, Genius, you'll get a kick out of it. You'll no longer want to escape to any past or future O'story and miss out on Here and Now, and you'll always want to get and stay connected."

"From up here," Shooter added, "it's easy to look and see, and become aware of the rest of the gifts that Here and Now offers you. You don't even have to look far. Start by looking at yourself."

"What *about* myself?"

"Rise up," he ordered.

Confused by this command, I remained still.

"Come on! Rise up," he repeated. "Elevate yourself!"

"I'm not a *star*, Shooter! I'm Human, remember? How do you want me to elevate myself? To where do you want me to rise up?"

"Upstairs ... to your bedroom."

I made no sound, wondering what Shooter meant.

He and Starry said nothing.

After a few moments, I thought and concluded, "I guess the message behind their silence is pretty clear. Maybe I'm starting to understand this mysterious 'language spoken beyond all Human words' after all. I guess I'll go upstairs."

I got up, walked up the stairs, and went into my bedroom.

"*Now* what?"

"Stand in front of your mirror," he said, "the same mirror you look at every morning and see your twinkles, your stuck-out stomach, and the veins on your legs that show from a mile away. Stand there and look at yourself.

"First, look at your face. Look at it until you can really see it."

Shooter paused for a moment, giving me a chance to look at my face, and then asked me a curious question.

"Do you see your face?"

"Yes, I do."

"Now snap a picture."

"I don't have a camera, Shooter!"

"Extend both your arms with your hands closed," he explained. "Open your thumbs and index fingers. Let the tip of your right index finger touch the tip of your left thumb and the tip of your right thumb touch the tip of your left index finger.

"Look at your face through this rectangle that you just created, like a photographer does. Frame it within your fingers as if it were all that existed in the room. Snap a picture and look at your face as if you were seeing it for the first time."

I stood in front of my mirror, looking at my face, and snapped a picture.

"You can also snap a picture by slowly blinking your eyes," he added. "Try it and you'll see."

I slowly blinked. I swear that I heard my eyes actually click like a camera does ... and I *really* saw my face!

"Observe each part and describe it in detail," Starry said. "Become aware of the abundant gifts that it offers you, and thank it out loud."

I looked at my eyes and described them. I became aware of the opportunities they give me to see the empty space and abundant life around me, the beautiful people—especially my loved ones—and the creatures and things.

I became aware of the opportunities that my eyes give me to see the empty space and the abundant life inside me and how, through them, I can express and communicate my thoughts, true emotions, and feelings. I became aware of the language that my eyes speak beyond all Human words ... *and I thanked my eyes!*

"When Old Teller dwells on a missing I-have," Shooter added, "try living, moving around, and working with your eyes closed or blindfolded for just five minutes.

"When you're deprived of one part of your body—in this case, your eyes *and* the twinkles around them—you'll be quickly reminded of how rich your body is, how many needs it satisfies, and how many I-haves it helps you collect. You'll also be reminded of the abundant life inside and around you with which your eyes connect you Here and Now.

"Try it, Genius. You'll see ... or not," he joked. "I'll bet that you would not want to exchange this part of your body for all the money in the world!"

"I would certainly not want to exchange my eyes for all the money in the world, Shooter. As far as my twinkles, I'm not so sure about *them!*"

"Wrinkles are the impression of the endless expressions and blessed emotions you felt throughout your life," Starry said. "Through a language they speak beyond all Human words, they tell stories of your living, your pain and joy, and your smiles and laughter. They are a confirmation of all the opportunities that helped you grow and glow along the way.

"Wrinkles are to the Being glowing through your eyes what twinkles are to a bright star!"

Starry stayed quiet for a moment, and I heard Shooter humming, *"Twinkle, wrinkle, little star ..."*

I smiled and looked at my face again.

I looked at my ears and described them. I became aware of how they allow me to hear the silence and the endless sounds of the abundant life happening around me, especially the voices of my loved ones telling me their words and stories, and the sound of their laughter. I became aware of how my ears let me enjoy music, this powerful *will* pill that instantly carries me to different and wonderful worlds ... *and I thanked my ears!*

I looked at my nose and mouth and described them. I became aware of how they give me life through every breath. I became aware of how my nose allows me to enjoy the endless scents, and how my mouth lets me enjoy an abundant variety of foods and drinks, and helps me express and communicate my every need, thought, emotion, and feeling ... *and I thanked my nose and mouth!*

Shooter invited me to look at the rest of my body and reminded me to keep snapping the pictures.

I looked, snapped the pictures, and described my body. I became aware of every sensation it gives me and every gesture and movement it makes. I became aware of how it helps me do my million things ... *and I thanked my body!*

"Become aware," Starry said, "of how every part of your body—every system, organ, and cell—takes and then genuinely gives back in return, accomplishing its unique mission.

"Then become aware of how all parts work together in total harmony as a well-synchronized and orchestrated team, accomplishing one common mission, which is to keep you happy Here and Now."

"Celebrate your body, Genius! Let your shower time be your daily ceremony where you become aware that your body loves you, and thank it out loud.

"Throughout the day—during your breaks—regularly move your fingers and wiggle your toes as an instant celebration and reminder of this love. Let those same fingers and toes, which made your parents happy on the day you were born, remind *you* to be happy Here and Now.

"Every time you catch yourself dwelling and complaining that Here and Now is unhappy, come into your bedroom and stand in front of this mirror. Snap the pictures and make sure that you look beyond your wrinkles, stuck-out stomach, and veins."

I looked at myself and was amazed at how long I have lived without *meeting* my body this way before. I had never thought of actually thanking it.

"You're amazed at meeting your body, Genius? Wait until you meet the abundance with which it connects you. Start meeting it right Here inside your bedroom.

"Look around you and become aware of everything you see. Count, name, snap pictures, observe, and describe. See, hear, smell, taste, and touch and feel.

"Let's meet abundance inside the rest of your house. Salute everything and say, 'Hello!' Be thankful and repeat out loud, 'Thank you for satisfying my needs and making me happy!'"

Shooter escorted me while I walked around the house. I felt like I was a tourist inside my own home, meeting it one room, one space, and one thing at a time. I looked at the empty space around each thing and between all things. I saluted and thanked everything.

"Become aware of every I-have you have earned over the years," Starry said. "Thank it for what it offers you, and thank yourself for having worked hard and collected it."

"You spend your life and energy-units collecting many I-haves," Shooter added, "hoping they will lead you to happiness. Then, you leave them there, like medals you hang on a wall and take for granted ... and off you go to your next race. Stop! Look at your medals and admire their shine!

"Celebrate your I-haves, Genius! Throw a party in their honor. Put on your party clothes and your hidden jewelry, and take out your special-occasion china, because Here and Now is a special occasion!"

After the "tour," I went back and sat at my kitchen table.

"Become aware," continued Starry, "of all your basic and not-so-basic needs that your house—or home—satisfies. Become aware of every I-have that the life happening around you—your neighborhood, town, city, country, planet, and world—offers you ... *and thank everything!*

"Treat every I-have of Here and Now kindly. Give it your undivided attention and show it respect and gratitude by staying with it. Do not ignore or take it for granted anymore. Instead, become aware of the effort it makes to satisfy your need and keep you happy.

"Watch it, instead of watching a distracting O'story describing a past that is gone or a future that may or may never happen. Listen to it, instead of listening to Old Teller comparing this I-have of Here and Now to one that belongs to your good old days or one that you wish and dream will later save you.

"Give your I-have of Here and Now love, and send a smile its way. Say 'hello' and 'thank you,' and watch a miracle happen! Watch how this I-have is encouraged to give you more, just like you are encouraged to give to someone who is thankful to you.

"Do not be shy or hesitate to take what this I-have of Here and Now gives you; otherwise, it will get confused and might interpret your hesitation with the fact that you do not really need or want it.

"Never refuse a gift, whether it is one that you offer to yourself, one that another Human offers to you, or one that life grants you. Always welcome a gift and humbly say 'thank you,' so the gifts keep coming."

✭

"Become aware of every I-have of Here and Now (product or service)," Starry continued, "which is a gift that one Human's talent and mind created, and one Human's hands and body crafted and offered to you through their hard work, in order to satisfy your need and keep you happy ... *and thank these Humans!*"

Shooter had a long list of people whom I would thank. He said that every time I feel that Here and Now is unhappy because someone should give me more, I go back to my Precious Box and read the Happy Lists I had created for them.

He reminded me that, while I'm reading my Happy Lists and being thankful, I can choose one cause that is close to my heart and serves my story and me, and help improve it ... one step at a time.

"Do not deny a giving Human the joy, pleasure, and satisfaction that their act of giving to you offers *them*," Starry added. "When you welcome their gift, you actually do yourself *and* them a favor. Receiving and taking from them becomes your gift to them.

"Your need gives them a chance to collect their satisfying I-have. It becomes *their* opportunity to grow and glow—do a favor, have a job, make a dream come true, and maybe even find and accomplish a life mission where, through serving you, many of their physical, mental, and emotional needs are satisfied.

"Your need, which another Human satisfies through the I-have they offer you, is a gift you offer them. In the same fashion, another Human's certain need is their gift to you."

"*Their* need is a gift to *me*?"

"One Human's need to receive allows you to satisfy your need to give," she said.

I thought about this for a second and then it hit me.

"Are you talking about my job? Please don't remind me that I have to go back to work tomorrow!"

"Hey, Genius, wait until you become aware of the gifts that your job offers you. Go back to your Needs chart and read it over; it will quickly remind you of them. No matter how much you despise it, and how many times a day you repeat and tell it that you hate it, your job keeps serving you."

"All the gifts in the world don't outweigh the horrible emptiness I'll be feeling tomorrow," I said.

"Your job keeps serving you, even through this emptiness," Starry kindly reminded me, "leading you straight back to your true story."

"Abundance, emptiness, true story or not, I don't *care*! I still wish that I didn't have to go back to work. I wish I could win the lottery and stay home!"

"Your job is obviously a source of income," Starry said, "which helps you satisfy your basic and not-so-basic needs to receive and give.

"Every I-have you offer through your job serves someone. It satisfies their need and adds to their comfort and well-being. It continues to make a difference way after your actual job has stopped. Put a little love ..."

"*Molto amore!*" interrupted Shooter. "It's Nonna's secret: *molto amore—a lot of love!*"

"Put a lot of love," Starry corrected herself, laughing, "into your job, thoughts, words, gestures, and actions.

"When you do, you will be able to see the Being inside the Human with whom you are interacting—the Being inside the boss, employee, collegue, client, case, file, number, contract, project, investment, connection, or source of opportunity and income into which this Human Being had turned.

"Become interested in the Human *and* the Being. Say nice words, make gestures, and do acts of kindness to show them that they are important and worthy. Offer them an I-have seasoned with a lot of love.

"When you learn to understand the language your job speaks beyond all Human words, your job becomes more interesting. Watch closely when it shows you, and listen carefully when it tells you, about all the help it allows you to offer every day, way after your words, gesture, or action have actually ended."

"It doesn't matter what your job is," Shooter said. "You could be at home cleaning and taking care of Dunia, or at work taking care of business. You could find a new job tomorrow. You could design something, manufacture a product, work at a bank, offer a service over the phone, serve food at a restaurant, work at the cash register at a grocery store, or sell a purse at a boutique. You could teach, research, drive a bus, repair cars, fly a plane, or fight fires. You could relieve someone's physical, mental, or emotional pain, or become the president of a small company or a whole country ...

"Whatever your job, put a smile on your face and repeat out loud, 'I am putting *molto amore* into my job, words, gestures, and actions, and into this I-have (product or service) that I am offering.'

"Your job then becomes fun, Genius, and you'll look forward to going to work every day, even if you *do* win the lottery!"

Shooter suggested that, every morning after I wake up and as I'm stretching my body and dancing, I repeat these words out loud:

- Today, I have a great day because no 'unhappy' Here and Now—no one, no thing, no problem, no small- or big-bite situation, no unmet need, no missing I-have, and no O'story—will ruin this day for me.

- Today, I celebrate my tomorrow's good old days that are Here *and* Now.

- Today, I enjoy Here and Now because every Here and Now is a precious moment.

- Today, I enjoy everyone—namely my loved ones—and every creature and thing.

- Today, I put *molto amore* into every product or service that I offer.

- Today, I put *molto amore* into every thought, word, gesture, and action.

Shooter then gave numerous examples of words, gestures, and actions seasoned with a lot of love:

I could be courteous on the road, wave "thank you" to someone who gives me the right of way, let someone go ahead of me, or let them take the parking space that I saw first.

I could say "hello," send good wishes, open the door and hold it, or help someone I know or a complete stranger.

I could shake someone's hand or give them a hug and a kiss, blow them a kiss from a distance, or send them a smile because smiles are contagious, and every smile will take them and me an "extra mile."

I could give them a compliment about their hair, face, clothes, house, car, or achievements.

I could ask how their day is going, how their weekend went, or about their next weekend's plans. I could ask about their work, health, family, parents, spouse, kids, or pet, and show interest and listen when they tell me about their life, including their dreams and ambitions, or troubles and problems.

I could genuinely approve of their feelings by saying, "I hear you," "I see," "I understand," "I agree," and "You're right," without analyzing, judging, or giving them advice, such as "You should," "You must," "You can't," or "You'd better"—even when my intention is to help them—unless they request it.

Shooter suggested that, every day and during one of my breaks, I select one name from my contact list and give that person a quick call—starting with Aunt Maryam—or send them a short, nice e-mail to say "hello," ask them, "How are you?," and wish them a nice day.

He proposed that, every day, I start by saying only one nice word or doing only one nice gesture or action. He explained that, at first, I might find myself making a conscious effort to say or do so. I might even feel uncomfortable or unauthentic, but that's okay.

On his famous 1-to-10 scale theory, my discomfort will score 10 the first time around, but that should not stop me. If I feel uncomfortable and unauthentic, I repeat out loud, "So what? Let me feel uncomfortable and unauthentic." Slowly, with time, patience, and practice, my discomfort score will become 9, then 8, and so on, until it eventually becomes 0.

✭

"Whenever seasoned with *molto amore*," continued Starry, "every word even if small, every gesture even if little, every action even if simple, and every service even if modest will keep affecting you *and* the other Human Being, and make you *and* them feel better, way after this word, gesture, action, or service has ended.

"The love inside the other Human Being wakes up, and they feel encouraged and inspired to put this *molto amore* out there in their turn. Remember that the Being glows through the Human's words, gestures, and actions.

"Every day, become aware of all the love inside the words, gestures, and actions that are exchanged among Human Beings: gifts from you to them and gifts from them to you!

"Feel the great energy of this love flowing between Human Beings who are coexisting, interacting, and complementing each other and sharing inside one family, one team, one community, one society, one planet, and one whole world ... *and thank this love!*

"Feel, become aware, and thank the abundance of receiving and giving.

"Feel, become aware, and thank the abundance of talking and listening.

"Feel, become aware, and thank the abundance of being helped and helping.

"Feel, become aware, and thank the abundance of being thanked and thanking.

"Feel, become aware, and thank the abundance of being loved and loving.

"Become aware and thankful for the I-haves that you offer to yourself, the I-haves that other Human Beings offer to you, and the I-haves with which nature constantly blesses you."

✦

"Nature! Now *there's* a source of endless I-haves. I wish you could see it from up here, Genius!"

Shooter paused for a moment, and then let out a deep and long sigh of envy.

"*Ahhhhh* ... I wish I could see it from where *you* are! I wish I could get closer and watch and see, hear and listen, smell, taste, and touch and feel ..."

"Celebrate nature's abundant I-haves," Starry said. "Go out there, sit comfortably, contemplate nature's majesty, and try to understand the language that nature speaks beyond all Human words.

"Let the deep sky show, tell, and remind you to go back to the deep stillness of your mind.

"Let the stars twinkle, and show, tell, and remind you to grow and glow.

"Let the clouds show, tell, and remind you that, no matter how thick they get, and even when you cannot see through them anymore, Shooter and I can always see you.

"Let the birds show, tell, and remind you to be happy for the only reason that every Here and Now is a brand new day.

"Let a butterfly show, tell, and remind you to travel light.

"Let a flower show and tell you how it blossoms ... one petal at a time. Let it remind you of the *molto amore* it has inside and generously puts out.

"Let a tree show and tell you how to welcome abundance and absorb it deeply, and then give back abundantly. Let it remind you that you are connected with the earth and sky and, through this connection, you are completely fulfilled and truly happy!"

Shooter said that when people, including myself, watch and see, hear and listen, and learn the language that nature speaks beyond all Human words and understand its messages, we will say "thank you."

We will learn to respect nature and, instead of taking it for granted, and neglecting, abusing, wasting, hurting, and destroying it, we will kindly take care of it and love it, just like it takes care of us and loves us.

✪

Starry and Shooter stayed quiet for a few moments, allowing me to feel nature's love, which they just described, before Shooter offered me a strange invitation.

"Hey, Genius! Step outside for a minute. I want to show you something you haven't seen in a while."

"Outside where?"

"Your backyard!"

"You want to show me something I haven't seen in *my* backyard?"

"Right! Now step outside."

I went outside, curious to see what Shooter wanted to show me.

"Do you see the swing?"

"Yes."

"Do you see the table and the chairs?"

"I see them, too."

"What about the fence?"

I started to lose my patience.

"*Shooter*!"

"Okay, okay. What about the pine tree?"

"What about it?"

"When was the last time you saw it?"

"The pine tree over *there*? The one I planted when Dunia was born?"

"*You* planted this tree? You plant *trees*? This is news to me!" he teased. "Yes, that one. When was the last time you *saw* it?"

I stood there, wondering, "When was the last time I saw this tree? When was the last time I even *looked* at it? What point was Shooter trying to make anyway?"

"Get close and look at it," he said.

I walked towards the tree and stood in front of it.

"What exactly am I supposed to be looking at?"

He said nothing.

I looked at the tree for a few seconds.

"How long am I supposed to look?"

"Look until the tree is the only thing you see and nothing else exists ... and snap a picture."

I looked.

I finally saw the tree.

"It grew so much!" I quietly thought.

It really felt as if I had not seen this tree in a long time.

I blinked and snapped a picture.

"Come closer," Starry invited. "Bring your body close to the tree. Touch the earth and sense the roots that grew deeply.

"Observe the trunk and describe it. Look up and let your eyes follow the path of each branch, one branch at a time, until they reach the tip of each needle.

"Count those needles, and observe and describe them, one needle at a time. Touch and feel them with your fingers. Rub them and let their scent invade your soul. Watch them bathe in the light of the setting sun. Watch how the breeze caresses and cradles them, and listen to their shy whisper.

"Look at the tree until you see and feel the energy of life flowing through it. Contemplate it until you feel the gifts of the earth—food and water—running through the roots, and reaching the trunk, branches, and needles."

"Hey Genius! Look until you see those two birds watching you!"

"Contemplate the tree," continued Starry, "until you see and feel its aliveness. Contemplate it until you feel every needle breathing life and welcoming the gifts of the sky—air, wind, clouds, rain, sun, and moon."

"... and the million stars, and you and me, Starry!"

"The million stars, and me and you, Shooter," she sweetly said. "Contemplate it until you see how the earth and sky become one, and how, through the tree, they offer themselves to you."

"Oxygen, food, scent, oil, shade, and beauty," Shooter added, "just to serve you and keep you happy ... and to serve those two birds and keep them happy, too.

"Hey, Genius! Can you get a little closer to the tree? Can you make your way to the trunk?"

"I think so."

"Watch out for the needles and be careful not to poke your eyes!"

"Am I close enough?"

"I don't know. Can your arms reach around the trunk?"

"I can try ... you mean like *that*? I feel as if I'm hugging the tree!"

"You are, Genius! Now stay."

"*What*?"

"Don't move," he ordered. "Just close your eyes and stay. Keep your arms around the tree and keep your body as close to it as possible."

I felt ridiculous, standing there and hugging a tree.

"Feel the aliveness," added Starry. "Feel the energy of the earth beneath your feet flowing through the roots, into the body of the tree, and then into yours. Feel the energy of the sky above you flowing through the needles, into the body of the tree, and then into yours.

"Feel how the tree is sharing its aliveness with you. Feel how you are sharing your aliveness with the tree!"

Endless minutes went by, and I kept hugging the tree, feeling its energy running through my body. I felt the miracle of life filling my soul.

I became one with the tree ... a connection beyond the description of any Human words!

"Okay, you can let go of the tree now, Genius! You're freaking out the birds!"

"The *birds*?" I thought, as I let go of the tree.

"The next time you want to hug a tree, make sure that no birds are watching. If there are, lean your back against it and feel the energy flowing from the tree into your body ... or you can shake hands with it; a handshake will do quite well."

"*Shooter*! Stop being silly."

"I'm serious, Genius! Grab a branch with your hand and shake it up and down."

I stood there, debating.

"Just *do* it!"

Despite my hesitation and fear of looking ridiculous—even if only to Starry, Shooter, and the birds—I chose a branch, held it in my hand, and shook hands with it. I actually moved it up and down!

"Keep doing it. Do you feel the energy of the earth and sky being passed on to you? Do you feel your connection with the earth, birds, wind, clouds, sun, moon, the million stars, and Starry and me?"

"I actually *do*, Shooter! I feel the energy of the sky above me flow into the needles and through the branches, and then reach my hand and arm and run through my body.

"I feel my feet sink into the ground, as if roots were growing out of them, digging deeply and trying to reach the heart of the earth beneath me.

"I feel the energy of the earth flowing through the roots of the tree, through the trunk and the branches, and then reach my hand and arm and run through my body.

"I feel connected with the sky ... I feel connected with the earth ... I feel connected with the world!"

"Become aware that you have the abundance of the whole world inside your hand right Here and Now ... at the tip of your fingers and toes!

"Come on, Genius, say it out loud."

"I am aware that I have the abundance of the whole world at the tip of my fingers and toes right Here and Now!"

My hand slowly released the branch.

Feeling an overwhelming, almost ecstatic sensation of fulfillment and happiness, I went back to the swing, which has become the signature place of my conversations with Starry ...

"... and Shooter!"

"... and my favorite Shooter!"

"Wherever you are and whatever you are doing," Starry continued, "blink and snap a picture. The pictures will remind you of the abundant life happening inside and around you, and will keep you connected with Here and Now. They will remind you to become aware and be grateful."

"I'm not sure that I'll always remember to snap the pictures. I don't know if I'll always remember to be aware and grateful."

"At first, you will remember every once in a while," she reassured me. "With time, patience, and practice, you will become more and more aware and grateful.

"One day, you will want to always get and stay connected with Here and Now, where you are completely fulfilled and truly happy!"

"I'll try to remember to snap the pictures," I finally agreed. "I'll try to become more aware and grateful, and get and stay connected with Here and Now ... but I know it will be hard. All it takes is *one* unhappy Here and Now for me to forget. I wish that God would make every unhappy Here and Now go away. I wish that He would remove each and every one of them."

"Do not be in a hurry for Here and Now to go away," Starry said. "You might miss out on something important.

"Remember that Here and Now loves you. Welcome it into your life, and give it a fair chance to satisfy its need to serve you and be your growth opportunity that it was born to be.

"Accept its presence, allow it to accomplish its mission to help you be the great Human Being that you are, and fulfill its purpose to make you happy.

"Let it show you what it wants to show you. Let it tell you what it needs to tell you. Through the language it speaks beyond all Human words, let it deliver its message to you, and let it help you discover the blessing under the disguise."

Shooter had precious words for me to repeat out loud:

- I am aware that Here and Now loves me and wants me to be happy.
- I am aware of how rich I am Here and Now.
- I trust, welcome, and accept Here and Now.
- I am happy Here and Now, being exactly where I am, and doing exactly what I am doing.
- I thank and then release Here and Now.

"When am I going to start discovering the blessings?"

"You already have, Genius!"

"Who's going to teach me this language that Here and Now speaks beyond all Human words?"

"*Grace* will!" Shooter answered, amused.

"When can I start? When can I meet grace? Where can I find it?"

"Grace will meet *you*," he said. "It will find you. Meanwhile, keep in touch with God and the angels, and don't worry about those times you forget ... Starry and I will remind you. Right, Starry?"

"Of course we will."

"Instead of begging God to remove every 'unhappy' Here and Now from your path," he added, "ask Him to help you understand what important message Here and Now has for you."

"Ask for the help of God and the assistance of the angels," Starry said. "They hold a 24/7 open answering and communication service. Knock at the door; it always opens. Call Them, like you often do, and become aware when you do. Tell your story and talk about anything; They always listen. Ask your questions; They always answer. Send your requests; They always grant them. They take pleasure in answering you and giving to you, just like you take pleasure in answering and giving to Dunia.

"God and the angels are always near, and always available and ready to assist you to grow and glow. When you want to have a long conversation, you can communicate better through the empty space, the loud silence, and the deep stillness.

"You can hear Them more clearly during times of retreat, meditation, and prayer."

"Pray, Genius! Prayer mysteriously connects you with God and the angels. It is a direct line to Them."

"Prayer soothes when and where other I-haves have failed," continued Starry. "Prayer helps you stay connected with God and the angels and, inside this connection, you are completely fulfilled and truly happy!

"Call upon God and the Angel of the Million Stars to remind you that Shooter and I are always near ... every time you 'look up here.'

"Call upon God and the Angel of the Blessing in Disguise to help you see beyond the disguise and discover the blessing of Here and Now.

"Call upon God and the Angel of the Language Spoken Beyond All Human Words to help you see, listen, learn this language, and understand the message of Here and Now.

"Call upon God and the Angel of Here and Now to help you get and stay connected with Here and Now.

"Call upon God and the Angel of Happiness to remind you that the ultimate purpose of your life is for you to be happy Here and Now.

"Call upon God and the Angel of Music to help you celebrate Here and Now, with every bird's song welcoming a glorious morning and every cicada's lullaby serenading a wise night."

The first cicada of the evening said, "Hello!"

The amber sun slowly went to sleep.

Soon, the million stars would shine and paint another marvel "*up there!*"

I lay on the swing and looked up. I knew that Starry was smiling down, always reminding me of the great Human Being that I am ... and Shooter, well ... still running around ...

I watched the empty space, listened to the loud silence, and felt the deep stillness.

I closed my eyes, and swung ...

*To the million stars in my life who inspired
and helped me write this book ... Thank you!*

*Through the language you speak through and
beyond all Human words, you help me grow
and glow ... a little more every day!*